DARK CITY

The perfect English murder as described by Orwell is the stuff of Agatha Christie – indeed, it is the stuff of fiction. It's neat and hardly messy. Whereas in wartime London, the killers who plied their merciless trade did so using more barbaric methods. They used gas, ropes and guns, corrosive chemicals and tin openers. Some operated under the cover of darkness, emerging when the city was at its most vulnerable; others simply struck whenever opportunity presented itself. At a time when Londoners were pulling together in the face of terrible adversity, these sinister individuals roamed the bomb-ravaged streets without fear of reprisal.

Indeed, the war gave rise to some of Britain's most infamous killers: John Christie, the monster of Rillington Place, and John 'Acid Bath' Haigh. There was Karl Hulten, the American GI who played the role of a vicious Chicago mobster, and Elizabeth Jones, his English stripper girlfriend whose greatest ambition was to be a mobster's dame. Harry Dobkin almost pulled off the perfect crime, and Gordon Frederick Cummins earned the sobriquet the 'Blackout Ripper' for his ghastly work with razor blades and knifes.

Dark City explores this gallery of rogues, a collective whose grisly work still sickens today. These killers went to their deaths at the end of a rope, but their violent legacies live on and continue to fascinate.

1

What the Psychic Saw

Tuesday, 8 April 1941. Madam Nerva led Rachel Dobkin into the living room of her small house on Underwood Road. Although it was a bright spring afternoon, the blackout curtains were drawn across the window. Madam Nerva motioned to a table and told Rachel to have a seat. A solitary candle in the centre of the table cast flickering patterns on the wall and bathed the room in a pallid light. Rachel sat down and anxiously drummed the tabletop with her fingers. For two years she'd been coming to see Madam Nerva for her special brand of guidance.

'Can you tell me something?' Rachel asked, watching the candle's flame replicate itself in the glass beads around Madam Nerva's neck.

'Give me an item,' the psychic said, 'and I'll try and get through.'

Rachel removed her wedding ring and slid it across the table. Madam Nerva traced the ring's circumference with a delicate forefinger before picking it up and gently pressing it between her palms. She mumbled quietly to herself, her brow creased in concentration as she gently rocked back and forth in her seat. Her eyes rolled under heavy lids, revealing just the whites. In her self-induced trance, Madam Nerva was no longer sitting at her living room table, but standing in a vast, grey empty space. In front of her, two forms slowly took shape: one was Rachel Dobkin; the other a building, its features not entirely distinguishable. An open door materialised in the building's façade and seemed to beckon Rachel Dobkin in. No sooner had Rachel passed through the entrance, it disappeared, trapping her inside. Madam Nerva shook herself partially free of the trance and returned to her physical self.

'You are worried and full of trouble,' she said, eyeing Rachel across the table. 'You are planning to go on a journey in a few days to meet someone. Don't go – leave it to the spirit friends and stay where you are. I see sadness for you. Will you promise you will not go?'

'I promise I won't go,' Rachel said, although she was supposed to meet her estranged husband on Friday to collect some money. Madam Nerva returned Rachel's wedding ring and urged her to simply stay at home. Rachel, sliding the ring back on her finger, said she would. She thanked Madam Nerva for her time and said she would come back the following week for another reading. The psychic saw Rachel to the front door and watched her walk down the small garden path, knowing she would never see the young woman again. Indeed, eight days later she answered a knock on her door to Polly Dubinski, a woman who introduced herself as Rachel Dobkin's sister.

'Mrs Nerva,' the woman said, 'my sister was here on Tuesday. You told her not to go see her husband, and she went – she hasn't returned yet. Could you go into a trance and tell me about her?'

Madam Nerva, first name Hilda, ushered Polly in and led her to the sitting room. She asked Polly if she'd brought any personal item belonging to Rachel, something she might touch to establish a psychic connection. Polly opened her handbag and retrieved a scarf and a jumper that Rachel had worn recently. As she handed them over, she told Madam Nerva she'd last seen Rachel at 4.30 on the afternoon of Good Friday, 11 April. Polly said she had filed a missing person's report at the Commercial Street Police Station the following day after her sister failed to return home. The on-duty sergeant took the report and entered the details on page 347 of the Metropolitan Police Department's

'Persons Missing Book'. Rachel had gone off wearing a fawn tweed coat with brown fur collar, a blue woollen jumper, two woollen cardigans – one dark blue and the other light blue – a navy blue skirt, black shoes and a brown hat. Madam Nerva said nothing and simply ran her hands over the scarf and jumper, which she laid across her lap. She closed her eyes and concentrated on the texture of the fabrics against her skin.

'I went into a full trance,' she later told investigators, 'and felt very funny.'

In her entranced state, Madam Nerva saw Rachel Dobkin standing alongside a stretch of river that wound its way through an open field. On whatever plain the two had made contact, Rachel failed to acknowledge Madam Nerva's presence. The psychic did, however, note that Rachel 'looked sad' and watched as the missing woman stared forlornly into the water rushing past. Observing the scene, Madam Nerva felt a tightening sensation around her neck, as though some invisible force were attempting to crush her windpipe. She struggled against the impending sense of suffocation, but to no avail. Gasping for breath, she shook herself free of the trance and returned to the more natural surroundings of her sitting room, where Polly Dubinski sat crying beside her. The distraught woman told the psychic what she had said in the trance about 'a strangling or choking sensation'.

'I may be wrong,' Madam Nerva said, handing back the scarf and the jumper, 'so come and see a medium who is a friend of mine.'

The two women paid a visit to Lydia Kain, a self-proclaimed 'spiritualist' who lived at 77 Luken Street, Commercial Road. A cleaning woman by trade at a chemist's office in London, Lydia had in recent years discovered her supposed ability to converse with the dead. She had developed her skills under Madam Nerva's tutelage after a chance meeting five years earlier at a West End séance. Like her mentor, Lydia described herself as 'a woman who can go into a trance, and when in this state, the spirits speak to me'. Unlike Madam Nerva, however, Lydia did not believe in capitalising on her gift, communicating with the spirit world only when close friends sought her advice. Now, on this Monday afternoon, Madam Nerva introduced the visibly distraught Polly Dubinski and asked Lydia if she'd attempt contacting 'the spirits' to ascertain Rachel Dobkin's whereabouts.

Lydia agreed and took the scarf and jumper from Polly. She closed her eyes and tightly clutched the garments. When she declared several minutes later that 'bad vibrations' were preventing her from establishing meaningful contact, Madam Nerva suggested Lydia try her luck with Polly's pearl necklace. Lydia took the pearls and draped them around her fingers. Again, she closed her eyes and almost seemed to drift off.

'There is a passing out,' she said in a thick voice. 'A sudden death.'

She opened her eyes and sat staring momentarily at some distant point only she could see. She handed the pearls back to Polly and said that while in the trance, she had been overwhelmed by a 'choking sensation'. Polly, weeping, gathered her belongings, bid the two mediums a good afternoon and left the house in a hurry. Madam Nerva, also clearly upset, thanked Lydia for her time and returned home.

'After that,' Madam Nerva later told investigators, 'one afternoon, I was lying down and I saw Rachel and I started to cry, as she looked so sad. She didn't give me a message, but just looked at me. Then I went to sleep.'

Fearing for her sister's wellbeing, Polly Dubinski returned to the Commercial Street Police Station at 5 o'clock on the evening of Tuesday, 15 April, and said her sister's estranged husband, Harry Dobkin, was responsible for Rachel's disappearance. She said Rachel had planned to meet Dobkin the day she vanished.

'She said that Harry had promised to give her a pound of onions as a present,' Polly explained, adding that she had little faith in her one-time brother-in-law. 'My sister's husband has been very cruel to her. She has received severe blows from him at different times and for the past few years has been unable to follow any employment on account of the treatment she received.'

Polly recounted one episode in particular when Rachel 'received a blow on her head from her husband in the street, when she met him'. The incident, having occurred four months ago, resulted in Rachel being hospitalised. 'This blow caused her to have a mental lapse,' Polly said. 'Shortly afterwards, we – her family – received a message from the police at Commercial Street to the effect that she was in St Clements Hospital, Bow. I went to this hospital . . . and seeing that it was a mental hospital and that my sister was perfectly sane, made an application for her release.'

It was unlike Rachel to simply run off and not tell anyone of her whereabouts, Polly said. So there would be no room for doubt, she told the on-duty sergeant she believed Harry Dobkin 'had some hand in Rachel's disappearance'.

The sergeant asked Polly if she'd ever heard Dobkin make threats against her sister.

'He has never threatened my sister in my presence,' Polly said, 'although he has frequently spoken very badly of her. I cannot say anything definite against him, but I do feel he knows something about her disappearance. None of the family have seen him since my sister disappeared.'

The sergeant typed up Polly's statement and had her sign it in front of Divisional Detective Inspector A. Davis of City Road Station, 'G' Division, who assumed the role of lead investigator. Davis escorted Polly out and offered her a few words of assurance before returning to his desk. His immediate thoughts didn't swing in any particular direction. In the chaos of a city at war, missing persons were hardly uncommon. Going by Polly Dubinski's statement, it seemed there was little incentive for the unemployed and routinely abused Rachel to stay in London. True, she had a son – but the lad, according to Polly, was now 19 and had recently registered for military service. Nevertheless, standard enquiries would be made at all London hospitals and casualty wards. Detectives would review air raid casualty lists, and a photograph of the missing woman would be forwarded to the Central Air Raid Casualty Bureau. In the meantime, Davis would focus his attention on the missing woman's estranged husband. He would have him brought in the following morning for questioning.

Night came and the lights went out. War Reserve Constable Charles Moore patrolled No. 16 beat that evening, covering Kennington Lane, Vauxhall Street, Black Prince Road and various side streets. Shortly after 2 in the morning, he noticed a red glow casting buildings far down Vauxhall Street in silhouette. He ran in the direction of what he immediately knew to be a fire and, at the junction of Vauxhall and Kennington Lane, saw flames clawing at the sides of a church. Moore broke the glass and pulled the bar of a nearby fire alarm. Joined by War Reserve Constable Alfred Remant, Moore ran toward the burning building and tried to gain entrance. As the two officers pulled boards from the bomb-damaged windows, they were approached by a stout, round-faced man, wearing a dark grey suit and a trilby hat.

'Come this way gentlemen, if you want to get in,' he said.

Moore assumed the man was the firewatcher assigned to the premises but failed to ask given the situation's urgency. The man led the constables around to the side of the building and approached what appeared to be two large garage doors, which he swung open with little effort.

'I'm glad you've come,' he said. 'What a blaze this is!'

The constables followed the man through the doors into a large room that appeared to be a storage space for various ledgers and deed boxes. The three men ran past rows of neatly organised boxes and leather-bound folders before passing through another set of doors, which opened onto the back of the church. It was immediately apparent to Moore there was nothing he could do. The flames had by now devoured the boards nailed across the windows. Thick columns of black smoke climbed skyward; from inside the church, came the sound of breaking timber. Along the front of the building, on Kennington Lane, members of the Auxiliary Fire Service attacked the blaze with their hoses. All Constable Moore could do was watch.

Police notified Herbert Burgess, the church's minister, shortly after 5 that morning. Burgess left his home in Montford Place and arrived at the church within the hour to inspect the damage. He entered the building through a small door that faced out onto St Oswald's Place and noticed a still-smouldering stack of charred wood lying on the floor. The church's schoolroom was separated from a larger room in the back of the church by a wooden partition, which, along with two American-made organs, had been completely incinerated.

Burgess said nothing as he stepped over the charred wood-and-brass remnants of the organs and moved into what had been the church's recreation room, built directly over the cellar. The fire had burned two large holes through the floor: one adjacent to where the gas fireplace had been, the other along the base of the wall of the main chapel area. Although no fire expert, it appeared to Burgess that flames had burned through the floor from underneath.

Curious, he made his way down to the cellar and saw a straw mattress lying in the middle of the floor. It was evident someone had ripped the mattress open using a sharp instrument; a small pile of heavily singed straw lay beside the mattress. Burgess had never seen the mattress before and guessed some individual had dragged it from one of the bombed-out houses nearby. The great oak beams directly above the mattress, which supported the floor of the chapel, were severely burned, arousing the minister's suspicions that the fire had been deliberately set. Wood panelling on the walls and floor was also charred; a portion of ceiling in the right-hand corner of the cellar had collapsed and caved in the floorboards. At 11 that morning – Wednesday, 16 April – Burgess paid a visit to the Fire Brigade Headquarters at Albert Embankment to find out what he could regarding the blaze. The cause of the fire, he was told, remained under investigation.

A short, round-faced gentleman with a thick neck and squat build, 47-year-old Harry Dobkin was brought in for questioning that afternoon, picked up by detectives at his home in Navarino Road. He came along without protest, not once expressing any concern at being summoned by the police. In the interrogation room at Commercial Street Police Station, he appeared totally indifferent to his surroundings. Davis entered the room, pulled up a chair and introduced himself by name and rank. He said he was making enquiries into the disappearance of Rachel Dobkin. The mentioning of his wife's name did nothing to alter Harry Dobkin's calm façade. The affable smile stayed in place without so much as a quiver and he willingly provided information when Davis began his questioning. He readily admitted to living a life of quiet desperation. Like his father before him, Dobkin worked a market stall, selling leather aprons and pockets. When the war arrived, business dried up. Only two weeks earlier, to supplement his diminished income, Dobkin had taken a job as a night watchman and fire-spotter – a job not intended for timid individuals.

Come nightfall, the bombers arrived and gutted great swathes of the city. The mournful wail of air-raid sirens warned of the coming devastation and dragged weary Londoners from their beds. They retreated to their garden shelters, or sought solace in the Underground, crowding the platforms, stairways, corridors and escalators, listening to the thunderous cannonade above. While others scurried for shelter, Dobkin – and the city's 3,500 fire spotters – did their best to direct emergency services to the flames. Even before the first bombs fell, London's skyline changed as observation towers appeared atop the tallest buildings. Each evening at 7 o'clock, Dobkin reported to the Vauxhall Baptist Church at 302 Kennington Lane. The schoolroom at the rear of the church was being used by a London-based firm of solicitors to store legal documents, and it was Dobkin's responsibility to ensure the place did not burn down in the event of a raid. German bombs had blasted the church and surrounding areas on the night of 4 October 1940, killing 100 people. The church, miraculously, had not caught fire – but the night before Dobkin was brought in for questioning, a freak blaze had broken out in the chapel.

His nocturnal duties aside, Dobkin was less than thrilled with his domestic situation. He had married Rachel Dubinski at Bethnal Green Synagogue on 5 September 1920. 'The marriage was arranged in the Jewish fashion by a marriage broker,' he said, 'and has been a failure from the start.'

The couple took up residence in a small flat in Brady Street, a location Dobkin thought was too far from his place of business. His insistence that they move resulted in a separation after only three days together. The 27-year-old Dobkin moved into his mother and father's house on Flower and Dean Street, leaving Rachel the Brady Street flat. The landlord, taking pity on Rachel, allowed her to live there rent-free. After three tumultuous months of matrimony, the couple agreed to a legal separation. Rachel Dobkin appeared before a magistrate at Old Street Police Court and secured a maintenance order against her husband for £1 a week.

'I have never had much at that rate,' Dobkin said, 'and got in arrears and was sent to prison. The order has been varied from time to time and at present stands at 10s per week. At the present time, I am not in arrears.'

Davis scribbled the information in his notebook and asked Dobkin to recount the last meeting he had with Rachel.

'Last Friday, I was walking along Navarino Road,' Dobkin said. 'I was going out to sell some aprons, when I saw my wife at the corner of Navarino Road and Graham Road. It was between 2 p.m. and 3 p.m., and it was obvious that she had been waiting for me.'

He continued, saying his mother had been ill that day, leaving him little patience to deal with his wife, whom he claimed took great pleasure in trying his nerves. He told Rachel to meet him at 5 o'clock outside Metropolitan Hospital in Kingsland Road. He spent the next 2 hours at Chapel Street Market, hawking his merchandise, before rendezvousing with Rachel at their prearranged spot. The two of them walked to a café across the street and took a table in the corner. Over tea and cakes, Rachel told Dobkin her brother was getting engaged that Sunday. Dobkin stared out the café's taped windows and muttered his congratulations, not caring one way or the other. He had never kept his dislike for her family a secret, which made it all the more surprising when Rachel invited him to the engagement party on the condition she and Dobkin reconcile. Dobkin balked at the idea.

'If you don't make peace with me,' Rachel hissed, 'I'll make trouble for you.'

'Now, calm yourself,' Dobkin said. 'I'll consider peace if you will calm yourself and go home.'

In the interrogation room, Dobkin sat back in his chair and shook his head, clearly annoyed by the memory. Davis asked him what happened next.

'She was talking in low tones but was a bit hysterical,' Dobkin said. 'She drunk her cup of tea and, as we left the tea shop, she said she didn't feel well and she was going to her mother's to hear the wireless. We walked together a little way up Kingsland Road. She again said she didn't feel well and that if I wanted to do so, I could go to her at any time. As she was still upset, I promised to consider returning to live with her. Then my wife got on the No. 22 bus going towards Shoreditch, and that was the last time I saw her. We parted on quite good terms.'

Davis nodded and asked Dobkin if he had actually planned on following through with his promise. Dobkin was incredulous.

'I had no intentions of making peace with her or attending her brother's engagement party, as I have had too much trouble with my wife before,' he said. 'I only met her to try and stop her coming round to Navarino Road. I know nothing about my wife's disappearance. I think she has gone out of her mind. If I can get any information about my wife, I will notify the police at once.'

Davis thanked Dobkin for his time and told him he would be in touch. A uniformed constable escorted Dobkin from the station, leaving the detective alone with his thoughts. Certainly, one could argue the case that Harry Dobkin had failed as a husband, but did that make him a murderer? Davis thought not, for Dobkin's relationship with Rachel had imploded two decades ago. 'It cannot be considered feasible,' Davis wrote in the case file, 'that the man would wait twenty years if he intended to do her harm.'

Davis ordered Police Constable Robert Woodland to pay a visit to Rachel Dobkin's home at 44 Cookham Buildings, Old Nichol Street, Bethnal Green. Woodland arrived at the address, a squat building of red brick, shortly before 1 in the afternoon and ascended the stairs to Rachel's flat. He knocked on the door and got no response, pounding several more times before turning to leave. Just by chance, he glanced down at his feet and saw what appeared to be a small, pink playing card lying by the door. He picked it up, turned it over and saw it was actually a picture card. The caption scrawled across the bottom in a loopy cursive read, 'My latest photo.'

The image above it was that of a skeleton.

At 7 o'clock that evening, Minister Burgess returned to the Vauxhall Baptist Church to again inspect the damage. He stood in the cellar and pondered the mattress for some time before ascending the small flight of steps into the church courtyard. There, he saw firewatcher Harry Dobkin picking up pieces of debris and piling them in a corner. Burgess approached Dobkin and asked what he knew of the fire.

Dobkin said he was making his normal rounds in the early morning hours when he noticed smoke coming up through the church's floorboards. He ran and fetched a pail of water from a nearby hydrant and returned to find the floor burning. He dumped the bucket on the flames. When that failed, he sounded the alarm and called the Fire Brigade. It was, he said, no doubt the work of neighbourhood children who had sneaked onto the premises to play with matches. An unconvinced Burgess nodded and eyed Dobkin's steel blue firewatcher's helmet. It glistened with a fresh coat of paint; several small pieces of straw adhered to the paint around the brim. Burgess, although adamant in his belief the fire was arson, did not believe children to be the culprits responsible. The tearing open of the mattress and the piling up of straw was far too deliberate and did not seem to be the actions of mischievous youth.

Whatever suspicions Burgess harboured, nothing came of them and the fire at Vauxhall Baptist Church was quickly forgotten in the wake of a devastating raid that befell the city that night. Nearly 700 bombers appeared in the skies above London, dumping incendiaries and high explosives, igniting more than 2,000 fires and killing 1,000 people.

Sitting at his desk the morning after, Divisional Detective Inspector Davis considered the previous night's enemy action. Police work in peacetime was challenge enough without the complications of war. For all he knew, Rachel Dobkin now lay buried beneath a pile of rubble somewhere. He had heard unsettling stories regarding the city's public air raid shelters: unsightly bunkers, made of brick and concrete with reinforced roofs, and 14-inch thick walls, which could accommodate up to fifty people. The government had sanctioned the building of such shelters in March 1940, but wartime demands depleted the supply of building materials several months later, resulting in numerous shelters of questionable quality going up. Rumours were circulating of communal shelters collapsing on their occupants, killing all inside. It was no wonder the majority of Londoners preferred the safety of the Underground, but even that was vulnerable to a well-placed bomb.

Only three months prior, on 11 January 1941, an armour-piercing explosive sliced through King William Street and detonated in the ticket concourse of Bank Station. The blast, channelled downward by the escalator shafts, devastated the

Central Line platforms and hurled people clear across the station. The explosion ripped a crater 100 feet wide 120 feet long in the street above the concourse, requiring a temporary bridge to be built across the chasm for traffic. Such catastrophes were not uncommon but were routinely kept from the public. On 17 September 1940, a high explosive scored a direct hit on Marble Arch Station. The blast's concussion ripped the tiling from the walls, fragmenting it like the shell of a hand grenade, killing seven people and wounding another thirteen. At Balham Station on the Northern Line just one month later, a bomb ripped a crater more than 27 feet deep in the street above the station and took out a city bus. Below ground, the blast collapsed Balham's northbound tunnel and ruptured the water and sewage mains. Muck and debris flooded the station's north and southbound platforms, killing sixty-five civilians and wounding another seventy. 'All you could hear,' remembered one air raid warden, 'was the sound of screaming and rushing water.'

Davis stared out of his taped office window at a gunmetal sky. It was easy to grow despondent about a case under such conditions, but the detective had never been one to surrender easily. He and his team had wasted no time the day before interviewing known friends of Rachel Dobkin and members of her estranged husband's family. Depending on whom they spoke with, the investigators heard very different takes on who seemed to cause the trouble in the relationship. Harry's sister, Annie Silverstein, lived with her brother and parents in Navarino Road and told police that Rachel routinely dropped by the house to cause a ruckus.

'The last time I saw Rachel was on 7 April at midday,' she said. 'She was in Navarino Road outside our house. I saw her call at several houses on the same side of the road. I went on the step but I did not speak to her, as I knew there would only be a row. I gathered she was out to cause trouble by telling our neighbours about her husband.'

Davis asked what sort of trouble Rachel caused.

'There is a maintenance order in force against my brother,' said Annie, whose husband was currently serving overseas in the Auxiliary Military Pioneer Corps. 'Mrs Dobkin has always alleged that her husband was unable to pay or increase the maintenance, as he spent it all on his family. She has called at all hours and kicked up a row … I have often heard Rachel threaten to make trouble for Harry because he wouldn't go back and live with her. Harry has lived with my family on and off for the last twenty years and whenever he is at home with us, Rachel comes round to cause trouble.'

Annie said it was not until Polly Dubinski paid a visit to the Dobkin residence on 13 April that she knew Rachel had gone missing.

'From what I personally know of my brother,' she said, 'I am certain he knows nothing about his wife's disappearance.'

Rachel's friend Dinah Epstein told Davis she'd last seen the missing woman on Thursday, 10 April, the day before she vanished.

'She called on me at about 6 p.m.,' she said. 'We had very little conversation as I was busy getting meals ready, but she seemed quite jovial and appeared in good spirit. I knew Rachel and her husband were not on friendly terms – she used to often tell me she was having trouble getting her money … I have not seen Rachel since she left me at 8 p.m.'

It was Dinah who told Davis that Rachel consulted mediums.

'About six months ago, Rachel took me to see Mrs Nerva, as she could tell us about the future,' Dinah said. 'We used to visit her every other week on a Sunday. She always used to tell Rachel not to have anything to do with her husband, as there would be trouble. The last time we went to see Mrs Nerva, she gave me a message from Mother, who died two years ago last September. She said my mother told her to tell me not to work so hard looking after other members of the family because I would get myself ill.'

For a man whose job it was to ascertain concrete facts, Davis had little time for so-called psychics and soothsayers – but going where the investigation led, he paid a visit to Madam Nerva. He maintained a look of polite interest while she babbled on about trances and mystic visions. For the past eight years, she said, ever since she discovered her ability, people had been coming to her to obtain some glimpse of the future or receive messages from deceased loved ones. She told Davis of Rachel's last visit, of the choking sensation that accompanied her vision, and her warning Rachel to stay clear of Harry Dobkin.

By the end of the week, Davis and his detectives had interviewed more than a dozen people. Vendors at the Cheshire Street Market recalled seeing Dobkin selling his wares the afternoon Rachel vanished, and the proprietress of the café on Kingsland Road told investigators Dobkin came in with a woman matching Rachel's description later that same day. They sat at a corner table and ordered tea and pastries. The couple appeared friendly, but the woman seemed to be the more talkative of the two and very animated when she spoke. From where the proprietress stood behind the counter, she couldn't make out the conversation but didn't think the two were arguing. The couple were in the café for no more than 45 minutes and left together in the direction of the bus stop.

'At this stage, I feel that the allegations against Dobkin have no foundation,' Davis wrote at week's end. 'If the woman has met her death, it is by her own hand. I really think she will ultimately be found, suffering from loss of memory, unless she has disappeared to cause trouble for her husband or has become an air raid casualty.'

On 23 April, a sergeant from the Guildford Borough Police Office contacted Davis to say a local resident had found Rachel Dobkin's purse in the Guildford General Post Office in North Street. Although the discovery had been made eleven days earlier, manpower shortages and the demands of policing in wartime accounted for the delayed notice. The purse was forwarded to Davis at the City Road Police Station, where its contents were catalogued. Along with the ration book, national identity card, comb and compact mirror, were two railway tickets, one being a return ticket issued at Kings Cross Underground Station and the other a ticket purchased at Westminster for a journey to Richmond. Although the dates on both tickets had been erased, Davis called the London Passenger Transport Board with the ticket numbers and learned both had been issued before 7.30 a.m. on Saturday, 12 April – one day after Rachel Dobkin's disappearance. Again, the evidence seemed to point to Harry Dobkin being innocent.

'If Dobkin's story is true,' Davis noted in the case file, 'it can now be assumed that Mrs Dobkin was alive on the morning of 12 April 1941. The only alternative being that she had been murdered and her handbag taken to Guildford and the tickets left in it to hamper any investigation.'

In his case report to the Superintendent's office on 2 May, Davis dismissed the disappearance as an act of spite, one perpetrated by a vindictive ex-wife to exact some sort of revenge on her hapless husband. It was his opinion that both Rachel and Harry Dobkin were pathetic characters. She was a constant troublemaker who routinely hounded Dobkin for monetary support, while he appeared to be a spineless individual incapable of standing up to his estranged wife's demands. The detective's assessment of the supposed victim was blunt:

> Exhaustive queries have been made to trace this woman, who, from statements we have obtained, seems to have been a believer in Spiritualism … who, in my view, is mentally unbalanced.

Likewise, Dobkin was not smart enough to hatch the perfect crime:

It appears that he is a man of low mentality. He does not appear to have sufficient intelligence to murder his wife without leaving some tangible clue as evidence, although that cannot be placed outside the bounds of possibility.

An extensive sweep of city hospitals had turned up nothing.

'Enquiries are continuing to trace the missing woman,' he wrote in conclusion, 'and a further report will be submitted in due course.'

The search for Rachel Dobkin, much like the war, dragged on.

2

A Skeleton in the Cellar

The inhabitants of London went about their business in as normal a manner as circumstances allowed, attending to their jobs and going to school, some still lugging their 'mandatory' gasmasks with them. They continued to volunteer for roles in Civil Defence and queued outside their local registration offices to have their ration books stamped. Women went to work in the factories and young men shipped off to foreign battlefields. By now, they had grown accustomed to the scarred landscape of a city at war. Air-raid trenches zigzagged their way through numerous city parks, and barbed wire surrounded government buildings. The statue of Charles I in Whitehall, and other monuments to history, had long since disappeared beneath great stone slabs. The shattered storefronts and piles of smouldering rubble, the yawning bomb craters and lumbering barrage balloons were as much a part of the city as double-decker buses and red telephone boxes.

At home, glass and valuable breakables remained packed away. Windows were taped – or covered in gummed paper – to prevent shattering in the event of a bomb blast. Vegetable patches were still planted in gardens alongside Anderson shelters to supplement the bland wartime diet. Meals continued to be a miserable affair, with swede and turnip often being the primary ingredients;

shredded carrots were routinely substituted for sugar. 'These were the times,' Winston Churchill later wrote, 'when the English, and particularly the Londoners, who held the place of honour, were seen at their best. Grim and gay, dogged and serviceable, with the confidence of an unconquered people in their bones, they adapted themselves to this strange new life, with all its terrors, with all its jolts and jars.'

While the war brought deprivation and destruction to the people of London, it opened numerous doors of opportunity to its criminals. For hustlers, thieves, black marketers, pimps and shady characters of more violent disposition, the wartime blackout and the destruction wrought from above meant good business. Looters routinely stalked the streets, picking through the ruins of shattered homes for anything of value. They often plied their unlawful trade during the raids, operating with little fear of capture. Between the first week of September and the end of November 1940, nearly 400 cases of looting had been reported to the police. Signs were soon affixed to damaged buildings:

WARNING! LOOTING
Looting from premises, which have been damaged by or
vacated by reason of war operations, is punishable by death or
penal servitude for life.

The dire warning did little to deter the roving safecrackers and common crooks willing to risk the bombs for a piece of swag. Clothing, jewellery, cutlery and anything else that may have survived a bombing was lifted from the ruins, even as the dead and wounded lay nearby. Shattered storefronts were picked clean of merchandise, whether it were women's corsets or fine goods; coal was pilfered from bombed churches and machinery parts swiped from wrecked factories. The police established anti-looting squads to combat the scourge and sought volunteers amongst the public to act as lookouts while the bombs fell. The more intrepid thieves volunteered as Air Raid Precaution Wardens, overseeing evacuations to the shelters before taking their pick of premises. What were once everyday items had now become valuable wartime commodities. Nylons, clothing, cigarettes, beef carcasses and countless other goods swiped from restaurants, warehouses and off the backs of lorries sold for a hefty price on the black market. On street corners, in his flashy suit with the sharp creases, the trilby hat, a cigarette dangling from the lips and rapid-fire banter, the spiv sold his pilfered wares from a battered suitcase.

Criminals of a more sinister calibre also took advantage of the wartime chaos. By the end of 1941, as police continued the search for Rachel Dobkin, Scotland Yard detectives were busy with four ongoing murder investigations. Homicides, challenging enough in peacetime, took on added complexity amidst bombings and blackouts. Many such investigations fell to the Yard's Murder Squad. Initially formed to assist rural authorities in the handling of complex crimes, the squad had built its distinguished reputation cracking cases worthy of any detective novel.

Seven hundred detectives worked the streets of London in 1907, while the remainder of the country had to make do with the meagre resources of local constabularies. 'The County Police, excluding a few large provincial cities, have no detective forces,' stated a Home Office memorandum that year. 'They deal well enough with the ordinary run of criminal cases, but when a case of special application arises, they almost invariably muddle it. Sometimes at a late stage, they ask for assistance from Scotland Yard, but by then the scent is cold and, moreover, the Scotland Yard detective gets very little help from the local men who regard his intrusion with great jealousy.'

Cases of 'special application' referred specifically to murder, a crime which most rural and county police departments were ill equipped to handle. Home Secretary Herbert Gladstone proposed Scotland Yard assume command of all murder investigations – and those of other violent crimes – in country areas, bringing big city resources to bear on cases that might otherwise go cold through lack of investigative experience and skill. Several detectives from the Yard's Criminal Investigation Department were placed under the command of the Home Office and dispatched accordingly when the need arose. While Gladstone proposed no name for this specialised unit, the public and press, fascinated by the grim nature of the crimes it tackled, christened it the Murder Squad. In April 1942, the squad was called upon to assist in the investigation of a brutal beating-to-death in its own backyard – a crime that took root over casual lunchtime chatter.

Two young men named George and Sam sat in a Shoreditch café, idly sipping their cups of tea and munching on their sandwiches. Their conversation covered the usual gamut of women and night-time entertainment before turning to serious business. Sam, leaning forward and lowering his voice, said he had recently come into possession of a gun. He cast a careful glance about the café and placed a silver revolver on the table, being careful to hide it under his paper serviette.

'I'm going to do a job,' he said.

'Where?' George asked through a mouthful of food.

'Anywhere. I don't care – as long as it is something.'

The two men finished their lunches, slurped the last of their tea and left. They wandered aimlessly in search of a score and turned down the High Street. They generally liked to work at night, under the cover of the blackout. But on this particular day – 30 April 1942 – they were both bored and eager for a bit of action. On a whim, they turned into Hackney Road and surveyed the various shopfronts.

'Remember,' George said, 'the gun is for only putting the frightening power in.'

They kept walking until they came across a pawnshop. It was early-closing day, and the elderly shopkeeper was lowering his blinds and preparing to lock up.

'We might as well go in and do this if you are coming,' George said.

'All right,' replied Sam, 'only no violence.'

'All right.'

The two men entered the shop and pretended to be last-minute customers. As Sam eyed the display cases, George turned around and casually locked the front door. The 71-year-old shopkeeper Leonard Moules, or 'Old Moules' as people called him, knew immediately what was happening. George, seeing the old man reach for his police whistle, bashed him once in the skull with the butt of his revolver. The old man slid to the floor, but clawed at George and tried to regain his feet. George pushed Moules back down and whacked him several more times. As he pushed the deadbolt into place, Sam heard the commotion behind him. He turned to see the old shopkeeper lying on the floor with blood pouring from a deep gash in his head.

'You silly sod!' cried Sam, 'What did you do that for?'

'I had to,' George said, the bloody .45-calibre revolver dangling at his side, 'he was going to blow a whistle.'

George knelt beside the unconscious man and used his overcoat to gently wipe the blood away.

'Well, we've done the damage,' he said. 'We'd better do what we came here to do.'

The pair took some rings from the display case and snatched cash from the open safe in the basement, where they dumped 'Old Moules' before fleeing the store. He was found bleeding and still unconscious shortly after 1 o'clock that afternoon. Police responding to the scene were surprised by the crime's brutality. The old man, in the words of one investigator, had been 'mercilessly clobbered'.

He was rushed to Bethnal Green Hospital, where doctors did what they could before placing him in a guarded room. For nine days, detectives kept a round-the-clock vigil by Moules' bed, hoping he might open his eyes and provide names or descriptions of his attackers. In the end, the old man died without ever regaining consciousness. The body was autopsied by Home Office Pathologist Dr Keith Simpson. A good-humoured man who took great pleasure in his work, Simpson had been assisting the police in their criminal investigations since 1934 and always looked forward to the next case. 'I have never lost the thrill of the sudden call to crime, of dropping everything, leaving a dinner party, even getting up at dead of night, to drive to some new case,' he wrote in later years. 'The life of a crime pathologist is so packed with colour and interest he has no time to get bored – hardly even to feel tired.'

Examining the corpse, Simpson saw that five heavy blows from a blunt instrument had split the man's head open. The wounds, he noted, were set close together and suggested Moules had most likely been restrained and unable to struggle. The man had been choked prior to, or during, the beating as evidenced by the heavy bruising of the neck muscles. There were no defensive wounds; no blood or skin scrapings under the worn nails. The old man had been an easy target.

The crime scene had little to offer. A wrench found on the floor near the body was initially believed to be the murder weapon, but a closer inspection revealed no hair or blood. While there were no usable fingerprints to lift, a palm print was found in the open safe tucked away in the corner of the basement. For Scotland Yard detectives, the finding was of little consequence, for the Yard kept only fingerprints on record, not palm prints. More than a decade prior, in 1931, the Yard found itself pursuing a burglar who had made off with a significant number of jewels from houses in Hendon, Watford and Staines. At one house, the intruder had left partial fingerprints while, at another, he left his palm print on a glass tabletop. Police eventually arrested John Egan for the string of break-ins and used the palm print and partial fingerprints to connect him to the crimes. Egan eventually pleaded guilty and was sentenced to fourteen months in prison. It was the first time a palm print had been used in Great Britain to secure a conviction. Burglary, however, was one thing; murder was something else entirely.

Charged with the Moules investigation was Divisional Detective Inspector Keen, who faced the daunting prospect of launching his inquiry without the benefit of a concrete lead.

Keen knew the area well and the various lowlifes who inhabited the back alleys and shady clubs around Hackney Road, Kingsland Road and Bethnal Green Road. Uniformed officers and undercover detectives fanned out through the area and began working the streets. Known gang associates, pickpockets and prostitutes were pulled in for questioning. No one seemed to know anything. In pubs and cheap cafés, undercover detectives simply sat and listened. Two weeks went by before a major break in the case developed. On 15 May, a detective sitting in a Bethnal Green café heard a soldier talking about the recent murder. He said that while lunching in another café around the time of the killing, he saw two men sitting with a gun between them at their table.

'It was George and Sam,' the soldier said. 'I will bet anything they did it.'

It did not take Keen and his detectives long to find out that 'George' was George Silverosa, a 23-year-old machinist who lived in Pitsea. Confronted by Keen, Silverosa made no claim of innocence and readily admitted to taking part in the killing. The gunman, he said, was 22-year-old Sam Dashwood, who had been discharged from the Army for his lack of mental acuity. Once taken into custody, Dashwood also confessed, telling detectives he pleaded with 'the old boy' to keep quiet before bashing him multiple times in the head to shut him up. The palm print found in the safe was matched to Silverosa's left hand. This evidence, when coupled with the pair's confessions, meant defence counsel's only task was to save the two men from the gallows.

At trial, Silverosa's attorney conceded his client had taken part in the robbery, but argued he had nothing to do with the murder. Dashwood caused quite a stir when he excused his court-appointed lawyers after they tried to introduce evidence suggesting he was mentally unstable. Deciding to handle his own defence, he made a shambles of the case. The jury, unsurprisingly, returned a verdict of guilty on 21 July 1942, and the pair was promptly sentenced to death.

Standing in the docks, the two men accepted their fate with a show of bravado. 'Hard luck, George!' cried a woman in the public gallery upon hearing the sentence.

'Don't worry,' Silverosa smiled as the bailiffs led him away. Dashwood, for his part, simply waved goodbye to those in the courtroom as he disappeared down the stairs to the holding cells below.

The two men were sent to Pentonville Prison to await their execution. A few days before the hangings, Silverosa obtained permission from the warden to burn his personal letters in the prison incinerator. As he watched the flames take hold of the paper, Silverosa grabbed a fire poker and attacked the two warders who stood watch over him. He severely injured both men but was still overpowered and dragged back to the condemned cell. On the morning of Thursday, 10 September, Silverosa and Dashwood both died at the end of a rope.

The same month police arrested Silverosa and Dashwood, the firm of solicitors Bulcraig and Davis relieved Harry Dobkin of his fire-watching duties at 302 Kennington Lane. The Vauxhall Baptist Church – or what remained of it – was scheduled to be demolished, prompting the lawyers to move their ledgers and deeds elsewhere.

The dismantling of the church ruins began in June with the clearing of loose debris around the site. On the morning of Friday, 17 July 1942, demolition worker Benjamin Marshall went to work clearing wreckage in the church's cellar. He piled large pieces of charred timber and broken masonry in the small courtyard before tackling the 8 inches of debris that covered the cellar floor. He set to work with a spade, shovelling away the detritus to expose the paving stones beneath. One stone felt loose underfoot. Marshall bent down and pulled the stone free, leaning it against the wall. Crouching on his haunches he peered into the shallow opening and saw skeletal remains lying in the damp earth. The legs had been removed and the bones doused in a powdery substance. Marshall scrambled from the cellar and called to several other workers in the courtyard. Together, using a tarpaulin as a stretcher, they lifted the body from beneath the floor, carried it to the chapel and called Kennington Road Police Station.

Within minutes, Detective Inspectors Frederic Hatton and John Keeling, 'M' Division, were kneeling over the skeletal remains on the church's stone floor. The lower jawbone was missing, as was the left forearm; some decaying tissue still clung to the torso. Judging by the skeleton's small size, Hatton initially believed the remains to be those of a 'very young person' killed during an air raid. The body was photographed and removed to St George's Mortuary. In the course of routine inquiries that afternoon, cross-referencing the church's location with missing-persons reports, Keeling learned 'G' division officers investigating the disappearance of Rachel Dobkin had searched the premises in April the previous year. In light of such developments, the detectives asked Dr Keith Simpson to examine the remains.

The pathologist, eager as always to start his work, arrived at the mortuary early the next morning. The remains, wrapped by the coroner in a brown paper parcel, lay ready for Simpson on a hospital trolley. A shrivelled womb revealed the sex, but there was nothing to immediately identify the remains as those of Rachel Dobkin. Like Hatton, Simpson at first believed the deceased to be the victim of a bomb blast, which perhaps accounted for the severed limbs and missing jawbone – and the bones did show signs of being burned: the left side of the skull, the front of the chest, the hips and limb extremities were all charred. The presence of soft tissue, riddled with maggots and fly pupae, Simpson told the detectives, suggested the deceased had died no more than eighteen months ago. A more detailed examination, he said, would be necessary to determine the precise cause of death and, hopefully, an identity.

With the coroner's permission, Simpson removed the body to his laboratory in the Department of Forensic Medicine at Guy's Hospital, where it quickly became apparent the victim did not

die in an air raid. Whoever buried the body did not want it identified, removing the eyes and slicing off the ears. The left arm
had been severed with a clean cut through the elbow; the right
arm had been removed in a similar fashion. Both legs had been
chopped off at the knees. All four amputations were far too 'clean'
to have been caused by a bomb. Decapitation had occurred post-
mortem at the point where the skull joined the neck. Saw marks
were clearly visible in the bone. Simpson reconstructed the skeletal remains to the best of his ability, piecing them together like
some grim – but incomplete – jigsaw puzzle. Taking the missing bones into consideration, and applying the formulas of his
trade to the left humerus, Simpson estimated the victim to be
5 feet 1 inch tall. Studying how the skull plates fused together, he
determined the woman's age to be 40 to 50 years old. Simpson
compared his numbers to those of Rachel Dobkin in the police
department's 'Persons Missing Book,' which listed her age as 44
and her height as 5 feet 3 inches. Although not conclusive identification, it was a start.

It was evening when Simpson focused his attention on the
cause of death. The torso and skull – aside from the missing lower
jaw – showed no signs of physical trauma, ruling out shooting
and stabbing. Having little else to work with, Simpson bent low
over the neck, a scalpel in hand. He gently dissected the voice
box and noticed the 'right corner horn of the thyroid bone was
fractured across the base,' resulting in the bone collapsing inward
toward the airway. Closer examination revealed the soft tissue
around the fracture to be almost black in colour, darkened by
what Simpson believed to be a blood clot, which do not occur
after death. Simpson knew such damage to the thyroid occurred
only in cases of strangulation. Although ruling fatal asphyxia as
the absolute cause of death was impossible because the heart and
lungs had decomposed, Simpson notified Hatton and Keeling
of his findings. The detectives arrived at Simpson's laboratory
within the hour and asked the pathologist how confident he was
in his theory.

'In my experience of more than 11,000 post-mortem examinations over the past fifteen years,' Simpson replied, 'I have never seen this fracture exist alone except from strangulation.'

He lifted the skull off the examination table and turned it over to reveal a large bruise on the decomposing skin that still clung to the back of the head.

'The broad nature of the bruising over the convex surface of the skull excludes the possibility of this injury being due to a blow from a blunt object,' Simpson said. 'It's most commonly seen following a fall to the ground, or resulting from the head being bashed against an unyielding wall or object.'

Simpson spent the next two days with Hatton and Keeling at Vauxhall Baptist Church, now a crime scene. Trench-coated detectives moved silently about the grounds, sifting through dirt in search of the missing limbs; uniformed constables stood guard around the premises. While no other bones were recovered, investigators found traces of yellow powder in the dirt similar to the substance smeared on the remains. The powder samples from the church and the body were handed over to Dr John Ryffel, Head of the Department of Clinical Chemistry at Guy's, on 20 July and proved to be slaked lime. The killer, intending to destroy all traces of his crime, had meant to cover the body in lime to hasten decomposition. Unfortunately for the culprit, slaked lime – lime mixed with water – has the opposite effect, proving destructive only to maggots and fly larvae, thus preserving much of the vital evidence.

It was not until the middle of August that Simpson confirmed the victim's identity through dental and medical records, and forensic photography. A portrait of Rachel Dobkin, provided by the missing woman's sister and copied by Simpson onto X-ray film, was superimposed over a negative image of the skull. The overlay revealed a near-precise match in all facial and cranial lines. Four teeth – three molars on the right and one on the left – remained in the upper jaw. Marks on the teeth showed the victim most likely wore dentures, and a thickening of the tooth-bearing border revealed a particularly heavy bite. Police tracked down Rachel Dobkin's dentist, who, on 2 August, examined the skull's dental work, recognised the fillings, bite patterns and denture markings, and excitedly proclaimed the remains to be those of his one-time patient. From his own records, the dentist drew a diagram of the missing woman's upper jaw, which 'corresponded in every detail' with that of the skull. Simpson's examination of the uterus had revealed a large fibroid growth, one any doctor would have discovered during a routine examination of the pelvic organs. A consultation with Rachel Dobkin's doctor at London Hospital confirmed the woman had been diagnosed with such a growth, yet resisted advice to have it surgically removed.

On 25 August 1942, Simpson confirmed the remains as being those of Rachel Dobkin, some sixteen months after she first went missing.

Detectives Hatton and Keeling paid a visit to the Dobkin residence in Navarino Road at 8.30 on the morning of Wednesday, 26 August. A bullish, thick-necked man met them at the door.

'Are you Mr Dobkin?' Hatton inquired.

'Yes, sir,' Dobkin replied, somewhat bewildered.

'We're police officers,' Hatton said, 'what part of this house do you occupy?'

Dobkin told the two men he lived in the front room on the first floor and asked if they cared to see it. More than willing to accept an invite in, the two investigators followed Dobkin up a narrow flight of stairs to his living quarters, sparsely furnished with two single-sized bedsteads and sacks of leather and webbing cuttings. The inspectors rifled through the sacks, looked under the beds and turned down the sheets, finding only a collection of Underground rail tickets. One of the men turned to Dobkin, who stood watching in a corner.

'In April 1941 and onwards, you were interviewed by Inspector Davis regarding your wife, who was reported missing,' he said. 'I am Divisional Detective Inspector Hatton of the Kennington

District, and as there has been a development in respect to your wife, I want you to accompany us to Southwark Police Station for further enquiries.'

'What have you found?' Dobkin asked, his voice registering surprise. 'My wife?'

'It would be advisable,' Hatton said, 'if you did not ask questions at this stage.'

The detectives escorted Dobkin out to their car and drove him to the police station. In the backseat, he chatted nervously, attempting to mine information from the two silent men up front. At the station, the detectives sat Dobkin in a drab interrogation room.

'In fairness to you,' Hatton said, 'I am now telling you that human remains were found in a cellar at a chapel next to where you were firewatching in April 1941, and we are satisfied that they are those of your wife.'

'I don't know what you're talking about,' Dobkin said, the words spilling into one another. 'I don't know of any cellar at the chapel and have never been down one there. In fact, I don't believe it is my wife – but if you tell me it is so, I suppose it must be so.'

Hatton nodded and left the room, leaving Dobkin to sweat it out for several minutes. When the detective returned, he was somewhat surprised when Dobkin slid a letter, scrawled on the back of a leather merchant's bill, across the table.

'Here you are, sir,' Dobkin said, 'this is what I've just written.'

Hatton picked up the piece of paper and read:

Dear Sir.

In respect to what you say that my wife has been found dead or murdered and that you say I know something that I am holding back from the Police. I'm sorry to say that I cannot say anything different to the statement at City Road Police Station … My statements are the same to anyone who is concerned.

Hatton smirked. He had said nothing to suggest Rachel Dobkin met with foul play, nor had he implied that Harry Dobkin was withholding information.

'You have told us you know nothing about your wife being dead, or her remains having been found in a cellar,' Hatton said.

'No,' Dobkin said. 'I have never seen a cellar.'

'Would you like to come with us?' Hatton asked. 'We will point it out to you.'

Dobkin accepted the invitation and the two men, along with Hatton's superintendent, drove to what remained of Vauxhall Baptist Church. They let Dobkin out of the car and walked him down to what was now the open-air cellar, the vestry above having been completely demolished and cleared. Hatton led Dobkin to a shallow hole in the ground.

'This is where your wife's body was found,' he said, 'under a stone slab. She was murdered by strangulation. Later, I believe, the cellar was set on fire.'

'I wouldn't strangle a woman,' Dobkin said, peering into the muddy opening. 'I wouldn't hit a woman – some men might, but I wouldn't. I didn't know the cellar was here, and I certainly have never been down here.'

Dobkin led Hatton to the adjoining house off the courtyard – formerly used by Bulcraig and Davis to store legal documents – and said he patrolled the building and courtyard three times a night while employed as a firewatcher. Hatton surveyed the courtyard from the building's entrance and noticed the short stairway leading to the cellar was clearly visible. No more than 20 yards from the stairwell, in a corner of the courtyard, was a pile of paving stones not unlike the one that concealed Rachel Dobkin's remains.

'Has your wife ever visited here?' Hatton asked.

'No,' Dobkin said, 'but she knew I worked here. I left here in May and have had no reason to come back since.'

Hatton nodded solemnly and said he had a witness who could place Dobkin at the church on the night of 4 August – three months after he was relieved of his fire-watching duties. Up until now, Dobkin had displayed no outward sign of emotion. He had not voiced remorse for his wife's violent passing, nor had he fallen victim to the nervous stammering of a guilty man who knows the game will shortly be up. But news of the mysterious witness triggered a minor irritation. Dobkin frowned and vehemently shook his head, insisting no such person existed – and if they did, he demanded to know who they were. The detective glanced at his superintendent, who left the courtyard and returned shortly thereafter with a war reserve police constable named Wakerly. Under Dobkin's cold gaze, the constable relayed the story he had told Hatton earlier in the day.

Wakerly patrolled Kennington Lane and the surrounding side streets on the night of 3 August. He finished his 8-hour shift shortly after 6 the following morning and, cycling back to the police station, saw Dobkin entering the church and peer through an upstairs window. The constable was in no doubt as to Dobkin's identity: he had chastised the man on several occasions for not drawing the blackout curtains across the church windows at nightfall. What Dobkin was doing at the church that morning, however, Wakerly couldn't say.

'That's a lie!' Dobkin screamed. 'I have never seen him before, and I wasn't there! He's lying!'

The officers returned Dobkin to the station and charged him with murder. He appeared in Bow Street Police Court the following morning, where Detective Inspector Hatton outlined the evidence and motive of the case. For more than twenty-three years, he said, Dobkin looked upon his estranged wife as a financial hindrance. The ongoing maintenance order against him 'was a constant drain,' resulting in his imprisonment on several occasions for failure to pay. No longer able to bear the pressure, he killed Rachel Dobkin on the night of 11–12 April to break free of the crippling financial constraints. To thwart investigators and put them on the wrong trail, he purchased two Underground tickets on the morning of the 12th and placed them in the deceased's handbag before leaving the bag at the post office in Guildford. Trains left Waterloo Station every hour for the 50-minute journey to Guildford, allowing Dobkin to get there and back before anyone noticed he was missing.

In citing evidence against Dobkin, Hatton referred to lime found on the body and a bag of lime found in Dobkin's resting quarters at the church, as well as the pile of paving stones in the courtyard. Dobkin told police he never knew of the church's cellar, but a statement obtained by detectives from 13-year-old Robert Cadby proved otherwise. Cadby lived several doors down from the church at No. 307, Kennington Lane. The boy told investigators he often hung around the church, chatted with Dobkin and saw him go into the cellar on at least one occasion. Detectives brought the boy to the scene, where he showed them the basement entrance he saw Dobkin use. Finally, there was Dobkin's curious hand-written statement on the morning of 26 August in which he said police were accusing him of withholding pertinent information.

'No such thing had been said,' Hatton told the Police Court, 'therefore was it a guilty mind raising a defence to a crime with which he had not then been accused? We have a collection of facts from which we have inferred that Dobkin was responsible for this crime and the points enumerated provide strong circumstantial evidence pointing to his guilt.'

The court agreed and arraigned Dobkin on the charge. The case went to trial at the Old Bailey on Tuesday, 17 November 1942. Dobkin testified in his own defence, insisting he knew nothing of his wife's disappearance, her subsequent death, or how she came to wind up in the cellar of Vauxhall Baptist Church. He maintained an air of arrogance on the stand, dismissing the allegations against him as ludicrous – but there was no dismissing Simpson's forensic evidence, which withstood a gruelling cross-examination by the defence. In its aftermath, the murder of Rachel Dobkin would become a textbook case for students of pathology. On the strength of Simpson's forensic evidence, the jury took only 20 minutes to find Harry Dobkin guilty. The judge pronounced the only sentence allowed by law: death by hanging.

A grey fog hung heavy over Wandsworth Prison in the early hours of Wednesday, 27 January 1943. That morning, after a shot of brandy to calm the nerves, Dobkin went to the gallows without protest. Afterwards, the very man whose testimony had condemned him to hang examined Dobkin's body. The execution, Simpson ruled, had been 'expeditiously carried out.'

The Dobkin case proved to be a career-maker for the young pathologist and established his reputation as one who could communicate with the dead.

'I was only thirty-five when I had the sort of case every young pathologist dreams of, "the case of a lifetime",' Simpson wrote in later years, 'It certainly had all the ingredients, and, but for the heavy shadow of a war that still hung desperately in the balance, it would have hit the news headlines as Crippen did.'

3

Murder in the Dark

Pathologist Bernard Spilsbury, dressed in a leather apron and with the grim tools of his trade arranged on a surgical tray, studied the body on the cold metal slab. Although slender, she appeared well nourished with high, pronounced cheekbones and long, black hair. An electrician walking to work shortly before 8 that morning had found the woman in a surface air-raid shelter on Montague Place, Marylebone, and notified police. The date was Monday, 9 February 1942.

There was no apparent motive for the killing, nor did investigators have any clue as to the woman's identity. She was found lying on her back in the gutter, which ran through the centre of the small, brick-built shelter near Regent's Park. The hands on her wristwatch had stopped at 1 o'clock. Her white undershirt had been torn away, revealing her right breast; the brown skirt she wore was bunched around her thighs. Even in the dim light of an early winter's morning, bloodstains were visible on her underwear and stockings. Her scarf covered her face and the swollen tongue protruded between her teeth. The killer had placed the victim's gloves palms-up on her chest, with the fingers pointing toward the face. Police found a tin of Ovaltine tablets near her body and a box of Master's safety matches.

Divisional police surgeon Dr Alexander Baldie arrived at the scene at 9.10 a.m. and examined the body before its removal. Snow had fallen the night before but had turned to slush by daybreak. The victim's arms and legs were cold, but her torso was still relatively warm. He noted heavy bruising and a number of pressure abrasions on the neck. Based on the partial onset of rigor mortis, he estimated the woman had been dead for several hours. He told the senior officer on scene, Divisional Detective Inspector Leonard Clare of Albany Street Police Station, 'D' Division, that cause of death appeared to be manual strangulation. Shortly after 10.30 a.m., the body was removed to Paddington Mortuary.

Spilsbury began the autopsy 4 hours later. He made note of her height, 5 feet 4 inches, and photographed her face to assist police in determining the woman's identity. He bent over the body and began his examination, a morbid routine he'd performed countless times in the service of the law. A 1935 issue of *Time* magazine had dubbed the pathologist 'His Majesty's Government's real-life Sherlock Holmes', for no one else seemed capable of deducing so much from the dead.

There were numerous markings on the woman's neck: abrasions where the skin had been chafed on either side, and heavy bruising just beneath the chin and around the Adam's apple. The skin along her right jaw line was a purplish-blue in colour, suggesting she had sustained a blow to that side of her face; a similar bruise ran below the left jawline. Toward the front of the neck was an indentation in the skin, curved like a fingernail. A patch of skin on the back of her neck had also been scraped away. Her lips and fingernails were livid, and a faint scratch mark about ½ inch in length was visible just above her left eyebrow. Haemorrhaging had discoloured the skin on her forehead, scalp and the lining of her eyelids. The whites around her dilated pupils were dark with blood. Spilsbury noted heavy bruising on the woman's legs and right temple. A 2-inch scratch – and a number of smaller cuts – had left the lower-right side of her breast red and raw.

Detective Inspector Clare looked on as Spilsbury picked up his scalpel and opened the body with two large incisions that began at each shoulder, converged at the base of the neck and ran down to the navel. The cricoid cartilage of the larynx had been fractured on either side of the neck; haemorrhaging was evident in the surrounding muscle tissue and the surface of the heart. Both sides of the tongue were badly bruised. Although a small amount of blood was present in the vagina, Spilsbury saw nothing to indicate forced penetration. In the stomach, he found some partially digested beetroot. Judging by the bruises on the victim's neck and the damage to the larynx, Spilsbury told Clare the cause of death was strangulation by hand. The clustering of bruises on the neck indicated the assailant was left-handed. Clare nodded and asked that the dead woman's photograph be sent to the Albany Street Police Station as soon as possible.

As Clare drove back to his office, Detective Chief Superintendent Frederick Cherrill, head of Scotland Yard's Fingerprint Department, busied himself with evidence taken from the crime scene. He had visited the mortuary earlier in the day to lift prints from the victim, dusting her fingers in black powder and capturing the prints with lifting tape. A constable when he joined the Fingerprint Department in 1920, Cherrill had rapidly ascended the ranks. His expertise in the field – his familiarity with the intricate mapping of whorls, arches and loops – was born of a fascination he'd harboured as a child reading detective fiction.

Cherrill took great pleasure in his work, for it played upon art and science, two of his great passions. A talented artist who sometimes rendered cartoon caricatures of his co-workers, Cherrill admired the aesthetics of fingerprints. The fact that no two fingers on earth shared the same print fascinated the scientist in him. 'The fingerprint expert,' he later wrote in his memoirs, 'must be able to state that he has personally examined thousands of prints taken from different fingers, and has made an exhaustive study of the unique markings which Nature has placed on each individual finger.' The Yard had amassed an immense catalogue of prints since 1900, the year it adopted fingerprinting as its primary method of identification. As a result, other agencies often called upon the Yard's Fingerprint Department to assist in various investigations, whether it be a simple burglary or complex murder. The department occupied a series of rooms in a building adjacent to Scotland Yard's gothic-styled headquarters on Victoria Embankment. Filing cabinets, card catalogues and bookshelves lined the walls and comprised a massive library of prints that numbered in the tens of thousands.

In his book-lined office, Cherrill hoped evidence from the morning's grim discovery would yield some telling clue. A police constable canvassing the area had found a woman's black handbag lying on Wyndham Street not far from the bomb shelter. Torn and soaked through from a night in the snow, it was unlikely it would surrender any usable prints – but Cherrill deemed it worth a try. Using a feathered brush, he dusted the bag's surface with white powder, keeping his wrist still, guiding the brush strokes with only his fingers. Fingerprints are the result of sweat and oil secretions from the skin coming into contact with a given surface. Fingerprint powder adheres to these secretions, producing a latent print.

Much to Cherrill's delight, several well-defined prints materialised against the bag's black leather. He took a picture of each print before applying lifting tape to the white, swirling patterns. Each piece of tape was stuck on its own black index card, allowing for easy study. He repeated the process with the tin of Ovaltine tablets and the book of matches found by the body. He studied each print under his magnifying glass, an accessory he never travelled without, then examined the prints from the morgue and soon realised, with a sigh of disappointment, the prints from the crime scene belonged to the victim.

The wife of a Blackpool farmer, Evelyn Oatley moved to London in 1936 with dreams of becoming a marquee name in the West End. Raising poultry had never been her life's ambition, and her husband willingly – albeit sadly – gave her up to the capital's neon dazzle. Evelyn, then 28, had in fact married Harry Oatley just months prior on the understanding she would leave Blackpool for London should she find farming disagreeable. But although the city beckoned, it did not embrace her. She worked the night-club circuit as a hostess but never seemed to ace an audition. The outbreak of war and the devastation wrought by the nightly raids destroyed any possibility of serious theatre work. Desperate for money, she turned to the streets.

She sometimes thought about returning to Blackpool and her husband's small cottage but could not reconcile herself to a life in the country. Turning her back on London – even in all its bomb-ravaged dreariness – was to admit defeat and surrender any chance she had of forging her own identity. Nevertheless, the decision pained her. Evelyn missed her husband, if only for his simple-natured kindness. In late 1941, she told him what she was doing to make money; his response had been to profess his love for her. It was too bad he couldn't accommodate the life-style she so desperately craved. And while she still longed for a meaningful relationship, she feared her capacity to love had been damaged beyond repair. She often struggled with intense feel-ings of loneliness and drank to find some measure of comfort. Sometimes, she could be found nursing a scotch in the King's Arms pub in Gerrard Street. And it was here, on the night of Monday, 9 February, that Evelyn Oatley downed her last drink.

The evening's street-side business had been slow, and the pub offered a warm respite from the cold anonymity of a darkened doorway outside. Evelyn sat at the bar, dressed all in black, and sipped her drink until closing time. She left the King's Arms at 11 p.m. and made her way to the Monico Restaurant, where other working girls had gathered to try their luck. Evelyn buttoned the collar of her wool coat and joined two girls she recognised for a smoke. Such scenes aggrieved London's Public Morality Council, a group of worried citizens who feared the war had corrupted the English sense of decorum. The matter, however, remained beyond their control. A woman in London could not legally solicit men for sex, but she could work as a prostitute. The muddled law did nothing to deter the profession; consequently, sex became a major blackout industry. Many women, whose husbands had been called to war, simply turned to prostitution to put food on the table. Some worked in the employ of a pimp or brothel, while the majority worked the streets for themselves.

From darkened alleys to surface air-raid shelters, nocturnal London offered no shortage of places to conduct business – even the open-air trench shelters that zigzagged through Hyde Park offered some measure of privacy. The arrival of the first American troops in Britain on 26 January 1942 further bolstered the trade. With their chocolate bars, gum and wallets thick with paper money, the Yanks were chagrined to find they were charged more than their British counterparts. It was not an American serviceman, however, who approached Evelyn on this Monday night outside the Monico Restaurant, but a British airman.

In the darkness, she could make out the crooked skew of his cap and an unruly head of hair. He lit a cigarette as he approached, the flicker of orange flame revealing pronounced cheekbones and a broad mouth. He introduced himself with a smile and asked Evelyn her name. He carried himself well, looking slim in his uniform, and spoke with an accent that struck Evelyn as being quite posh. When he asked if she had a place nearby, she took him by the arm and led him away.

A simple dividing wall of two folding doors separated Evelyn's living quarters at 153 Wardour Street from those of her neighbour, Ivy Cecilia Poole. A fun-fair attendant in Leicester Square, Ivy had enjoyed a night off work and spent the evening at the Phoenix Theatre on Shaftesbury Avenue. She returned home shortly before 10.30 p.m., switched on the wireless and brewed some tea. She washed her hair and listened to the 11 o'clock European news. At 11.40, as the broadcast ended, she heard someone enter through the building's street-level door. She peered out of her apartment and saw Evelyn coming up the stairs with a man in tow. The two women exchanged pleasantries before Evelyn disappeared inside her flat. The man, however, dressed in a blue overcoat with the collar turned up, said nothing and kept his head down.

Ivy knew full well what Evelyn did to make money; how could she not living in such close proximity with minimal privacy? The two women, however, enjoyed a casual friendship, often sharing light conversation over a cup of tea. Whatever the pitfalls of Evelyn's occupation, she was a pleasant girl who tried to be a considerate neighbour. She always turned on her radio whenever she brought a man home to conceal the sounds of sex on her side of the folding doors. Every night from Tuesday, 3 February, to Saturday, 7 February, Evelyn's wireless had stayed on well past 11. She had taken last night, Sunday, off to wash her hair and go to bed early. Tonight, it appeared to be business as usual.

Ivy returned to her kitchen and made another cup of tea. From Evelyn's side of the partition, came the murmur of quiet conversation. The talking never seemed to last long, and within minutes Ivy heard Evelyn turn the wireless on. Ivy finished her brew and got ready for bed, climbing beneath the sheets at 12.20 a.m. She usually had no problem tuning out the sound of Evelyn's radio, but on this occasion it seemed to be louder than normal. Although annoyed, she chose not to complain and left the couple alone.

It was quite some time before the radio went silent.

Tuesday, 10 February. Catherine Jones, manageress of a boarding house at 76 Gloucester Place, answered the knock on her door shortly after 9 that morning to a trench-coated detective. He introduced himself as Detective Inspector John Freshney and asked Jones if she might have a moment to answer a few questions. When Jones said yes, Freshney pulled a photograph from his coat pocket.

'Have you seen this woman before?' he asked.

It turned out the woman had rented a room only two nights ago. She had checked in at 10.30 p.m., put her suitcase in an upstairs bedroom and asked if any nearby restaurants served late-night dinners. Jones told Freshney she had recommended Lyon's Corner House near Marble Arch. The woman had left and never returned; her suitcase was still upstairs. Freshney, his morning spent knocking on countless doors, pocketed the photograph and asked Jones if she knew the woman's name.

'Evelyn Hamilton,' said Jones, inviting Freshney in to look at the case.

He went up the stairs and down a hall, into a room sparsely furnished with a bed, night stand and bureau. Freshney pulled the suitcase from underneath the bed and gently sifted through its contents, seeing nothing but clothes. Someone had written 'E. Hamilton' in a feminine scrawl on the luggage tag wrapped around its handle. Freshney moved to the room's only window and pulled aside the blackout curtains. Bleak morning light, the colour of slate, flooded the room. Everything in London seemed grey these days, from the surly pillboxes that dotted Victoria Embankment to the anti-aircraft guns pointing skyward. He looked out the taped window and cast his gaze down the street. The bomb shelter where the body had been found was no more than a block away.

Armed with a name, Freshney and Divisional Detective Inspector Clare drove later that morning to Lyon's Corner House on the west end of Oxford Street. The place boasted four floors, multiple dining rooms and a large tea bar. Unsure where to start, the detectives pulled aside a young waitress and asked if she'd been serving tables on Sunday night. When the girl said yes, they showed her Evelyn Hamilton's picture and asked her if the woman looked familiar. The waitress, balancing a tray of food, nodded and said the woman had come in alone around midnight on Sunday.

'She didn't sit in my section,' the waitress said. 'I'm not even sure what time she left the restaurant.'

Remembering the contents found in Evelyn Hamilton's stomach, Clare asked the waitress to list the dishes served on Sunday night. She rattled off a number of unsavoury platters, the primary ingredients of which were partial-meat products and root vegetables. The last item mentioned was a beetroot stew. The detectives thanked the waitress for her time. They now had a name and some sense as to Evelyn Hamilton's movements the night of her murder. But when and where did the killer select Evelyn as his target – was it in the restaurant, or as she walked back to the boarding house?

Two meter readers for the Central London Electric Company discovered the body of Evelyn Oatley shortly after 8 that morning. The men entered the darkened flat when no one answered their knock on the partially opened door. The blackout curtains were still drawn across the window, but light from one of the men's electric torch revealed Evelyn Oatley, her throat slit, lying diagonally across the bed. Blood from the neck wound had dripped to the floor and flowed in a thick rivulet across the room. The men fled the building in search of help and came across Police Inspector John Hennessy walking his morning beat on Wardour Street.

Hennessy ran to the scene, looked in the flat and signalled the West End Central Station to send a divisional surgeon and divisional detective inspector. Dr Alexander Baldie, who had examined the body of Evelyn Hamilton in the air-raid shelter the previous day, arrived at 8.50 a.m. He opened the blackout curtains and knelt beside the bed. On the sheets, to the left of the woman's head, lay a bloodied Ever-Ready razor blade and a blood-spattered pair of curling tongs. A torch, its white-metal handle covered in blood, protruded from the vagina; a blood-stained tin opener lay between her legs. Baldie estimated the woman had been dead for no more than 4 hours. The body was cold to the touch. Rigor-mortis extended to the elbow in the right arm. He reported his findings to Detective Inspector Clarence Jeffery of the West End Central Station, 'C' Division, the senior officer on scene. Jeffery asked Hennessy, who stood guard in the hallway, to notify Scotland Yard Superintendent Frederick Cherrill.

Shortly after 9 a.m., Detective Inspector Charles Gray arrived at the flat and assumed command of the crime scene. He found a box of Ever-Ready razor blades on a washbasin in one corner of the room and ordered they be bagged as evidence. Between the washbasin and electric fireplace stood a large wardrobe, which appeared to have been forced open. Its lock lay in two halves on the bed and floor. The wardrobe contained a few pieces of cutlery and some clothes. More clothes – a dress, slip, brassiere, skirt and a pair of stockings – were draped across a chair by the fireplace. Scattered across the cushions of a sofa that faced the fireplace were the contents of Evelyn Oatley's black leather handbag: two Post Office Savings Bank books and a wallet with no money in it.

As Gray inventoried the scene, Cherrill entered the apartment with his magnifying glass at the ready. He had only just arrived at the Yard that morning when word of the murder reached him. He canvassed every object and surface in the flat, even dropping to his knees to examine the blood on the floor. He passed his magnifying glass over the bloodied razor, curling tongs and tin opener on the bed and ordered they be sent to his office for closer inspection. In the victim's handbag, he found a broken piece of looking glass and asked that it, too, be forwarded to the Yard's Fingerprint Department.

Cherrill was busy examining the wardrobe for bloody prints when Bernard Spilsbury arrived. He pulled on a pair of rubber gloves and moved toward the bed. The killer had sliced a 6-inch gash in the right side of the neck, cutting deep down to the back of the throat and severing a large vein. The torch, still protruding from the woman's vagina, had been pushed almost 4 inches up inside her. The pubic region had been stabbed a dozen times but had not bled heavily. Spilsbury theorised the killer had inflicted the wounds after cutting the woman's throat. Heavy bruising was evident around the victim's neck. Spilsbury told Gray the killer had tried to strangle the woman first, but more would be known after an autopsy. He removed his gloves and got to his feet.

In the hallway, two morgue attendants waited with a stretcher, ready to take Evelyn Oatley to the Westminster Mortuary.

In his office later that afternoon, Cherrill reviewed Spilsbury's pathology report.

The cause of death was major haemorrhaging from the neck. The first act was that of strangulation, which continued until she was unconscious. Her throat was then cut in the position in which she was found with her head hanging over the side of the bed.

Her larynx had been crushed before the killer slashed her throat with a razor blade. He had stabbed the genitals with a blunt cutting edge, most likely the tin opener. There were no defensive wounds on Evelyn's body and no skin or blood beneath the fingernails. In the vagina, there was blood but no trace of semen. Spilsbury noted the killer had probably forced the torch into the victim after she died.

The barbarity of it all shocked even Cherrill, a veteran of countless morbid crime scenes. He put the report aside and turned his attention to the items taken from Evelyn Oatley's apartment. With a gloved hand, he removed the tin opener from its evidence bag and applied fingerprint powder to the battered metal handle. Almost immediately, a series of swirling patterns took shape along the handle's length. There had been nothing to suggest the murders of Evelyn Hamilton and Evelyn Oatley were related. The cause of death and circumstances surrounding each crime were quite different. Whereas Evelyn Oatley had been stabbed and violated with a metal object, Evelyn Hamilton had been strangled but not sexually abused. The only similarities between the two cases were the victims' first names – but perhaps the slayings shared a more significant link.

Cherrill stared at the patterns in the dust. The print of an index finger, to the untrained eye, may appear no different than the print of a middle finger. To Cherrill, however, the shape and characteristics of individual prints were wonderfully unique. Examining the opener's handle under his magnifying glass, Cherrill deduced which finger left which print and thus determined how the object had been held. He put his magnifying glass down and leaned back in his chair, exhilarated by what he saw. The positioning of the prints revealed them to be those of a left-handed individual. Just to rule out the obvious, he compared the prints with those taken from Evelyn Oatley in the morgue. He found no match. He reached for the piece of looking glass found in Evelyn's handbag and ran his feathered brush over the smooth surface, revealing a thumbprint in one broken corner. He studied the print's intricacies beneath his magnifying glass. Its diagonal placement on the mirror meant that a left-handed individual had also handled it.

Cherrill pushed himself away from his desk and moved to one of the large chest of drawers that housed the print index. Prints lifted from crime scenes are often smudged or incomplete; the perfect print is a rarity. Because the broken piece of looking glass had a smooth, flat surface, the partial thumbprint Cherrill found was relatively clean and well defined. And so he began his methodical searching of left thumbprints in the Yard's print collection, looking for the proverbial needle.

4

A Secret Life

He seemed perfectly normal to those who knew him. Indeed, if the RAF men who bunked with 28-year-old Gordon Frederick Cummins at St James's Close voiced any opinion regarding their fellow officer-in-training, it would have been some snide comment ridiculing the man's pretentious demeanour. His nickname around the billet was 'The Duke', a less-than-flattering acknowledgement of the man's upper-class accent and perceived snobbery. He never seemed to be short of money and often made sure someone noticed when he pulled a wad of notes from his pocket and started counting. Like the other men, however, he enjoyed drinking and the company of women.

His wife, Marjorie, whom he married on 28 December 1936, at the Paddington Register Office, believed him to be a loyal and devoted partner. They had met seven months earlier at Empire Air Day in Hendon. She now lived in a flat on Westmoreland Road, Barnes, while he completed his training. He phoned her on a regular basis and promised to return home whenever he could. But on nights when he was free to do as he pleased, he preferred the pubs of Soho to the small flat Marjorie shared with her sister. On the occasions he did make it home, he always seemed to be short of cash and borrowed money from his wife.

Those with whom Cummins served wondered why he ever bothered getting married. He had joined the RAF as a Flight Rigger on 11 November 1935, after failing at a succession of jobs. Military life did nothing to soothe his appetites. His early years in the RAF were spent with the Marine Aircraft Experimental Establishment in Scotland until the outbreak of war, when he was transferred to No. 600 Squadron, stationed at Helensburgh, Dunbartonshire. He became a regular in the local pubs, a Player's cigarette constantly hanging from one corner of his mouth and his arm always around a woman. It was here he earned the nickname 'The Duke' for his dandified way of talking and the intoxicating effect it seemed to have on the local ladies.

When the RAF transferred him to Colerne, Wiltshire, in April 1941, Cummins took the nickname and ran with it, referring to himself as the Honourable Gordon Cummins. He told those who listened that he was descended from aristocratic stock but had willingly turned his back on a life of privilege to serve his country. He befriended a local farmer and often borrowed the man's horse to ride into town, cutting quite the debonair figure as he dismounted outside the White Hart, the local pub. His tendency to buy drinks made him popular with the locals. The money he flashed around only leant credence to his claims of family wealth. It was, he explained, his 'family allowance', which never seemed to last more than a day or two. Leaning against the bar, nursing his Canadian rye whisky – his drink of choice – and his ever-present cigarette, Cummins would tell stories of his life before the war, of how he mingled with the West End's champagne crowd. He did have a theatre connection: his wife, Marjorie, worked as a producer's secretary.

He never voiced any yearning to visit his wife on leave and never expressed remorse at being separated from her for so long. Instead, he would find a car to borrow and drive into Bath, where he displayed a prowess on the dance floor at a local hotel and seduced other men's wives. Cummins craved sex and often frequented a café in town called The Hole in the Wall, where working girls plied their trade. Cummins's superior officers had made it perfectly clear on multiple occasions that the establishment was strictly off limits to all military personnel, but Cummins shrugged off the warnings. He'd leave base dressed in his uniform, change into civilian clothes on the drive into town and visit the café without drawing attention to himself.

It was while Cummins was stationed in Colerne that an airman attacked a woman one night in the neighbouring town of Ford. Someone accosted her in the darkness, grasping at her neck with one hand and trying to remove her clothes with other. She fought him off, kicking and screaming, but could not describe him when she reported the incident to investigators. Two more women were attacked by an airman shortly thereafter in Bath. Again, the victims were unable to describe their assailant and the cases went unsolved.

In September 1941, after he had amassed 1,000 hours' flying time, Cummins took a pilot's test in front of the RAF selection board. He was notified several days later of his stellar performance and ordered to report to the Air Crew Receiving Centre at Regent's Park on Monday, 2 February 1942. He spent Sunday, 1 February, with his wife, and reported for duty the next morning as ordered. Before leaving home, he told Marjorie he would visit her when he could but expected pilot training to monopolise his time. The following night, he picked up a girl near Oxford Circus and spent the rest of the evening between her thighs. When Cummins awoke on the morning of Wednesday, 11 February, it was his plan to do more of the same that evening. He was inoculated in the afternoon and stopped by the YMCA on Avenue Road shortly after 6.30 p.m. He called his wife at 9 p.m. and told her the inoculation had made him ill; he planned to spend the night in.

'When will you be home again?' she asked.

'I'll try and visit next weekend.'

He hung up the phone, lit a fresh cigarette and counted the money in his pocket: £25, more than enough for a night on the town. He put on his coat and headed for the door.

On Wednesday, 11 February, with two murders possibly committed by the same individual in a two-day period, investigators established a command centre at the Tottenham Court Road Police Station. A map of Central London with two coloured pins marking the crime scenes dominated one wall. Against another wall hung photographs and biographical sketches of the two victims. The contents of Evelyn Hamilton's suitcase recovered from the boarding house in Gloucester Place had been booked as evidence but yielded nothing to assist investigators with their task. Divisional Detective Inspector Leonard Clare and his men, however, had managed to track down the woman's younger sister, Kathleen, a nurse in the family's hometown of Newcastle.

She told detectives Evelyn had always been a solitary figure, one who favoured intellectual pursuits over social engagements. 'As far as I know, she has never had a man friend,' Kathleen said. 'All her holidays were spent with various fellowships and worker educational societies … Her one hobby was to improve her knowledge and mind on all subjects.'

She studied chemistry as a teenager and spent several years working as an assistant in local pharmacies before obtaining her chemist and druggist degree from Edinburgh University in October 1938. She took a job the following month as the manager of an Edinburgh pharmacist but left two years later, deciding she wanted some sort of change. Indeed, Evelyn always seemed to be searching for something not fully defined, some elusive experience. After working a succession of unsatisfying jobs – her most recent being manager of the High Street pharmacist in Hornchurch – she decided to try her luck in London. At 7.20 p.m. on Sunday, 8 February 1942 – her 41st birthday – she purchased a ticket for London at Hornchurch Railway Station and told booking agent William Whatford she hoped to find something in the city to appease her restless spirit. She arrived in London on the 10 o'clock train at Baker Street Station. A porter spotted Evelyn on Platform 2 with her travel case and offered to carry it up the stairs. On blacked-out Baker Street, he hailed

Evelyn a taxi and placed her bags in the boot. She got in the backseat and gave driver Abraham Ash the address of a boarding house on Gloucester Place. Hours later, she was dead.

Patrolling the area where the murder occurred that night was War Reserve Constable Arthur Williams, working the No. 13 beat out of the Marylebone Police Station. He passed the bomb shelter at 11.20 p.m., shone his torch inside and saw nothing out of the ordinary. 'I think if anyone had been lying on the floor, I would have noticed them. It was a very quiet night with very few people about and no moon. It was very dark,' he said in his statement to police. The only people he saw that night were several soldiers enjoying a few precious hours of leave. He passed by the shelter three more times that evening but never noticed anything out of the ordinary.

War Reserve Constable Kenneth Begley, who also worked the area that night, encountered nothing more insidious than a few drunken servicemen. One airman in particular seemed to be in a hurry after, what Begley assumed, was an evening of debauchery. He spotted the man just before dawn outside the National Registration Office – between Baker and Glentworth streets – walking quickly from the direction of Edgware Road. He carried his respirator case over his shoulder and walked with his head down. When he looked up and saw Begley standing just a few feet away, he came to an abrupt halt and stared. The constable estimated the airman to be about 5 feet 8 inches tall with a slender yet powerful build. In the faint, pre-dawn light, the airman managed a smile and asked Begley if he knew the way to King's Cross Station. He spoke with an upper-class accent, his tone of voice slightly agitated. Begley gave the airman directions and watched him hurry off.

Begley's statement, along with all others taken in connection with the Hamilton murder, were copied and sent to Detective Chief Inspector Edward Greeno, a good cop with a tough reputation and a fondness for the drink. When responding to crime scenes outside London, he routinely stashed a bottle of whiskey away in his Murder Bag, a standard piece of kit with tweezers, magnifying glass, rubber gloves and other essentials carried by all detectives assigned to Scotland Yard's Murder Squad. The Home Office on this Wednesday morning had assigned Greeno the task of coordinating the Hamilton and Oatley murder investigations.

Described by one associate as the 'Edward G. Robinson of the Yard', Greeno brought sharp analytical skills to the job and an unabashed enthusiasm for physical confrontation. With a bulky – yet powerful – build, he thought nothing of smacking around the occasional lowlife. He often made a show of such beatings, removing his jacket and asking a bystander to make sure it didn't get creased while he dispensed with some rough justice. Greeno was not a timid man and enjoyed the inherent danger of police work. He had always sought out excitement and, in his younger years, took great pleasure speeding around London on his over-sized motorcycle. During the First World War, he served as a radio operator on an ammunition ship. The fact such vessels were prime targets for German torpedoes only appealed to his sense of adventure. When the ship docked at night in the various ports on England's south coast to load cargo, Greeno would mount his motorcycle and race off to London, opening the throttle wide on the country lanes and pushing the machine to its limits. In the city, he pursued pleasures craved by young men who don't expect to live long.

But survive Greeno did – and upon completing his military service, he joined the police. His streetwise demeanour and physical courage earned him a formidable reputation among those on both sides of the law. He made a name for himself in the 1930s on Scotland Yard's Flying Squad, taking down high-profile street gangs and notorious safecrackers. On the job, he developed a vast network of criminal informants. From Cockney pickpockets and Soho mobsters, to jewel thieves and pimps, Greeno took pride in the underworld sources he cultivated and used them to his advantage. Now on the Murder Squad, he hoped his contacts would continue to prove beneficial.

Since the discovery of Evelyn Oatley's body on Tuesday morning and Cherrill's subsequent findings later that same day, investigators had immediately begun cross-referencing the backgrounds of both women in search of a common thread. They found none. Hamilton's lonely existence and Oatley's promiscuous lifestyle were worlds apart.

Greeno increased the number of foot patrols in the Paddington and Soho areas. Female officers were placed undercover and put on the streets in an effort to draw the killer out. Detectives worked street corners and questioned prostitutes, asking if they had noticed anyone peculiar in recent days. Most women approached seemed more amenable to the idea of taking their chances with a killer than talking to police. Pimps with violent criminal records were pulled in for questioning; men seen fraternising with streetwalkers ran the risk of a police interrogation.

Greeno reviewed Cherrill's fingerprint evidence. If the same man had indeed committed both murders, he would surely kill again. The passing of mere hours between the two slayings, coupled with the sexual nature of the crimes, suggested a killer driven by a compulsion not easily satisfied. Greeno, who had set up his office at Tottenham Court Road Police Station, studied the wall map of Central London. The murders had occurred within a square-mile radius, indicating the killer's familiarity with – or close proximity to – the area. It was unlikely he would stray, but isolating the hunting grounds did little to assist Greeno in his investigation.

The murder of a prostitute, by the simple nature of her work, presented unique challenges even in peacetime. London's influx of military personnel, now the primary consumer of the city's sex trade, complicated matters. Countless trains rolled into London on a daily basis, transport ships steamed into its harbours, all disgorging soldiers, sailors and airmen who sought some relief from the constraints of military life. Consequently, Piccadilly Circus and all of Soho had become a bustling marketplace for sex.

The suspect pool was in a constant state of flux – and with no solid leads to follow, all Greeno could do was wait.

Margaret Lowe believed one had to rise above their circumstance.

The other women simply referred to her as 'The Lady' because of her debonair manner. She preferred long, elegant dresses to the more revealing attire worn by some of her street corner compatriots. On winter nights, she wrapped herself in a long coat and never stepped outside without donning her black felt hat. She often began her evenings with a drink at the Excelsior Pub in Charing Cross before making her rounds on Oxford Street. For fifteen years, she had worked the West End, never telling her now-deceased husband what she was really up to on her frequent 'shopping trips' to the capital. She and Fred had lived in Southend-on-Sea, where he owned a fancy goods store that ultimately went bankrupt. He died in 1932, leaving Margaret with a 5-year-old daughter to look after.

In 1934, she decided to make London her full-time home. She enrolled her daughter in a boarding school and moved to the city, setting up residence at 9/10 Gosfield Street. She had once pursued housecleaning as a more legitimate line of work, but preferred the financial benefit of working the streets. She knew the risks, of course. A Canadian soldier had roughed her up the month before, ransacking her flat when she refused a particular request. Not until she screamed 'Murder!' did he run from the building. When a neighbour appeared in her doorway and asked if the police should be called, Margaret had simply shrugged.

'What's the point?' she said, 'I'm sure he's got away by now.'

On this Wednesday night, she lit a cigarette and sauntered through Piccadilly Circus. The large neon signs, which in peacetime flashed and dazzled, clung lifelessly to the sides of buildings. Even the statue of Eros had retreated from view, concealed beneath large concrete slabs that loomed black and featureless in the dark. Margaret made her way toward Shaftesbury Avenue. Outside the Eros News Cinema, she stopped and spoke briefly with several women she recognised. The police, they observed, seemed to be out in greater numbers tonight – no doubt in response to the recent killings. Although the papers had yet to break the news, word of the slayings had spread from street corner to street corner. When the women in the group suggested Margaret stick with them for the evening, Margaret declined. She preferred working alone; she lit another cigarette and sauntered off, a solitary figure making her way down Shaftesbury Avenue.

Mary Heywood noticed the airman leaning against the bar, whisky in hand. He swirled the liquor in his glass, downed its contents in one gulp and ordered another. When he cast his gaze in her direction, she averted her eyes and stared at her watch. It was nearly 8 o'clock on the evening of Thursday, 12 February. The British Army officer she had met three months ago was on leave and had called her earlier in the afternoon to arrange a date.

She had arrived at the Universelle Brasserie in Piccadilly Circus several minutes early to ensure they got a table. Tobacco smoke hung grey and heavy over the crowd of American and British servicemen who jostled for space at the bar. Women, who Mary presumed were of questionable reputation, loitered nearby, angling for dates. Indeed, many men who entered the restaurant alone soon left with a willing companion for the night. Mary, sitting by herself, had already been solicited once this evening by a passing solider. In a rather cold tone, she had explained she was not in that line of work.

She glanced again at the time. When she looked up, the airman from the bar was standing beside her table. He was handsome in a hard-looking sort of way with a sharp chin and pronounced cheekbones. His eyes were creased in a smile beneath a crown of scruffy nut-brown hair. He looked slender but fit in his tunic, and Mary – herself 30 – guessed him to be somewhere in his late 20s. Assuming the airman's intentions, Mary explained she had a date.

The airman seemed not the least bit bothered and offered to buy her a drink. Somewhat taken back by the man's confidence and apparent determination, Mary surprised herself by accepting. He voiced his approval and sauntered back to the bar. He returned with two whiskies and took a seat. Mary thanked him and had a sip. The airman downed his with a quick flip of the wrist and asked Mary if she'd care to join him for dinner at the Trocadero. Mary stared into her glass and told him again she was waiting for someone. The airman didn't seem to mind.

'Oh, I'm sure we have plenty of time,' he said. 'In any case, I have to be back at my unit by 10.30.'

Mary took another sip of her drink and felt the airman's eyes all over her. He lit a cigarette and offered her a smoke – the very act bristled with confidence. When she looked up, he arched his eyebrows in an anticipatory gesture. It only seemed to add to his rakish charm. Mary glanced at the wall clock above the restaurant's entrance. Her army officer friend was nearly ½ hour late. She polished off the contents of her glass, made up her mind and nodded. The airman laughed and clapped his hands. He retrieved his overcoat, cap and respirator from the cloakroom and escorted Mary outside.

They walked in darkness across Piccadilly Circus to the Trocadero and ordered whisky in the cocktail lounge. The airman took a long pull on his drink and asked Mary where she lived. When she told him Wembley, he seemed disappointed and asked if she knew of any place nearby where they might have more privacy. Mary answered no.

'Are you a naughty girl?' he asked.

'There's nothing like that about me!' Mary said, her temper flaring.

The airman played his ace. He pulled a roll of cash from his tunic and began arranging the notes on the table, but the move failed to impress. Whatever curiosity had compelled Mary to accept this man's invitation had succumbed to a sense of regret. She grabbed her coat from the back of the chair and stood up, reminding the airman she had a date to keep. For the first time, he seemed to register Mary's apparent disapproval. He stood and urged her not to leave, saying he had £30 to finance a night on the town. His personality had suddenly changed. Gone was the cocky self-assuredness; he now seemed nervous, like a schoolboy addressing his first crush. Mary found something charming in this sudden change of demeanour and dismissed the previous display of bravado as an act. The nature of his smile had also changed: it was now more inquisitive than certain. Mary relented once more and scribbled her phone number on a paper serviette.

She flashed a sympathetic smile and headed for the door. The airman pocketed the phone number, followed her outside and offered to walk her back to the brasserie. The blackout had wreaked havoc with Mary's sense of direction and she blindly followed his lead, recognising her surroundings only when they crossed Piccadilly Circus along the west side of what she believed to be Haymarket. They turned down another dark block that seemed to be taking them in the opposite direction of the brasserie. When Mary protested, the airman said he wanted to find an appropriate place to kiss her goodnight. She scoffed at the idea and told him he needn't bother, but against her better judgement she followed him down another street. Passing what she recognised as the Captain's Club on St Alban's Street, the airman grabbed her by the arm and pulled her into a nearby doorway. He shrugged the respirator case off his left shoulder and wrapped his arms around Mary, pulling her close. She did not resist when he kissed her on the mouth, but struggled to break free when she felt his hands slide between her thighs.

'No,' Mary gasped.

When she tried to push him away, he slipped his hands further beneath her skirt. Mary lashed out with both arms and struck the airman on the wrists. He released his grip without comment and stepped aside but forcefully cupped her face in his hands when she tried to leave. In an instant, his hands dropped to her throat and began to squeeze. Mary opened her mouth to scream, but no sound came out. The airman tightened his grip and eyed her with a blank stare. His features betrayed no emotion and seemed almost lifeless. Mary clawed desperately at the airman's hands, but his grip remained steadfast. She pummelled his chest and brought her knee to his groin, but the lack of oxygen had drained her strength. The airman's face began to blur.

Then, there was nothing.

A nudging on the shoulder brought Mary Heywood back around.

A young man knelt over her with one hand on her shoulder. The other hand held a burning match, which cast a pallid glow down the length of her sprawled body. She lay with her feet pointing toward the street and her head propped upright by the door behind her. She could see her dress hiked above her thighs. The young man asked if she was okay. Mary opened her mouth to speak but could muster no more than a moan. When she tried to push herself up, she found her limbs numb and uncooperative. The taste of blood sat heavy on her lips. The Samaritan edged away to give her some room and passed the flickering match over the strewn contents of Mary's bag. The sight of her possessions scattered about the ground drew Mary fully into the present.

'What has he done?' she said, her voice cracking.

The man helped Mary to her feet before lighting another match and gathering up the contents of her handbag. As he reached for a compact mirror, he noticed a respirator case lying nearby and asked Mary if it belonged to her. When Mary answered no, he grabbed the case and suggested they notify the police. He took her arm and slowly helped her out of the doorway, mindful of her unsteady legs. It was 9.50 p.m. when they approached the corner of Haymarket and Piccadilly Circus, where Police Constable James Skinner happened to be passing by on his beat. Looking down Haymarket, Skinner saw a woman who appeared to be drunk, leaning against her date. Approaching the couple to see if they needed assistance, Skinner saw the situation was more dire than a drink too many. He asked the young man, holding the woman up, what had happened.

John Shine, an 18-year-old night porter, told Skinner he was walking around the back of St James's Market when he heard two people scuffling in a nearby doorway. As he drew closer to investigate, a man in uniform ran out in front of him and disappeared around the street corner. It was then, Shine said, that he first noticed the woman's legs lying across the doorway.

Skinner appraised the shaken woman and asked if she wanted to go to the hospital or provide investigators with a statement at the station.

'The police station,' the woman said, her voice barely registering above a whisper.

The couple met with Detective Sergeant Thomas Shepherd at the Savile Row Police Station and gave their statements. After ordering a constable to escort Mary to the nearest hospital, Shepherd took possession of the respirator case. He examined the exterior for traces of blood and found none. Opening the case, he noticed an RAF Regimental number – 525987 – printed on an inside label. A few phone calls to the RAF Service Police and a check of Air Ministry records matched the number to Gordon Frederick Cummins, a 27-year-old cadet of 14/32 Flight attached to A Squadron at St James's Close in Regent's Park.

The airman approached Catherine Mulcahy outside Oddendino's in Piccadilly Circus shortly before 10 p.m. Taking a long pull on his cigarette, he admired her curvaceous figure and dark-blonde hair, and asked her if she lived nearby. £2, she said, would buy him a good time in her room near Marble Arch.

The airman agreed to the terms, fished £2 out of his pocket and hailed a taxi. They rode in silence for several blocks, which made Catherine feel somewhat uneasy – most men at least attempted small talk. She liked to engage in some conversation, believing it leant a warm touch to an otherwise cold process. More importantly, it often revealed something about the man's character. Surviving in her line of work meant Catherine had to get an early read on people, but she was unsure what to make of the airman. He flashed her a smile, but it seemed to be nothing more than a façade; his eyes conveyed no emotion. Without saying a word, he slid off the seat and manoeuvred himself between Catherine's legs. He pushed up her skirt and began kissing her inner thighs, pushing his face hard against her flesh. Catherine tried to push the airman's head away and straighten her skirt.

The airman ignored Catherine's objections and kissed her down the length of one leg, stopping at the top of her black leather boot. His breath felt hot against her skin. In the front, the taxi driver seemed oblivious and kept his eyes on the road. Catherine continued pushing against the airman's forehead and pulling at his hair, asking him to stop. He groped her with rough hands and once more thrust his face between her thighs, and then he simply stopped. He retrieved his cap, which had fallen by Catherine's feet, and once again took his seat beside her. Staring out of the window, his face expressionless, the airman said nothing as Catherine pulled her skirt down around her knees. The taxi turned a corner and passed Hyde Park, its rolling greens now scarred by open trenches and anti-aircraft guns. When the airman suggested they stop and 'have some fun' in the park, Catherine demurred.

'Don't be silly,' she said. 'We'll be at my room soon.'

The taxi turned down a side street near Marble Arch and stopped in front of an anonymous redbrick building. Although Catherine roomed near Piccadilly Circus, she brought clients here to avoid revealing where she lived. The airman paid the driver and followed Catherine up to her room, a drab box with a bed in its centre and a small kitchenette. Discovering she was short a shilling for the electric meter, Catherine lit the gas fire. It crackled silently in its rusty grate and cast a flickering pattern on the worn carpet. She walked into the kitchen and placed the evening's take in an old biscuit tin. When she returned to the bedroom, the airman was undressing. Catherine undressed, keeping on only her boots and a bead necklace. She moved to the bed and pulled back the sheets. The airman shook his head and told her to lie on the floor. When Catherine refused, the airman crouched beside the bed and ran his hands along her bare legs. This he did for several minutes without saying a word before he jumped onto Catherine and brought his knees down hard on her stomach.

Her head shot off the pillow in a startled reflex and made an easy target of her neck. The airman gripped Catherine's throat with both hands and applied crushing pressure to her wind-pipe. Fighting to maintain consciousness, Catherine managed to bring one knee to her chest and thrust it forward, driving her boot into the airman's gut. He cried out and fell sideways off the bed, winded. Catherine sprang from the mattress and charged toward the door. She fled screaming into the hallway and banged on the door of the flat opposite. It was 11 p.m. Kitty McQuillen, a barmaid at a local pub, having just returned home from work, opened the door on her frantic neighbour, unsure what to make of the spectacle. From her doorway, Kitty could see what appeared to be a naked man in Catherine's flat, picking himself up off the floor.

'Save me! Please!' Catherine screamed. 'This man is trying to kill me! Send for the police!'

Kitty let Catherine into her flat just as the airman called out from the dark and politely asked for a match.

Kitty grabbed a book of matches off a table beside her front door and threw them across the hallway. Both women watched the man fumble for the book and strike a match. He dropped to his knees and began scavenging about the floor, looking for his clothing, asking Catherine at one point if she'd seen his boots. Catherine said nothing and remained standing behind Kitty. All the while, the man continued rooting around the flat in no apparent hurry. From their position in Kitty's doorway, the two women could hear the airman speaking to himself, but the words drifted across the hallway as a nonsensical mumble. When the match he was holding went out, he cursed loudly and lit another.

He eventually got dressed and moved into the bright light of the hallway.

The airman blinked and pulled £8 from his pocket. He dropped the notes in Kitty's doorway, mumbled his apologies to Catherine and fled the building.

5

Secrets to the Grave

Doris Jouannet waved her husband off at Paddington Station shortly after 9.30 p.m. After watching the train pull away, she returned to their nearby flat at 187 Sussex Gardens. Rain had fallen dark and slow for most of the day before giving way in the early evening to a light snowfall. Entering the flat, Doris ruffled the damp from her hair and hung up her coat. She walked down the hallway and past the dining room, ignoring the dirty dishes from that evening's dinner, which still sat on the table. In the bedroom, she took off the long dress she wore for her husband's benefit and put on a number that hung just below the knees. She threw on a matching shirt and pulled her favourite black coat from the wardrobe. Examining herself in the bureau mirror, she realised the snow would wreak havoc with her hair. She retrieved a black hat from her dresser drawer and pinned her hair beneath it. She gave one last appraising look in the mirror and left the room.

Henry Jouannet may have loved his wife, but trust was not a cornerstone of their relationship. He had married Doris at the Paddington Register Office in November 1935, a mere two months after he first propositioned her for sex at an Oxford Street bus stop. He had seen her about town before and knew, as he later told investigators, that Doris worked as a prostitute. Henry's job as manager of the Royal Court Hotel in Sloane Square kept him away most nights, though he tried – whenever possible – to have dinner with his wife. On those evenings, he would return home from work at 7 p.m. and enjoy the vegetable soup Doris always had waiting for him. At 9.30 p.m., he would walk back to Paddington Station and catch the train to Sloane Square. The short ride always gave him time to think. When he married Doris seven years earlier, Henry had hoped the ensuing stability would forever keep his wife from returning to the streets. But Doris – 35 years younger than Henry – had decided after several months that marriage was quite dull. While her husband worked nights at the hotel, Doris turned tricks in their Sussex Gardens flat.

'I'm living with an elderly gentleman who keeps me and pays the rent,' she said one evening to a street-corner friend. 'The money he gives me isn't enough, so I have to come out here and earn a few extra shillings. Of course, he doesn't know that I come out here to pick up men – and when I do, I can't go out until late in the evening.'

Henry returned to the Royal Court at 10 p.m. on the night of 12 February and retired to his room on the fourth floor. As Henry got into bed and turned out the light, Doris strolled down Tichbourne Street, near Edgware Road. The unpleasant weather had left the streets mostly deserted, but the airman who eventually approached seemed more than willing to part with his £2.

Margaret Lowe lay on the bed in her Gosfield Street flat with the blankets pulled up to her chin and a pillowcase draped over her face. It was 6 o'clock on the evening of Friday, 13 February. Detective Sergeant Leonard Blacktop slowly pulled back the sheets and grimaced at what he saw. Pink froth rimmed the dead woman's mouth and nose; a stocking was wrapped around her neck and tied in a knot just beneath the angle of her right jaw.

Police discovered the body after neighbours called the Tottenham Court Road Police Station to say a package had been sitting on Lowe's doorstep for the past three days. Blacktop had acquired a set of keys to Lowe's flat from a neighbour down the hall and let himself in. He moved slowly down a narrow hallway, past a small sitting room, into the kitchen. When he tried opening a door on the far side of the room, he discovered it was locked. Unable to find a key, he kicked the door in and found the bedroom beyond flanked in darkness. He fumbled for a light switch and saw the covered mass beneath the blankets. In a flat next door, neighbours were comforting Lowe's 15-year-old daughter, Barbara, who had just arrived in town from her Southend boarding school for a weekend visit.

Greeno and Cherrill arrived at the flat shortly after 6.30 p.m. The investigators made their way into the bedroom and inspected the scene. The room had a few sticks of furniture. A night table sat in one corner and a worn rug lay in front of a small fire grate. Divisional Police Surgeon Alexander Baldie kneeled beside the bed, examining the body. The woman lay on her back with her legs apart but her knees drawn up. A jagged, 5-inch gash in her abdomen had laid her intestines bare. A gaping wound measuring 10 inches in length ran along the right side of her groin. The killer had stabbed the victim once just above the vagina and shoved a wax candle inside her. Two large knives, covered in gore, lay across the dead woman's thighs; two more lay on the sheets between her legs alongside a fire poker with a broken handle. Baldie estimated the time of death, based on body temperature and the onset of rigor mortis, to have been sometime in the early morning hours.

While Greeno observed the body, Cherrill moved about the apartment with his magnifying glass at the ready. He found several prints on the base of a candleholder sitting on the bedroom mantelpiece. Partially smudged impressions were also found on a nearby beer glass. Both items were bagged as evidence, along with a nearly empty bottle of Hammerton's Oatmeal Stout found on the kitchen table. In the kitchen, Greeno found three ration books – all in the name of Margaret Lowe – scattered on a countertop. The cutlery drawer was open and disorganised. It was from here, Greeno surmised, the killer had found his weapons of choice. Pushed between a wooden tub and large cardboard carton on the floor, Greeno found Lowe's handbag. Unlike the Hamilton and Oatley crime scenes, the killer had not taken any money. Two folded pound notes sat near the top of the bag and another two were in a side pocket. Greeno jotted down the notes' serial numbers and asked Findlay to see if any of it could be traced. Greeno sifted through the remainder of the bag's contents: a handkerchief, two cigarettes and a pillbox. All of it was bagged for fingerprinting back at the Yard.

At 8.30 p.m., Spilsbury arrived at the flat to take possession of the body. He pulled on a pair of surgeon's gloves and removed the candle. He noted the whites of the eyes were flushed with blood and the nose clogged with blood and mucus. Lying in a pool of congealed blood between the victim's legs, Spilsbury found a used male contraceptive. Over his shoulder, he told Greeno the cause of death appeared to be manual strangulation.

Divisional Detective Inspector Leonard Clare stood in the bedroom at 187 Sussex Gardens. Having returned home at seven that evening for dinner, Henry Jouannet had alerted police after finding the bedroom door locked and his wife unresponsive to his increasingly frantic knocking. Police Constable William Payne arrived at the flat within minutes, kicked the door in and made the gruesome discovery.

Payne called his commanding officer from a neighbouring flat at 7.50 p.m. and told him to notify Scotland Yard's CID. Ten minutes later, Divisional Detective Inspector Leonard Clare arrived on the scene. In the bedroom, a small electric fireplace cast a flickering puddle of weak, orange light on the floor. Doris Jouannet, wearing an open, black nightgown, lay diagonally across the bed against the opposite wall, the sheets dark with blood. The killer had wrapped a silk stocking around her neck and draped another across her right thigh. Her right arm lay at a sharp angle from her torso; her left arm was draped across her upper left thigh with the hand resting between her legs. She was tall, at least six feet, and thin. She had been stabbed repeatedly in the pubic area and slashed across the left breast. A patch of skin had been removed from her left cheek. A 6-inch vertical wound ran from below the navel to the vaginal entrance, and there was another deep cut on the left side of the groin. Studying the gruesome scene, Clare noticed a bloodstained razor sitting on the bedside table.

Greeno was still in Margaret Lowe's flat when a motorcycle messenger, dispatched by Scotland Yard, arrived to inform him another body had been found in Sussex Gardens. From one murder scene to another, Greeno reached the Paddington address shortly after 10.30 p.m. with Spilsbury in tow.

Cherrill arrived at the scene approximately 30 minutes later. For the past 2½ hours, he had busied himself, dusting the evidence taken from Margaret Lowe's apartment, lifting prints and trying to find corresponding matches in the Yard's print index. The placement of prints he found on the base of the candleholder was indicative of a right hand, meaning who ever grasped the holder had removed the candle found in the victim with their left hand. Now, armed once more with his magnifying glass, he steeled himself for a long night.

Spilsbury autopsied the bodies of Doris Jouannet and Margaret Lowe at Paddington Mortuary on Saturday, 14 February. In both women, he found haemorrhaging in the linings of the larynx. The cause of death in both cases, Spilsbury told Greeno, was strangulation by ligature. The knife wounds inflicted on the two bodies were post mortem.

Greeno returned to his office at the Tottenham Court Road Police Station and called Cherrill, who had discouraging news: the prints found on the mirror, wardrobe and bedroom door in Jouannet's bedroom all belonged to the victim. Greeno hung up the phone and leaned back in his chair. Four coloured pins, one for each murder, now marked the large wall map of Central London. When the phone on his desk rang, he half expected it to be news of another body. Instead, it was a detective from the West End Central Police Station with word of an arrest.

Having arrived back at his barracks in St James's Close at 3.30 that Saturday morning – more than 4 hours past curfew – Gordon Frederick Cummins was caught by a sentry as he tried to sneak into his billet. When told by the on-duty orderly sergeant that police had called to say his respirator had been recovered at the scene of a crime, Cummins was incredulous. He said he drank the night away at a party and misplaced the respirator at a pub afterwards.

The sergeant told Cummins the police wished to speak with him and ordered the airman to wait in his billet. At 5.45 a.m., Detective Constable Charles Bennett arrived at St James's Close with orders to bring Cummins to the West End Central Police Station for questioning. Cummins was summoned to the orderly sergeant's room and found Bennett – accompanied by a uniformed constable – waiting to bring him in. The detective told Cummins he was not under arrest and led him to a waiting patrol car. The three men rode in silence to the station, where Cummins was searched and relieved of his wallet, cigarette case and a comb with missing teeth.

At 8 a.m., Detective Sergeant Thomas Shepherd arrived at the station. Before interviewing Cummins, who sat waiting in an interrogation room, he went through the airman's wallet and found Mary Heywood's phone number scrawled across a folded piece of paper. It was 9.30 a.m. when Shepherd sat down with Cummins and advised him of his rights.

'You answer the description of an airman who assaulted a woman in St Alban's Street, Haymarket, at about 9.45 last night,' Shepherd said. 'A service respirator with your regimental number was left behind by the person responsible.'

Cummins seemed not the least bit perturbed. He smiled and told Shepherd he had hit the town somewhat harder than normal the previous night, downing numerous drinks at various pubs before winding up at the Universelle Brasserie. There, at the bar, he consumed several more brandies and whiskies before chatting up some young woman. After that, he said, the evening's events were lost to an impenetrable haze.

'I don't remember what happened after I left the restaurant with the woman,' Cummins said. 'I certainly don't remember leaving her. I deeply regret what has happened, and I am willing to pay her compensation.'

Shepherd nodded and got to his feet.

'I'm arresting you,' he said, 'and charging you with assault.'

Shepherd drove to St James's Close to search Cummins's billet. In a jacket hanging from the bedpost of Cummins's bunk, the detective found a gold fountain pen engraved with the initials 'D.J.' A kit bag sitting at the foot of the bed contained a crumpled shirt and white towel, both of which had what appeared to be several blood splatters on them. He returned to the West End Central Police Station and ordered a constable to deliver the towel and shirt to the police laboratory in Hendon. Armed with the pen, Shepherd again questioned Cummins and asked him to explain the initials, informing the airman the body of a woman named Doris Jouannet had been found the night before. Cummins, still exuding a calm demeanour, said the pen wasn't his. How it got in his jacket, he insisted, was a mystery.

It was at this point Shepherd left the interrogation room and notified Greeno of Cummins's arrest.

On Sunday, 15 February, Greeno dispatched detectives to interview members of the suspect's family. Marjorie Cummins refused to accept the charge filed against her husband. She described Gordon to Detective Sergeant Thomas Mead as a caring man who returned home at every opportunity. She was unaware of his nightly sojourns into Soho and his fraternising with prostitutes. Likewise, Cummins's father – an official with the Home Office who oversaw a school for juvenile delinquents – voiced his disbelief when confronted by investigators. His son, he said, had never displayed any violent tendencies while growing up, nor was there any family history of mental instability.

Greeno, meanwhile, paid a visit to the barracks at St James's Close and questioned Cummins's bunkmates, who described the airman as being 'cheerful and normal', and quite a rogue with the ladies. A search of the premises turned up a cigarette case stashed in the back of a cupboard in the barrack kitchen. The initials L.W. were engraved on the case's lid. Victim Evelyn Oatley had also gone by the name Leta Ward. Inspecting the outside of the barracks, Greeno saw the building offered easy access to Prince Albert Road in the front and St James's Mews along the back, meaning a cadet could theoretically sneak in and out as he pleased. All cadets were required to sign in and out in the billet's entry hall when coming and going. Greeno examined the 'booking-in' book and saw Cummins had signed out on the nights of the murders and signed back in by the 10.30 p.m. weekday curfew. The entries, however, had been made in pencil and would therefore have been easy to manipulate in the event of a curfew violation.

The case against Cummins took another damning turn that evening when Henry Jouannet identified the fountain pen found in Cummins's barracks – and the watch and broken-toothed comb removed from his tunic at the West End Central Police Station – as belonging to Doris. He had last seen the pen and comb, he said, sitting on the night-table in their bedroom.

Doris had been wearing the watch the last day he saw her alive. A call to Evelyn Oatley's estranged husband in Blackpool confirmed he had given her a cigarette case matching the description of the one found in Cummins's barracks to his wife just weeks before her murder.

On Monday, 16 February, Greeno, along with Divisional Detective Inspector Leonard Clare and Sergeant Alexander Findlay, interviewed Cummins at Brixton Prison. The airman greeted his inquisitors with a smile when they entered the interrogation room. Greeno introduced himself and immediately got down to business, foregoing any customary pleasantries and demanding Cummins detail his movements over the past week.

Cummins shrugged and said he had ventured out on multiple nights the week before, drinking heavily with friends and taking pleasure in the company of several women. He was unable to provide details, however, saying too much drink had clouded his memory. He said he remembered meeting Mary Heywood in the Universelle Brasserie but could not recall anything that transpired between the two of them after leaving the restaurant. When he finished speaking, he leaned back in his chair and watched Greeno place Doris Jouannet's fountain pen, comb and watch on the table, along with Evelyn Oatley's cigarette case. Cummins said none of the items were his, but could not explain how they wound up amongst his possessions.

'As a result of the inquiries I have made,' Greeno said, gathering up the items on the table, 'you will be brought up to Bow Street Police Court tomorrow morning and charged with murder.'

Cummins, as he always did, took the news with no outward sign of emotion.

On Tuesday, 17 February 1942, one day short of this 28th birthday, Gordon Frederick Cummins was charged with the murders of Evelyn Oatley, Margaret Lowe and Doris Jouannet at Bow

Street Police Station. Although Greeno believed the airman to be responsible for the murder of Evelyn Hamilton, there was insufficient evidence to charge him in the case. Cherrill fingerprinted Cummins following the arraignment. When Cummins signed the fingerprint card, he did so using his left hand.

Cherrill rushed back to the Yard and compared Cummins's prints with those taken from the various crime scenes. Specifically, Cherrill was searching for 'points of similarity' between the impressions, or certain characteristics in the crime-scene prints that appear 'in the same position and relation to other ridges on the suspect's prints'. Comparing the print of Cummins's right ring finger to those lifted from the candlestick holder in Margaret Lowe's flat, Cherrill found sixteen points of similarity. More than three dozen other points of similarity were found between prints left on the bottle of stout and beer glass in Lowe's flat and Cummins's right thumb, forefinger, little finger and middle finger. Likewise, multiple points of similarity were found between the prints left on the tin opener and broken piece of mirror in Evelyn Oatley's apartment, and the little finger and thumb of Cummins's left hand.

Cummins's trial commenced on Monday, 27 April, at the Old Bailey before Mr Justice Asquith, with Christmas Humphreys and G.B. McClure representing the Crown Prosecution Service, and John Flowers and Victor Durand appearing for the defence. The trial was an unspectacular affair, lasting just a day and a half. Both Greeno and Cherrill testified, detailing the evidence stacked against Cummins and offering the defence little to work with. Cummins himself took the stand and prattled off the story he'd told from the start, saying he had been too drunk to recall the events of the evenings in question. His performance did not impress the jury.

The twelve-man panel convened at 4 p.m. on Tuesday, 28 April, to consider the evidence and took a mere 35 minutes to reach a verdict: 'Guilty of murder.' Cummins stood at the bar, his features having taken on a pallid hue. Behind him, in the public gallery, his wife sobbed loudly. The court clerk approached the bench and placed upon Justice Asquith's head a black piece of silk, the symbolic cap all judges wore before handing down a death sentence.

'Gordon Frederick Cummins,' Asquith said. 'After a fair trial you have been found guilty, and on a charge of murder, as you know, there is only one sentence which the law permits me to pronounce, and that is that you be taken from this place to a lawful prison, and thence to a place of execution, and that you be there hanged by the neck until you are dead. And may the Lord have mercy upon your soul.'

Cummins spent the last two months of his life in a dank cell with stone walls and floor just 20 feet from the gallows. Interviewed by the prison psychiatrist and allowed to meet with family, he never once confessed to the killings or offered a motive for his crimes. Investigators, meanwhile, suspected Cummins of murdering 19-year-old Maple Church the previous year but were unable to conclusively link him to the crime.

Children found the girl's partially clad body in a bombed-out house less than a mile from Cummins's billet on the morning of 13 October 1941. Maple, who worked as a prostitute in the Soho area, was reportedly last seen in the company of a man wearing a military uniform. She had been beaten and strangled with a ligature; wounds on her hands and arms suggested she had put up a fight. Examining the bruises on the girl's body, pathologist Bentley Purchase determined that the killer's left hand was stronger than the right. Although detectives pursued numerous leads, the case went nowhere.

On the morning of his execution – Thursday, 25 June – Cummins sat down and penned a letter to his wife, saying he had no recollection of committing the crimes for which he was about to die. 'Although I don't know, I think I must be guilty,' he wrote. 'The evidence is overwhelming.' His end came at 8 o'clock just as the air raid sirens across London began to howl. The man the papers dubbed the 'Blackout Ripper' went to the gallows without uttering a word of remorse, taking the reasons for his murderous rampage with him to the grave.

6

The Luton Sack Murder

A grey fog hung low over the murky surface of the River Lea at Luton on the afternoon of Friday, 19 November 1943. Two corporation sewer men walked along the river's soggy banks, not paying much heed to the refuse that always seemed to litter the shallow riverbed. Near the Vauxhall Motor factory, the workers descended the embankment and approached the shore to measure the water level. As they set up their equipment, they saw what appeared to be a large bundle lying among the reeds, partially submerged in 6 inches of water.

One of the men waded through the shallows and pulled the bundle closer to shore, surprised by its considerable weight. Whatever the object, it had been wrapped in four large potato sacks, which the workers began to remove out of natural curiosity. Pulling away a sodden layer of burlap, they were startled to see the battered face of a dead woman. A ghastly cut down the side of one cheek sent both men scrambling back in horror and running to find a police call box. It was 2.15 p.m. Officers arrived on the scene within minutes and removed the sacking, revealing the naked body beneath. The woman's wrists and ankles had been bound together and her knees tied up around her chest. The killer had gone out of his way to make identification of the victim all but impossible. The woman's face had been mercilessly battered, resulting in heavy swelling. In addition to the wound down the cheek, another gruesome gash stretched the length of her brow. One ear clung to her head by a thin strip of skin. The wounds were so severe, the face almost looked inhuman.

'Whatever rings she may have been wearing had been removed,' noted Chief Superintendent Frederick Cherrill. 'Nor was there any feminine adornment, such as a necklace, which might have provided some clue. Even her false teeth were missing.'

Questioned by police at the scene, the two sewer men said they had tested water levels in exactly the same spot at 4 the previous afternoon but had seen nothing out of the ordinary. Whoever dumped the body, then, had done so only recently – most likely the night before, or sometime in the pre-dawn hours. Vauxhall factory workers had noticed the bundle lying in the reeds early that morning but had thought nothing of it. Inspector Finch of Luton CID, pacing the scene, saw no evidence to suggest the murder had occurred alongside the river. Indeed, the killer most likely trussed the body to move it with minimal hassle.

Finch, a trench-coated figure in the afternoon fog, marvelled at the killer's audacity. Just 4 feet up from the water's edge, a public walkway traced the path of the river. At any time of day you could find couples ambling by or cyclists pedalling past. Workers came and went from the Vauxhall factory at regular shift intervals, meaning the area was never entirely free of people. Either dragging or carrying his heavy load, the killer would have had to climb down the 4-foot embankment to the shoreline to dump the body. Deciding the mere nature of the case warranted outside help, Finch asked his chief constable to contact Scotland Yard.

At the time of the murder, the Yard was composed of four primary departments. 'A' Department covered administrative and general duties, which included everything from maintaining crowd control and security at sporting events and royal processions, to cracking down on the scourge of illegal street gambling.

'B' Department – the largest of the four – handled road safety and enforced traffic laws. 'D' Department oversaw the Yard's general organisation, while 'C' Department (Criminal Investigation) handled crimes of a violent nature: the murders that made headlines and other nasty offences the press deemed not so glamorous. More than 1,000 plain-clothed detectives worked within 'C' Department, assigned to Special Branch or manning the 'Flying' and 'Murder' squads. One such man was Chief Inspector William Chapman, known by many on the force as 'Cherub' due to his portly physique and permanently blushed cheeks.

It was dark when Chapman arrived at the scene with Home Office Pathologist Dr Keith Simpson. He walked down the embankment, squinting against the glare of arc lamps set up along the water's edge. Mist swirled and danced in white cones of light. Finch approached and introduced himself. He told Chapman tyre tracks had been found near a bridge no more than 20 yards from where the body was found. Casts were being made, as officers continued canvassing the area for clues. Chapman nodded and walked to where the body lay. Simpson appeared beside him as he bent low over the woman, grimacing when he saw the severity of the wounds. 'I don't think her own mother would recognise her if she had one,' Chapman said, watching as Simpson began his cursory examination.

The pathologist gently moved an arm and found full rigor mortis had set in. The skin – though goose-bumped – was not yet wrinkled, suggesting the body had been submerged in the water for a relatively short period of time. Simpson placed a hand against the woman's torso and slid another under her back to roughly gauge the body temperature. He mentally ran through some calculations and got to his feet. The estimated time of death, he told Chapman and Finch, was somewhere between 12 and 24 hours before the two workmen made their discovery. He would know more following a full autopsy and asked that the body be taken to Dunstable and Luton Hospital. There, the next morning, Simpson sought to ascertain the cause of death. The victim was a well-nourished woman, no more than 35 years of age, with dark brown hair and eyes. He cut the cords bounding the woman's wrists and ankles, untied her knees and stretched the body out to its full length of 5 feet 3 inches. Bruising where the cords had been fastened around her legs suggested she was still alive when the killer tied her up.

Simpson examined the woman's head. She had been struck with tremendous force by a blunt instrument on the left side of her face. The bones were shattered and the jaw was fractured in multiple places; the blow had loosened her skull bones and bruised the brain. Simpson gently turned the woman's head and studied the less-severe bruising on the right side of the face, which he believed to be the result of her falling to the floor after being attacked. He attributed a split running up the back-right side of her skull to her head possibly hitting a piece of furniture as she fell. She was undoubtedly unconscious and bleeding when her killer bound her with rope.

Based on the amount of blood around the wounds, Simpson estimated the woman died about 40 minutes after being struck. Heavy bruising around her neck suggested the killer had tried to strangle the woman with his right hand before delivering the fatal blow. Cuts and bruises on the front and back of her hands, coupled with dark bruising on her elbows and shoulder blades, told the pathologist the woman – although pinned to the floor – had fought for her life. She had borne at least one child and was almost six months pregnant at the time of her death. Aside from a surgical scar on her abdomen, there were no physical abnormalities that could assist in identification.

Her fingerprints were taken and sent to Cherrill at the Yard in the hope of ascertaining her name. Cherrill set about the task with his usual degree of thoroughness, carefully mapping each of the victim's prints and making note of the distinguishing characteristics in the loops and whirls. 'The first object in any murder inquiry,' Cherrill later remarked, 'is to establish the identity of the victim as soon as possible. This enables one to check with relatives or friends and trace the movements of the victim prior to the crime.' He began sorting through the Yard's print index and comparing those on file with those of the woman in the morgue, hoping she may have had some previous encounter with the police. Meanwhile, on another forensics front, the sacks used to wrap the body were sent to the police laboratory in Hendon for chemical analysis. Lead investigator Chapman, waiting for science to do its thing, ordered the woman's face be photographed and released to the public before decomposition further altered her appearance. Plaster casts were made of her jaw in the hope of procuring her identity through dental records.

With nothing else to go on, Chapman pushed forward with his investigation. His team of detectives began reviewing missing-persons reports and checking with dry cleaners to see if any women had failed to pick up their laundry in recent weeks. Detectives stood outside the Vauxhall factory and questioned workers coming and going. As investigators pounded the pavement, the woman's post-mortem photograph began appearing in shop windows and newspapers across the country. The gruesome image even appeared on the screen at cinemas, accompanied by a plea: 'Murder: Police are still anxious to establish identity of this unfortunate woman. Here is her picture. If any person can help please communicate with Police immediately.' Sitting in a London cinema one afternoon when the image appeared between newsreels was the victim's daughter, who failed to recognise as her own mother the large, battered face looming over the audience.

When Cherrill reported back to Chapman and said the woman's fingerprints had failed to yield an identity, the lead investigator hoped the sacks used to wrap the body would point detectives in the right direction. At the police laboratory, chemical analysis revealed only that the sacks, previous to the murder, had held sugar, soda and potatoes. One sack, marked with the name of a local produce dealer, seemed to offer a promising lead. The trail, however, led nowhere after the dealer told Chapman he had no way of checking what individual sack went where. Analysis of the rope also proved disheartening: it was of a common variety and easily available to the public.

The tyre tracks found near the scene proved to be a dead-end when investigators traced them to a milk van that drove through the area each morning on its daily rounds. Now, weeks into the investigation, Chapman had seemingly hit a dead end. Although the ongoing review of missing-persons cases had thus far resulted in numerous 'missing' women being tracked down and ruled out as the victim, it had done nothing to bring the team closer to identifying the woman in the mortuary.

The case presented the occasional odd glimmer of hope, but circumstances never panned out. Nearly forty people asked to view the body, believing the woman might be a missing relative. Nine people identified the victim as being a loved one, but follow-up inquiries by the police revealed the identifications to be honest mistakes. Across London, the woman's battered features continued to adorn shop windows.

Two boys, aged 14 and 15, stopped one afternoon outside a tobacconists to gaze at the image. It was both hideous and slightly familiar. The eyes were closed, and the immense swelling gave the woman a somewhat bulbous appearance. A large, black contusion was clearly visible above the right eye. The boys stood fixated for several minutes, struck by the woman's uncanny resemblance to their mother, who had left home some weeks earlier and not come back. They returned to their house in Regent Street, Luton, and told their father what they saw. The man told his sons they were being silly; their mother had simply gone away to spend time with their grandmother. He had been telling the same story to friends and acquaintances.

Chapman and his men continued canvassing neighbourhoods. Detectives, armed with photographs of the mystery woman, went from door-to-door without success. When one officer called at the house on Regent Street, a young boy answered the door. The detective introduced himself and asked the boy if he recognised the woman in the picture. The boy shook his head, not mentioning it looked like his mother who seemed to have recently disappeared.

Just as the days had stretched into weeks, the weeks now stretched into months. Chapman, with no worthwhile leads and no new angles to explore, found himself growing increasingly desperate. The woman had since been confined to a pauper's grave, and the killer – for all Chapman knew – was a military man now serving somewhere overseas. For several weeks, officers had been scouring rubbish tips, gutters and dustbins for bloodied clothing the killer might have thrown away. The result of their efforts was a giant pile of filthy, rotten clothing in a London police garage. Short on ideas, Chapman ordered his men to once again sift through the pile and search every inch of detritus to see what may have been missed the first time around. Anxious for any sort of lead, he joined in the search of a rubbish tip in Luton one overcast morning in February.

His hands thrust deep in his pockets and his collar turned up against the cold, Chapman watched his men scour mountains of rubbish for anything that might put the investigation on track. Not far from where he stood, he eyed a dog sniffing about, nudging wastepaper and empty tins with a curious nose. The black-and-white mutt paid no attention to Chapman but seemed most interested in a random scrap on the ground. The dog pawed furtively at its find and gave it a good sniff before scraping it up and trotting off with the dark-coloured scrap hanging from its mouth.

Perhaps out of curiosity, or maybe police instinct, Chapman followed the dog and watched it run up to a young girl, who took the piece of rag from the dog's mouth. The detective approached and asked the girl if he could see what the mutt had found. She passed over a piece of black fabric, covered in canine drool, which Chapman took between thumb and forefinger. It appeared to have been torn from a coat and bore a worn inch of tape with 'V 12247' written across it. Chapman immediately recognised it as a dry cleaner's tag.

'If ever the long arm of coincidence reached out in bringing a murder to justice,' wrote Cherrill after the event, 'it was in the Luton mystery.'

The number on the tape led police to Sketchley's, a dry cleaners in Luton, where they learned the strip came from a coat dropped off by one Mrs Rene Manton several months prior. The store clerk checked his records and provided the woman's address in Regent Street. The information was relayed to Chapman, who reviewed the casebook and saw Regent Street – and the Manton house in particular – had already been canvassed by his men. Realising he had nothing to lose and everything to gain, he called on the Manton residence himself. He knocked on the door one grey afternoon and was rendered momentarily speechless when Manton's 8-year-old daughter opened it. The detective, struck by the girl's uncanny likeness to the dead woman, knew his prey was near. Chapman showed the girl his identification card and asked if her mother was home.

'No,' the girl replied, 'she's gone away. Is anything wrong?'

'I'm just making some enquiries,' Chapman said before asking the girl if he could see a picture of her mother. The girl disappeared and came back a moment later, a framed photograph in her hands. Chapman struggled not to show any reaction when he saw, smiling up at him from behind the glass, the woman now lying in an anonymous grave. The detective offered the girl a warm smile and asked where he might find her father. Bertie Horace William Manton, she said, worked as an engine driver at the National Fire Service Station in Luton. Chapman arrived at the station later that afternoon and asked Manton where police might find his wife.

'She left me some time ago,' he said, 'and is working somewhere in London.'

'Why did she leave?' Chapman asked.

Manton sighed and said the marriage was a combative one on account of her fraternising with men in uniform and his dalliance with a local barmaid. Tensions had finally boiled over, he said, on the evening of 25 November. Each accused the other of being unfaithful, prompting Rene to pack a bag and storm from the house. Where she went, exactly, Manton couldn't say. He told Chapman she was either staying at her mother's or visiting a brother in Grantham. Chapman jotted the information down in his notebook and pulled from his coat pocket the woman's postmortem photograph.

'Is this your wife?' Chapman asked.

Manton stared briefly at the picture and shook his head.

'No, that's not her,' he said. 'She still writes to me.'

He produced several crumpled envelopes and passed them to Chapman, who studied the postmark on each and saw they'd been sent from Hampstead between December 1943 and February 1944. Each letter appeared to have been read more than once. On the envelope, Chapman noticed Hampstead had been spelled without the 'p.' When the detective asked him to write the word 'Hampstead' on a piece of paper, Manton penned 'Hamstead' in a shaky scrawl.

Chapman, convinced he had his man, called Scotland Yard and asked Frederick Cherrill to come and dust the Manton residence. Cherrill soon arrived with his bag of brushes and powders, and set to work. What he needed was a well-defined print – one to compare with those taken from the dead woman that would confirm or disprove her identity. 'I decided that the kitchen would be the best place to look,' Cherrill later recalled, 'for that is the usual realm of the housewife.'

In 1902, when the Yard cracked its first case through fingerprint detection and analysis, its print index had been confined to a single filing cabinet. Breaking into a home in South London, Harry Jackson had climbed through a window and left a thumbprint on the freshly painted sill. A detective sergeant named Collins had discovered and photographed the print, and compared it to those of known criminals in the Yard's small index. Through visual comparisons, he was able to match it to Jackson, a 41-year-old labourer and small-time thief. Police nabbed Jackson, who pleaded not guilty at the Old Bailey to charges of stealing billiard balls. A jury found him guilty based on the fingerprint evidence and sentenced him to seven years in prison.

Three years later, fingerprint evidence played its first role in a capital case. Thomas Farrow was found murdered alongside his severely bludgeoned wife in the back of their oil-and-colour shop on Deptford High Street. The cashbox, emptied of its contents, bore a thumbprint on the lid. The print was photographed and compared to others in the Yard's 80,000-print catalogue, but investigators were unable to find a match. The case stumbled along until witnesses came forward and reported seeing two brothers, Albert and Alfred Stratton, hanging about the store the morning of the robbery.

The brothers – well acquainted with police – were taken into custody and fingerprinted, resulting in Scotland Yard matching Alfred's right thumbprint with the one found on the cashbox. When the case went to trial, Detective Inspector Charles Stockley Collins of the Yard's Fingerprint Department showed the jury side-by-side enlargements of the two prints and their eleven points of similarity. Collins went so far as to fingerprint a member of the jury and compare the prints in the witness box.

Caught out by a fingerprint, the brothers went to the gallows on 23 May 1905. The 'Deptford Murders' as the case came to be known – or 'The Mask Murders,' because the killers wore black stockings to try and hide their identities – established the legitimacy of fingerprint identification and secured Scotland Yard's reputation in the field. Consequently, the Fingerprint Department never seemed short on work. Police departments across the country routinely sent the Yard prints for analysis, and overseas law enforcement agencies sought the Yard's advice on all aspects of the burgeoning science. It was work that never ceased to fascinate Cherrill.

Since the days of Harry Jackson and the Stratton brothers, Scotland Yard's Fingerprint Department had evolved just as rapidly as the science in which it specialised. Its catalogue of prints, once limited to those of known criminals operating in London, had become a national database of various swirls and loops, the right combination of which could possibly reveal the killer's identity.

Now, with his trademark magnifying glass in hand, Cherrill systematically swept every surface in the Manton kitchen. He opened drawers and cupboards, examining pots, pans, cutlery, glassware and dishes. He passed his eager eye over ornaments on shelves and pictures hanging on the wall. The results were extraordinary: 'Every article had been carefully cleaned and polished. The crockery gleamed from repeated washing and scouring,' he noted. 'Cupboards, shelves, and every nook and cranny in all the various rooms were tested by every means known to us, without results.'

The absence of prints in the kitchen, far from ruling Manton out as a suspect, only aroused Cherrill's suspicions. He opened the door to a storage space beneath the stairs and saw several shelves cluttered with glass jars and bottles. Upon closer inspection, he noticed something strange: although the walls and shelves were covered in a thick layer of dust, the jars were spotless. He powdered each jar in search of prints and, as expected, found nothing. While it was obvious someone had gone to great lengths to remove all traces of fingerprints, that alone was not enough to warrant an arrest in the case.

Cherrill shone his torch into the dark recesses of the cellar space and saw one jar – a pickle jar – sitting back from the others. Immediately, he saw that whoever wiped the house down had missed this particular item. He picked the jar up by the edges of the lid, being careful not to disturb the grime-covered glass. With a steady hand he applied powder to the brush and dusted the jar, revealing on its side a thumbprint. Cherrill rolled lifting tape over the swirling pattern and pressed it gently onto a white index card. He slipped the print and the jar into his bag and returned to the Yard, where he compared the print to those taken from the victim. It did not take long for his experienced eye to identify more than enough points of similarity between the print from the jar and that of the victim's left thumb. Three months after the gruesome discovery, the dead woman had a name.

Manton was promptly taken into custody.

'I killed her, but it was only because I lost my temper,' Manton said, sitting in the charge room of the Luton Police Station with a cigarette clenched between trembling fingers. 'I didn't intend to. She left me about last Christmas twelve months, and was away for five months … I persuaded her to mend her ways and come back to me for the children's sake.'

As Chapman took notes, Manton detailed the events surrounding his wife's death. Their reconciliation had not been a happy one on account, he said, of her dismay over being pregnant again. The truth was that husband and wife had long ago fallen out of love with one another. Manton only wanted his wife to return home for the sake of their children. Tensions in the house built over time, as he and Rene bickered over the slightest irritation. The animosity between the two reached a flashpoint on the afternoon of Thursday, 18 November 1943.

The children were out of the house and the couple had finished dinner. He brewed a pot of tea and brought it out to the sitting room, where they both sat and drank by the fire. As he poured himself another cup, Manton told Rene he was heading down to the pub that evening to help behind the bar. Rene exploded, accusing him of wanting to sneak off and spend his last night on leave from the National Fire Service with the barmaid. She leapt from her chair and threw a cup of hot tea in Manton's face.

'I lost my temper, picked up a heavy wooden stool and hit her about the head and face several times,' Manton said. 'She fell backwards towards the wall and then on to the floor. When I came to my senses again, I see what I'd done. I saw she was dead and decided I had to do something to keep her away from the children. I then undressed her and got four sacks from the cellar, cut them open and tied her up in them. I then carried her down to the cellar and left her there. I had washed the blood up before the children came home to tea. I hid the bloodstained clothing in a corner near the copper.'

The children had their supper, Manton said, and left the house again to meet friends and spend the evening at the cinema. After sunset, and with the house to himself, Manton brought his wife's body up from the cellar. He tied the unwieldy bundle to the handlebars of his bike and pedalled off down the street in the direction of the river. He approached the edge of the bank along Osborne Road. A thin veil of mist rolled off the water. The pathway that followed the river's edge was deserted, as he untied his wife's body from the handlebars. With considerable effort, he carried Rene to the shoreline and rolled her into the water, believing she would somehow be carried away. He got back on his bike and rode through Luton's darkened streets toward home. He considered what he'd done and the impact it would have on his children. What would he say when they asked where their mother was? 'The first thing in my mind,' he recalled, 'was to keep it from the children.'

He went through the house when he got home and found his wife's false teeth sitting on a countertop in a glass of water. He disposed of them, making sure there was nothing about the house that might arouse the suspicions of his children.

'Where's Mum?' the youngest asked later that evening.

'Oh,' Manton replied, 'she's gone to London to stay with Grandma.'

The following morning, Manton woke up early and burned his wife's dress and teeth in the copper fire. He cut up her coat, which she had recently dyed black for her brother-in-law's funeral, and put the shreds in the dustbin. To lend credence to his cover story, he penned several letters, signed them in his wife's name, and posted them to himself from Hampstead. He made several such trips over the proceeding months to maintain the illusion that Rene was away but still concerned for the children. The heavy wooden stool he used to crush his wife's skull did not stay in the house for long. Noticing a split in the stool, the result of its violent impact with Rene's head, Manton asked one of his sons to chop it up for firewood. Manton signed his statement and resigned himself to his fate.

'He looked,' remembered Cherrill, 'such an inoffensive little man.'

He went on trial at Bedford Assizes in May for murder. Although he had made a name for himself in his earlier days as a light-heavy boxer, Manton looked frail in the witness box. He spoke softly and looked nervously about the courtroom as Crown counsel Richard O'Sullivan, KC, attacked the veracity of Manton's statement to police. Forensic evidence, Sullivan reminded the defendant, showed Rene Manton was choked and put up a struggle before the fatal blow.

'Yes, sir,' Manton replied. 'I remember taking hold of her throat and pushing her against the wall. I may have grabbed her twice, but that was in my temper.'

A 'crime of passion' the killing may well have been, but Manton's actions after the murder – removing all jewellery from the body, scrubbing down the house, dumping the victim in the river, omitting from his statement to police that he choked Rene before beating her – suggested a more calculating mind at work. The jury showed no mercy in their deliberations. Although members could have convicted Manton of manslaughter, thus sparing him from the gallows, they instead found him guilty of murder on 17 May 1944. The mandatory sentence of death passed down, Manton was shipped off to Parkhurst Prison to await his fate.

If not for Chapman's encounter with the dog that February morning, Manton may have got away with murder. As it was, the public took pity on the Manton children who had already lost one parent. A public petition for clemency garnered 30,000 signatures and persuaded the Home Secretary to commute Manton's sentence to life in prison.

A sick man, Manton died behind bars three years later.

7

Dreams of Molls and Mobsters

The Palm Beach Bottle Party in Soho was a drinking club tucked away in the basement of 37, Wardour Street. Members of the 'Italian Mob' routinely gathered within its cramped and smoky confines to talk business and plunder the depths of a bottle. Manager Antonio Mancini, a 39-year-old Italian immigrant, watched over the premises from his perch alongside the bar. A street tough respected for his prowess with knuckles and blades, Mancini was better known to his associates as 'Babe'. The mob had chosen Mancini to run the Palm Beach because of his fearsome reputation. Brawls at the club, generally the result of rival gang members trying to gain admittance, were a frequent occurrence. On such occasions, Mancini was not afraid to mix it up with his underworld rivals and excelled at inflicting physical harm.

Late on the evening of Monday, 21 April 1941, Edward Fletcher approached the club's basement entrance and tried to push pass the doorman. Fletcher was a member of 'The Hoxton Gang', a Soho street faction at war with the Italians over control of the neighbourhood's lucrative gambling clubs. When the doorman refused to step aside, Fletcher turned violent and threw a punch. Sitting at the bar, drink in hand, Mancini heard the ruckus and, going to investigate, walked into a full-scale brawl.

With considerable force, he separated the two combatants and banned Fletcher from the premises.

'I'll get you for this, Mancini,' said Fletcher, straightening his suit before retreating down the blacked-out street. Mancini dismissed Fletcher with a wave of his hand and returned to the bar. In the underworld of illicit clubs and battles for street supremacy, such threats were commonplace – and one reason that Mancini went everywhere armed with a 7-inch, double-edged blade.

Ten days later, on Thursday, 1 May, Fletcher returned to the Wardour Street address with fellow gang member Harry Distleman. Known as 'Scarface', perhaps in deference to American crime lord Al Capone, Distleman was a member of the West End Bridge and Billiard Club, which occupied the floor above Mancini's establishment. More than two dozen members of the Hoxton Gang were there that evening, playing cards around the green baize tables. Illicit gambling was big business for London's rival gangs and a pestilence not easily controlled by the police. The occasional undercover operation would shut down one club only to see another card room open in its place. The men who owned such establishments were rarely on the premises, relying instead on henchmen to oversee the business and take the fall when the law barged through the door.

Fletcher and Distleman found two chairs at an otherwise crowded table and watched the dealer shuffle the cards. As the hand was being dealt, members of the 'Italian Mob' entered the club. The casual banter stopped as all eyes turned towards the door and took in the unwelcome guests. Tensions, already high between the two gangs, now exploded and anything that wasn't fastened to the wall or floor became a weapon. Billiard cues were swung and chairs were thrown. In his club downstairs, Mancini could hear the maelstrom above but stayed put. Why go looking for trouble when he assumed it would find him sooner or later? The fight lasted no more than several minutes, but wrecked the card room from one end to the other. Tables and chairs lay in splintered ruins, and broken glass and liquor covered the floor. Among the mess lay the bruised and battered, Fletcher among them, bleeding from several wounds. Distleman, nursing his own cuts, heaved Fletcher to his feet and took him to Charing Cross Hospital.

Down in the Palm Beach Bottle Party, Mancini tended to his own business. Only when he was sure the club upstairs had cleared out did he venture to have a look. He traipsed through the ruins, righting tables and assessing the damage. Two other Italians – Joseph Colletti and Albert Dumes – hovered near Mancini's side in the event any Hoxton Gang member returned to settle a score. At Charing Cross Hospital, his wounds stitched and bandaged, revenge is exactly what Edward Fletcher had in mind. Discharged hours later, he returned with Distleman to Wardour Street. It was nearly 4 in the morning when the two of them entered the club and found Mancini there. Fletcher didn't hesitate.

'There's Babe,' he screamed. 'Let's get him!'

Mancini unsheathed his dagger and lunged forward. He sunk the blade into Distleman's left armpit, slicing through artery and vein. Distleman screamed and staggered backwards. He made it to the door and stumbled down a flight of stairs onto the street, where he collapsed in a widening pool of blood.

'I'm stabbed,' he choked. 'Get me a taxi. Babe done it!'

Upstairs, Mancini backed a terrified Fletcher into a corner and lashed out with his blade, swiping through Fletcher's arm and cutting the limb down to the bone. Fletcher pushed his back against the wall and steeled himself for the final blow when, over Mancini's shoulder, he saw several uniformed constables and a plainclothes detective rush through the door. They grabbed Mancini, pulled him away and wrestled the bloody knife from his grip. Fletcher was hurried from the building and taken once again to Charing Cross Hospital. On the pavement outside the club, a constable knelt over Distleman's lifeless body. Mancini was taken into custody and charged with the attempted murder of Edward Fletcher and the wilful murder of Harry Distleman.

Mancini's cohorts, Colletti and Dumes, were charged with attempted murder.

A jury found Mancini guilty of murder when he went to trial two months later. His execution at Pentonville Prison on 17 October 1941 was notable not only for launching the career of hangman Albert Pierrepoint, but also for the condemned's chipper manner on the gallows. Standing on the trap door, the white hood over his head and the noose around his neck, Mancini's final word was a jovial 'Cheerio!' just before he dropped.

From protection rackets and gambling outfits, to black-market deals and random acts of thuggery, organized crime thrived in wartime London. It lacked, however, the perceived glitz and glamour of its State-side counterpart in cities like New York and Chicago. Mancini and his ilk weren't a patch on the likes of Al Capone and John Dillinger, men of fearsome reputation bolstered by flamboyant news coverage and smooth Hollywood depictions. Indeed, it was Tinsel Town's stylish portrayal of the violent American dream that inspired a Young GI and his English girlfriend to commit wartime London's most infamous crime.

The body, wet and pale in the early morning grass, resembled a porcelain mannequin from a distance. Only when Robert Balding, an auxiliary fireman attached to the National Fire Service, approached the corpse on his way home that October morning, did he realise the true nature of his discovery. It was Saturday, 7 October 1944. He ran across Knowle Green toward Kingston Road in search of a police officer, attracting by sheer chance the attention of passing Metropolitan Police Inspector William McDougall, who ran with Balding back to the body. McDougall examined the corpse but didn't touch it, placing Balding in charge of the scene while he went off to call for assistance.

It was 40 minutes later, at 9.45 a.m., when Detective Inspector Albert Tansill took Balding's statement and relieved the fireman of his grim duties. Bounded by the River Ash to the south and an aqueduct to the east, Knowle Green is a small piece of land in the Thames-side town of Staines. A railway line ran along the northern edge of the green and rolling grasslands came to an abrupt halt alongside Kingston Road to the west. A small gravel driveway, which dead-ended at the railway, provided the only vehicular access from the Kingston Road. The body lay in a ditch north of the driveway and 440 yards from the main road.

At 10 a.m., Richard Elven – the divisional police surgeon – arrived on the green and climbed into the ditch with Tansill to examine the body. The dead man lay on his stomach with his face, cold to the touch, turned slightly to the left, the blank eyes staring off into nowhere. The deceased wore a thick navy coat, its collar pulled up high over the back of his head. Elven gently rolled the body over, revealing bloodstains on the victim's white shirt just above the waistband of the trousers and in the middle of his chest. The outer edge of his left hand, the fingers slightly clenched, was also wet with blood. Rigor mortis was in partial onset and post-mortem lividity had turned the right side of his face a dark-purple hue. A thin trickle of bloody saliva slowly ran from the right corner of the mouth and down his chin. With a gloved thumb, Elven pulled down the man's lower lip. Although blood was present behind and between the teeth, Elven saw no damage to the mouth's interior. Based on his cursory examination, Elven estimated the man to have been dead somewhere between 4 to 10 hours.

By now, Detective Inspector W. Tarr, 'T' Division, and Percy Law from Scotland Yard's Photograph Branch had joined the two men in the ditch. Elven returned the body to its original position as Law bent down low, framed the scene in his viewfinder and captured it in black and white. Tarr clambered out of the ditch with the others behind him and surveyed the surrounding topography. On the grass, just north of the gravel roadway, he saw two parallel tracks running diagonally from the roadway and stopping about 9 feet short of the ditch. Two more sets of parallel tracks, heading off in a right angle back toward the roadway, began where the first set ended. Torn grass and kicked-up soil suggested a vehicle had recently traversed the area; closer inspection by Tarr revealed three large oil-stained patches of grass between the tracks. Tansill ordered the tufts of grass to be dug up and preserved as evidence.

Tarr followed the tracks and, near the edge of the gravel driveway, found an oil-smeared spring lying in the grass. He bent down and picked it up, noting one side showed signs of rubbing while the other was clotted with mud and grass. A mechanical fellow, he knew it to be a 30-coil spring, often used to assist in the release of old, mechanical brakes and to prevent brake rods from rattling. It was a heavy gauge spring and one not commonly used on private cars. Tarr again eyed the area and saw there was little ground clearance where the gravel driveway verged onto the grass. A typical car, he thought, would severely damage its engine sump or rear-axle casing if it tried to manoeuvre from one surface to the other. Weighing the spring in his hand, Tarr ordered the tracks be measured for future reference.

At 6 o'clock that evening, after police had processed and catalogued the crime scene, Tarr oversaw the removal of the body to Feltham Mortuary. He helped pathologist Dr Robert Teare remove and inventory the dead man's clothing. In the pockets of the navy overcoat, the inspector found a white, blue-bordered handkerchief, a latchkey and a pack of cigarettes. A pocketknife and a phial of pills were all the victim had in his trouser pocket; there was no wallet, money or identification of any kind. On the back of the navy coat, about 9 inches below the collar, Tarr noticed a small hole. Inspecting the front of the jacket, Tarr saw a larger hole about 9 inches below the lapel of the coat. Removing the rest of the man's clothes, Tarr and Teare discovered the victim's pullover, shirt and the inside lining of his grey flannel jacket were soaked in blood. The man had been shot in the back, the bullet passing through his body and blowing a hole in his chest.

The entry wound, measuring ⅕ inch in diameter, was 1 inch to the right of the spine and just about level with the sixth rib. The large exit wound was about 2 inches to the right of the centre of the chest, about level with the third rib. Opening the body, Teare traced the bullet's trajectory for Tarr. The slug had perforated the spine and the right lung before grazing the sixth rib in the back and the third rib in the front. The bullet had maintained a perfectly straight trajectory, cutting through the body at a slightly downward angle and exiting just right of the body's horizontal axis. The cause of death, Teare said, was haemorrhaging resulting from the exit wound to the chest. Whoever fired the shot, the pathologist continued, had done so while standing above and slightly to the left of the entrance wound, the nature of which naturally precluded suicide.

'In my opinion,' Teare concluded, 'death occurred between 11 last night and 6 this morning. The deceased was probably placed where he was found within 2 hours of his death.'

It took police two days to identify the victim. John Marshall, a garage proprietor in Lambeth, recognised the picture of the deceased man on a police bulletin and notified authorities. He told Tarr the body was that of George Edward Heath, a taxi driver whom he had known for ten years. Heath's wife, he said, lived in Surrey with the couple's two young sons, ages 8 and 5. Investigators traced Winifred Heath later that evening to a small house in West Street, Ewell, and brought her at 7.30 p.m. to the mortuary. With Tarr standing beside her, she nodded slowly when the pathologist pulled away the white sheet to reveal the pallid features of her husband, naked from the abdomen up. She turned to Tarr and said her husband had walked out the previous autumn but still sent her £4 a week. She had last seen him alive in July.

Tarr thanked Winifred for her time and arranged for a constable to take her home. He looked again at the dead man, not realising the death of George Edward Heath would prove to be wartime London's most notorious murder.

It all began in a small café on Queen Caroline Street, Hammersmith, on the night of 3 October. They met by chance, the young American Army officer and the British showgirl. He wore the uniform of a second lieutenant with the 501st Parachute Regiment of the 101st Airborne Division. She wore her blonde hair down over her shoulders and introduced herself as Georgina Grayson. He, cherub-faced and smitten, said his name was Ricky Allen. Neither one would know the other by their real name until after their arrests. Both were loners and lived in a vibrant dream world, one that would soon turn exceedingly violent. In reality, neither one had lived up to the expectations they set for themselves.

Her real name was Elizabeth Maud Jones, an 18-year-old with aspirations of being a dancer. Her career peaked with various striptease gigs in London at the Panama Club in Knightsbridge and the Blue Lagoon in Carnaby Street, taking it off for military men who drank and hollered. She was born on 5 July 1926 in Glamorgan and caused trouble from an early age. Her father, a member of the Territorial Army since 1934, joined the Royal Artillery in August 1939 and left 13-year-old Elizabeth in the care of her mother.

Six months after her father's departure, she decided to run away from the family home in Neath, Wales, and stole money from her mother's purse to finance the adventure. Local police quickly picked her up and brought her home. When asked why she ran away, the girl simply shrugged and said she didn't know. Several months passed before she gave it another go, prompting police to stick her in Northenden Road School for Girls in Cheshire. Elizabeth's mother visited her regularly, and her father made trips to see her whenever his military duties in the south of England allowed. The visits were cordial affairs, and Elizabeth expressed her desire to return home as soon as possible.

'She remained in this school until she was 16,' her father later recalled. 'She seemed quite happy at the school, although I believe she ran away from it once or twice ... Betty was an intelligent girl, and the principal of the school told me that she was really too old for her years.'

Upon Elizabeth's release from the school, her parents hoped the discipline and regimented routine had dulled her rebellious streak. They were at a loss to explain her past behaviour, and she seemed unwilling – or unable – to shed any light on the matter. She returned home and seemed, much to her mother's relief, to have mellowed. She helped around the house and did as she was told, but the good-girl routine proved to be short-lived and she soon reverted to her troublesome ways. Although just 16, Elizabeth considered herself an adult and asserted her independence. She stayed out until all hours and fraternised with older men. Many evenings were spent at the local cinema, where she lost herself in a Hollywood-inspired fantasy world.

Removing herself from the bleak reality of bombings and rationing, Elizabeth, sitting in the darkness of the cinema, imagined herself on the flickering screen, immersed in a world of smooth-talking, gun-toting wiseguys. She craved a certain kind of highlife, one not found in the drudgery of wartime Britain, but in a world of sophisticated fashion, elegant nightlife and a little mob violence. The hardboiled life of American gangsters, with their women dipped in furs and jewels, fascinated her to no end. In her imagination, she cast herself as a gunman's moll, sipping highballs in a smoky Chicago nightspot and enjoying various luxuries financed by jewel heists and bank jobs. But when the end credits rolled and the cinema lights went up, she couldn't help but bristle at the reality of her situation, returning home late at night to stern lectures from her mother and an endless list of household chores. Desperate, she sought her own means of escape.

On 26 November 1942, at the Neath Register Office, Elizabeth married 26-year-old Stanley Jones, whom she'd known for some time. Her father, training with his unit in the Orkneys, could not attend the ceremony but implored both his daughter and Jones to reconsider the union, arguing Elizabeth was too young to handle the responsibilities of marriage. The couple brushed the concern aside and moved in with Elizabeth's family. Stanley, serving with an anti-tank unit in the Royal Artillery, spent very little time at home. When the couple were together, the relationship proved less than harmonious and – on at least one occasion – physically violent when he beat her on their wedding night. He accused her of fraternising with other men while he was away on training, and she did little to convince him otherwise. In the end, the marriage was short-lived.

He shipped off to war in 1943 and was reported missing in September the following year, a casualty at Arnhem. Elizabeth had by then moved to London to pursue dreams of stardom and casually shrugged off the loss. She focused instead on her dancing career with the intent of making a name for herself. This she did, but fame would ultimately elude her in favour of infamy.

Karl Hulten was born in Stockholm, Sweden, on 3 March 1922. His father left home when Hulten was still an infant, prompting his mother to seek better opportunities for the family in America. The Hultens arrived in the United States in December 1923 and settled in Massachusetts, where Mrs Hulten took a housecleaning job with a Boston family. He grew up on the East Coast and settled with a wife in Cambridge, Massachusetts, before joining the US Army on 24 March 1943. In October that year, he applied for naturalisation as an American citizen and came to Britain as a private with the 501st Parachute Infantry Regiment, 101st Airborne Division.

Stationed in Reading, he distinguished himself only through poor conduct, going absent without leave on 14 July 1944 to enjoy London's various entertainments. He was not alone: the capital swarmed with American, British and Canadian military men who forsook their duties to pursue a more subversive lifestyle. Toward the end of the war, London authorities estimated one-tenth of the city's crime to be the work of deserters. With limited resources and few places they could go, they robbed, beat and burgled to make ends meet. Some joined criminal gangs, while others hawked their uniforms and military paraphernalia to pawnbrokers and black marketeers for extra cash.

Hulten got by, spending the night with the occasional 'commando' (prostitute), slumming it in public places and dining in cheap cafés – but his adventure lasted barely a month. American and British military police routinely raided pubs, dance halls and other hotspots where deserters were known to congregate. They challenged random servicemen on the street, demanding to inspect valid identity cards and service passes, promptly arresting those unable to produce the required documentation. They nabbed Hulten in such a manner on 12 August and returned him to his camp in Reading. He appeared before a Summary Court Martial six days later, was fined $20 and placed under twenty days' restriction for carrying a concealed handgun with a live round in the breech. That very evening, however, he managed to sneak away from camp. Outside Reading, he stole a 2-ton, 10-wheeled US Army truck belonging to the 101st Airborne and drove back to London.

In the city, he parked the truck at the abandoned Old Gaumont Car Park, a bombed factory site, in Sussex Place, Hammersmith Broadway. He purchased a second-hand Class A American officer's uniform of a second lieutenant and deposited a duffel bag with extra clothes in left luggage at the Metropolitan Line Tube Station. He spent his days wandering aimlessly about the capital, sneaking into cinemas, hanging around in cafés and grabbing the occasional drink in various pubs.

He returned to the car park at night and slept in the back of the truck under two bed sheets. On the afternoon of Sunday, 1 October, he dressed in his lieutenant's uniform and sneaked into a picture at the nearby Gaumont Theatre. In the lobby after the show, he caught the eye of a young woman. He followed her outside and watched from under the theatre awning as she ducked into a nearby doorway to get out of the rain. He followed her lead and was soon huddled alongside her, shaking the rain from his officer's cap. She introduced herself as Joyce Cook. He shook her hand and said his name was Ricky Allen.

'We talked for a short time,' he later said, 'and just as she was leaving, I made a date to meet her in the same doorway at 1900 hours. She kept this date, and we went to the Broadway Theatre.'

They emerged from the show shortly after 10 p.m. Outside, the rain still fell. Hulten told Joyce he had an army truck parked nearby and could drive her home, but Joyce said she preferred to walk. The two ran to her family's home on Lurgan Street, ducking in and out of doorways, laughing as they splashed through puddles. Mrs Cook greeted the two as they walked through the front door. Joyce introduced the well-dressed gentleman as 'Lieutenant Richard Allen' to her parents and asked if he could stay for supper. The parents agreed, and Hulten dined with the family. He bid them farewell shortly after eleven and walked back to the truck. Hulten met Joyce the next two evenings at Oliver's Bakery in Hammersmith, where she worked, and took her to a show. Both dates concluded with dinner at Joyce's home and a lonely walk back to the Old Gaumont Car Park.

Prior to picking Joyce up from work on the night of Tuesday, 3 October, Hulten stopped by the small café in Queen Caroline Street for a cup of coffee. Sitting at a corner table, he saw Len Bexley – an acquaintance he knew from his various wanderings about town – chatting with a young, blonde-haired girl. 'I took another seat,' Hulten recalled, 'but [Bexley] asked me to come over and join them, which I did.' Bexley, who knew Hulten as Lieutenant Ricky Allen, introduced him as such to the young woman, who smiled and said her name was Georgina Grayson. The two shook hands and, in that instant, forged a relationship that would soon be front-page fodder. 'We were there a while in the cafeteria, and afterwards we all got up and left together,' Hulten subsequently told police, '[Georgina] and I walked towards the Broadway. I asked if she would care to come out later on.'

The couple arranged to meet at 11.30 that night outside the café. Hulten, smiling, went off to spend the evening with Joyce, while an excited Jones hurried back to her small flat at 311 King Street to prep for the late-night rendezvous. Sitting in front of her bureau mirror, she revelled in the delight of nabbing herself an American serviceman. They walked with what she perceived to be a Hollywood swagger, the result on her part of perhaps seeing one too many films. Her knowledge of Americans and their country was based entirely on celluloid fantasy, a carefully crafted image of glitz, glamour and violence. The more dismal her circumstances became, the more such a lifestyle appealed to her desire for escape. Life in London had thus far proved to be a disappointment. She had failed at being a waitress and a hostess, and was currently in between burlesque jobs.

At the arranged time, she stood outside the café, huddled in her coat against the cold and growing increasingly despondent as the minutes ticked by. Was it possible the young lieutenant had stood her up? She glanced at her watch, illuminating its face in the glowing end of her cigarette. A ¼ of an hour had passed and he still hadn't shown. Her patience exhausted, Jones turned toward her rented room – but as she started walking, a rumbling sound made her glance over her shoulder.

In the blackout, she just made out the large truck lumbering in her direction; its covered headlamps revealing only thin slivers of light. The truck pulled up along the pavement and paced her as she continued walking. Inside the truck, Hulten rolled down the window and hollered Georgina's name. He apologised for being late and asked her to get in. Jones quickly shrugged any hard feelings aside and clambered into the truck. With no particular place to go, Hulten put the truck in gear, pulled away from the kerbside and started driving.

Jones slid across the bench seat and nestled herself against Hulten's side. She shrugged when asked what she wanted to do and gazed silently out the window. Instead of blacked-out shopfronts and the ruined spaces where buildings once stood, she imagined a street lit by neon lights and glittering windows. She pictured herself riding not in the darkened cab of an army truck, but cushioned in the leather-lined luxury of some snazzy automobile with her mob-hitched lover behind the wheel.

She turned her gaze from the bleak cityscape and looked at Hulten, who, aiming to impress, told his date they were joyriding in a stolen truck. Hulten's bad-boy act instantly appealed to Jones's mob-inspired fantasies, and she confessed her desire 'to do something exciting like becoming a gun moll, like they do in the States'. Hulten, who, in wearing a lieutenant's uniform was seeking to rise above his own bland pedigree, flashed Jones a grin, slipped a hand into his tunic and withdrew a Remington automatic. Rising to the occasion, he said he 'carried a gun for the mob' and had been sent by gangsters in Chicago to muscle in on the various Limey rackets in London. And why not? The press carried frequent reports of gangland activity in the capital. Some gangsters, like Billy Hill, even acquired a certain level of fame.

Born in 1911, Hill had started small-time by breaking into houses as a teenager before advancing to more daring smash-and-grab raids. He ran protection rackets in the West End, going so far as to extort money from merchants who sold birdseed in Trafalgar Square. A man who enjoyed action, Hill developed a reputation for brazen robberies, driving up to shopfronts, smashing the windows while leaning out of his car's sunroof before speeding off with the loot. He had made headlines on 26 June 1940, while trying to rob Hemmings and Co., a jewellery store off Bond Street. Outside the store, the bumper of Hill's car caught on the pavement as it jumped the kerb, rendering it immobile. Hill leapt from the vehicle and into another car, driven by one of his associates. The driver, however, stalled the saloon when a constable responding to the commotion threw his truncheon at the car and shattered its windscreen. Hill took off running but was quickly nabbed and eventually sentenced to two years in prison. Fortunately for him, the war proved to be a long one and would accommodate his various other business ventures upon his release, including selling forged documents to AWOL servicemen and hawking petrol on the black market.

To someone like Jones, the star of her own delusional fantasy, individuals like Hill were the stuff of Hollywood. Whether she truly believed Hulten's gangster story, or simply wanted to believe it, is open to speculation. Whatever the reality, the young, failed soldier and the burnt-out teenage stripper embraced their mobster alter egos and searched for a victim as the truck barrelled into the night.

It was coming up on 1 o'clock in the morning of Wednesday, 4 October, when Hulten and Jones turned the truck into a narrow lane that wound its way around a small village outside Reading. The stretch of road was deserted except for a lone cyclist, a young woman riding toward the village. Hulten passed the girl on the bike and drove up the lane before pulling over to the side and climbing out the driver's door. He loitered near the side of the truck, as if inspecting something, and waited for the woman on the bike to draw near. He lit a cigarette and lunged towards her, his arms outstretched, as she rode past. The bike toppled sideways and sent the girl to the ground with a bruising thud. She scrambled to her feet and ran off screaming, leaving her handbag tied around the bike's handlebars. 'I took the pocket book and threw it up to Georgina before I got back in the truck,' Hulten recalled. 'We drove back toward Hammersmith.'

They drove for the first few minutes in silence. Jones, holding a torch between her teeth, rummaged through the handbag. Their first 'hit' scored nothing more than five shillings and a few clothing coupons, but the two were nevertheless exhilarated. Now, fully in character, Hulten claimed assault and robbery were nothing compared to some of his past deeds. They were notorious fugitives on the run, matching wits and bravado with the G-men on their tails. If cornered, they'd go down shooting. They arrived back in London, left the truck in the Old Gaumont Car Park and walked to Jones's one-room hideout in King Street to split the spoils. Hulten pocketed the clothing coupons and gave the 5s to Jones. Both slept well that night and met Len Bexley the following morning at the café in Queen Caroline Street. Not saying where they came from, Hulten passed the clothing coupons onto Bexley, who, realising he could make a few quid off them on the black market, paid Hulten a couple of shillings.

Early that evening, Hulten met Joyce at the bakery and took her to a show, not bothering to mention Georgina or the previous evening's adventure. The night concluded, much like their previous dates, with a late-night dinner at the Cook home. He left shortly after 11 p.m. and walked to Georgina's, where he spent the night. He slept in late, not waking until the early afternoon of Thursday, 5 October.

'I had arranged to meet Joyce at 1500 hours as it was her half day,' he later told investigators. 'I called at her home at about 1430 hours and told her that I couldn't keep the date as I had to go to camp.' It was, of course, a lie. He returned to Georgina's room, and the two of them took the tube to Victoria. They whiled away a couple of hours at the cinema and watched Deanna Durbin in *Christmas Holiday,* the dark story of a femme fatale who falls in love with a man she knows to be a killer. They emerged from the cinema at 10 o'clock, had dinner in a nearby café and returned to the car park in Hammersmith.

Hulten opened the truck's passenger door for Jones and told her as she climbed in he was in the mood to rob a pub. They drove to the village of Sonning in Berkshire and came to a stop outside a small country pub. Because blackout curtains were drawn across the pub's windows, it was impossible to tell how many customers were inside. The last thing Hulten wanted was someone deciding to play hero. He pulled the gun from his tunic and kissed Jones, who eyed him with admiration. He checked the gun's breach, took a deep breath, grasped the door handle but never left the truck. At the last minute, he pocketed the gun, slammed the truck in gear and sped away from the pub. A clearly annoyed Jones voiced her displeasure.

'Why are you leaving?' she whined.

'I think,' Hulten said, glancing in the truck's side mirror, 'we're being watched.'

Jones peered excitedly out her window. She hoped to see someone following them, but all she saw in the truck's wake was darkness and empty road. She slumped back in her seat and kept silent as Hulten drove back to the city. Instead of returning to Hammersmith, Hulten drove to Marble Arch in search of a new adventure. It was Jones who first suggested they rob a taxi, pointing one out as it drove past. Hulten turned the truck around and began following the car. In the taxi, driver John Strangeway kept an eye on the US Army truck behind him. Such vehicles were commonplace on the road these days, but this one appeared to be keeping close distance. He said nothing to his passenger, George McMillan Reeves, a lieutenant in the US Army Air Force. He watched in his driving mirror as the truck pulled into the adjacent lane and accelerated, overtaking him on High Road, Kilburn. When the truck had cleared the front of the taxi, it pulled abruptly in front of the car, cutting across the road at a sharp angle and forcing Strangeway to slam on the brakes. The taxi came to a screeching halt, stopping just inches from the truck.

Hulten, brandishing the Remington automatic in his right hand, leapt from the truck and, leaning into the taxi, stuck the gun in Strangeway's face.

'Let me have your money,' he screamed.

'I don't have any,' Strangeway calmly replied, 'I've just started for the evening.'

Hulten stood there, pondering what to do next, when he caught sight of the American officer sitting in the back seat. Panicked, he shoved the gun in his tunic and ran for the truck. He scrambled into the driver's seat, gunned the engine and sped off toward Marble Arch. It had just gone 2 in the morning. For the aspiring Bonnie and Clyde, the evening's take had thus far proven abysmal. They drove around aimlessly and discussed what to do next. Both remained intent on robbing and went in search of a victim. It didn't take them long to find one.

8

The Cleft-Chin Murder

Eighteen-year-old Violet May Hodge was not thrilled with her situation. She had come to London from Bristol, arriving on the midnight train, hoping to spend the night with a friend. When those plans fell through at the last minute, Violet found herself stuck in the city without a place to stay. She ate a late-night dinner of tea and cakes at the Paddington Station Buffet and left there shortly after 2 in the morning in search of a hotel. She knew of a boarding house nearby and hoped to find a room available.

Though her present circumstances were less than ideal, Violet enjoyed being on her own. She had spent the past two weeks living with her aunt following a noisy quarrel with her mother. She came to London when she could to enjoy the simple thrill of being in the midst of it all. Now, she left the station with her suitcase in hand and turned left on Edgware Road, searching for a boarding house at 23 Cleveland Place. She walked for several minutes, unsure of her stepping in the pitch black, arm extended, feeling for lampposts and postboxes. It soon dawned on her she had no idea where she was and asked a passing gentleman for directions. Told she was heading the wrong way, she turned around and proceeded back toward the station. Violet heard the truck before she saw it, rumbling in her direction. It was a large, army-type vehicle with a white star painted on the side.

In the cab, Jones spotted the girl walking alongside the road and told Hulten to stop. He pulled the truck over, rolled down his window and asked where she was heading. 'Paddington,' the girl replied.

'Would you like a lift?' Hulten asked.

'Yes,' the girl said, as Hulten hopped out of the truck to help her in. He put her suitcase in the back and returned to the cab. Hulten put the truck in gear and made casual conversation with the girl, asking what brought her to London. Violet explained her situation and said the earliest she'd be able to catch a train back to Bristol would be 9 that morning. Hulten smiled and suggested she ride with him and his wife to Reading. Although the couple never made formal introductions, they referred to themselves as 'Ricky' and 'Georgina'. Violet guessed the young American officer wasn't much older than herself. He appeared dashing in his brown, leather jacket and army tunic, which accentuated his slim yet powerful build. She found him rather attractive, with his dark complexion and thick, black hair combed straight back.

The young woman in the passenger seat also spoke with an American accent and said she was from the States. Her blonde hair was done up and framed in a black hood. Violet thought the girl was older than she appeared – probably 23 or 24. She wore an oversized fawn coat done up in a tie belt. She chatted amicably about London, saying she was robbed on her last visit to the city and only ventured into the capital when absolutely necessary. Pointing to Ricky, she said the two of them would be celebrating their third wedding anniversary come January. Ricky simply nodded and kept his eyes on the road.

'We continued on,' Violet recalled. 'Being a stranger, I did not know any of the districts we passed through. Most of the conversation was between the woman and myself, the man saying very little.'

They left the city and continued in the direction of Windsor. Driving along the Thames through Runnymede, where King John signed the Magna Carta in 1215, Hulten told the girls there was something wrong with the truck. One of the tyres, he said, felt soft. He pulled off the road onto the grass shoulder and opened the side door, explaining he had hit a tree three days ago and had probably done some damage. Jones scrambled over Violet's lap and got out with Hulten. Violet followed and stood on the wet grass, watching the couple trudge around the truck and inspect the wheels. Several minutes passed before Hulten circled back around the front of the vehicle and told Violet he'd have to change the tyre when they got to their destination. The three climbed back in the cab and continued on their way. They drove no more than a mile before Hulten began shaking his head.

'It's no good,' he said, 'I'll have to take the wheel off.'

He turned the truck around and returned to the grass verge where he had pulled over minutes before. The three of them once again slid out of the truck into the damp night air. Hulten lit a cigarette and passed the packet to Jones, whispering in her ear to keep the girl distracted. Jones nodded, lit her smoke and offered one to Violet, who noticed Hulten disappear momentarily behind the back of the truck. He returned a minute later with a crowbar and asked Jones to grab the wheel blocks from behind the front seat. As Violet watched Jones reach into the cab, Hulten swung the crowbar and smashed her in the left side of the head. The blow didn't knock her down, but staggered her on her feet. She screamed and stumbled toward the truck, reaching desperately for the door. Hulten hit her again and succeeded in knocking her to the ground. Still conscious, Violet screamed for help and tried to claw her way toward the main road. Hulten dropped the bar, threw himself on top of her and wrapped his right arm around Violet's neck.

Violet thrashed beneath him. Hulten buried his right knee in Violet's back and grabbed her throat with both hands. Even as he squeezed, Violet continued to struggle and throw punches over her shoulder. Jones watched mesmerised from the truck, thrilled and terrified by the spectacle, as Violet clawed desperately at Hulten's hands. When the woman screamed Georgina's name and begged her to help, Jones simply laughed and urged her lover on. Hulten squeezed harder and yelled at Jones to come and help him. She leapt from the truck and knelt in front of Violet, holding Violet's arms to the ground, laughing as she did so. Hulten felt the girl's body begin to go slack beneath him.

Her screams subsided to whimpers, then choking gasps, then nothing. Her body went limp, and it was over. Hulten rolled off the prostrate form, lay on the wet earth and listened to his own breath come and go in heavy rasps. Beyond the dark silhouettes of nearby trees, the Thames could be heard gently slapping against its banks. Hulten got to his feet, grabbed the body under the arms and told Jones to take hold of the legs. They heaved the body off the ground, lugged it to the river's edge and dumped it in the water. Hulten ran back to the truck, retrieved the crowbar and disposed of it in a similar fashion.

The couple, secret players in their own private movie, watched the rippling surface for a brief moment then turned to leave. Violet's suitcase remained in the back of the truck; her handbag lay on the seat in the front. In the cab, the couple embraced and kissed like Hollywood lovers. Back in London, they parked the truck on King Street and carried the suitcase and handbag up to Georgina's room. As Jones rifled through the case's contents – pleased to find orange satin pyjamas and four pairs of silk underwear – Hulten examined himself in the bureau mirror. He saw no evident change in his physical appearance, nor did he feel any different than when he woke up the previous morning. He appeared, despite what he had done, to be the same person he had always been. What he did notice, however, was the girl's blood splattered on his leather jacket and pink officer's trousers.

The cold overwhelmed everything. Violet Hodge opened her eyes and found herself floating 'in a pool of water'. How long she'd been out and managed not to drown, she couldn't say. When she tried to plant her feet on the bottom, she found the water was too deep. Her limbs felt like lead, numbed by the freezing temperatures. Treading water required nearly more energy than she currently possessed. Her eyes adjusting, but vision still blurred, she saw the branches of a nearby tree bowing to the water's edge. She struggled toward the nearest branch and grabbed hold. Kicking with aching legs and pulling with burning arms, she hauled herself out of the water.

As she lay on the bank and struggled to catch her breath, she felt the deep ache slowly creep into her head. When she got to her feet, she moved carefully, not wanting to attract the attention of her assailants. She reached the edge of the road and was relieved to find the truck gone and went in search of help. She walked for several minutes and kept close to the trees. Clearing a bend, she came to a house just off the main road and, sobbing with relief, walked up its front path and pounded on the door. When her cries went unanswered, she knocked and screamed louder, eventually giving up and moving on.

She was eventually taken in by the occupants of a nearby lodge, who called Surrey police and took her to Windsor Emergency Hospital. Doctors admitted her with a deep gouge to the left side of the head, numerous bruises and abrasions, and a haemorrhage in the left eye. It would be six days before she was able to provide a statement to police and a week before she was released.

Hulten slept until 3 in the afternoon. It was now Friday, 6 October. In the early morning hours, before returning to Jones's flat, the pair had abandoned the army truck on the side of King Street in Hammersmith, the vehicle having sufficiently served its purpose. He now got up, examined the bloodstained clothes and told Jones they would have to get rid of them. He asked her to retrieve his bag from the Metropolitan Line tube station and gave her the claim ticket. When Jones returned, Hulten dressed in a clean tunic and a green pair of officer's trousers. He bagged the soiled clothing and gave it to Jones, who said she would sponge out the blood and take the stained trousers and jacket to be laundered. He kissed her and walked to the door with plans to return later that night.

He met Joyce at the bakery and took her to a movie. She remained oblivious to his other activities and his relationship with Jones. Around Joyce and her parents, Hulten was soft-spoken and polite, almost shy. He betrayed nothing in his voice or manner to suggest a violent nature. Certainly, he lied to Joyce. He used an assumed name and never once mentioned his wife and child back in the States, but he felt no compunction when with her to lash out as he did in Georgina's company. The allure of both women pulled him in two very different directions. He enjoyed the stability of the Cook household and Joyce's gentle nature, but he revelled in Georgina's unpredictability and the secrets they shared. When he was with one, he often found himself thinking of the other, a quandary that left him feeling rather unsettled. And so Hulten stayed with Joyce until eleven that evening, when he left the familial warmth of the Cook household and returned to the cold squalor of Georgina's rented room. Reaching King Street, he decided not to go up to her room, and instead stood beneath her window and whistled loudly. A thin sliver of light appeared on one side of the blackout curtain as Georgina peered into the street. Minutes later, the two of them were strolling toward Knightsbridge.

The evening was cold and damp and threatened rain. The wind picked up as they walked and forced them into a doorway along Hammersmith Road opposite Cadby Hall, a large factory and office building. The time was 11.30. Roughly 10 minutes passed before Georgina, lighting a cigarette, saw the grey Ford saloon approaching from the direction of Hammersmith Broadway. She stepped to the kerbside, arm raised, and yelled, 'Taxi'.

Behind the wheel of the Ford was 34-year-old George Edward Heath, who had survived Dunkirk only to see his army career end when he suffered injuries in the Blitz. Invalided out of the service, he now worked as a 'private hire' driver – basically, an unlicensed cabbie – picking up illicit fares to make a few quid.

The car – a 1936 Ford V-8, registration number RD 8955 – belonged to a Mr Knowland Hawkins, from whom Heath was considering purchasing the vehicle. Hawkins had loaned Heath the car for the evening on the stipulation he return it in time for the races at Ascot the following morning. By 11.30 that night, Heath had already picked up some business outside the Strand Palace and Regent Palace hotels, and was most likely driving back to Hawkins's place in Sunninghill, Berkshire, when the young woman flagged him down. Heath pulled over and rolled down his window.

'Are you a taxi?' the woman asked.

'Private hire,' Heath responded.

Jones told the driver to wait one moment and scurried back to Hulten, who stood watching from the doorway. When Jones said there was no one in the car other than the driver, Hulten nodded. The two slid into the Ford's backseat, Hulten positioning himself behind Heath.

'Where to?' Heath asked.

'King Street,' Hulten said.

Heath quoted a price and turned the car around. Hulten gazed out the window and watched the first drops of rain hit the glass. The few people who remained on the street seemed no more real to him than those on a movie screen, certainly no more real than his present situation. The weight of the Remington automatic holstered in his waistband and the smell of Georgina's perfume assured him of the grim reality. Lest Georgina deem him a laughing stock, there was only one thing he could do to preserve his tough guy reputation. Of course, he could tell Heath to stop the cab and simply walk away, leaving Georgina and her gun-moll fantasies in the backseat. Neither decision seemed to be an easy one to make. In his reverie, Hulten lost track of where they were.

Heath shot a glance in the back seat. 'We've passed King Street,' he said. 'Where do you want to go?'

'It's further on,' Hulten said, quickly making up his mind and gripping the gun beneath his tunic, 'I don't mind paying more.'

Heath, clearly annoyed, grumbled something under his breath but kept driving. There was no attempt at small talk. In the silence, everything seemed amplified: the sound of the wheels on the road, the rhythmic slapping of the Ford's windscreen wipers. The car soon came to a roundabout.

'This is the Great West Road,' Heath said.

'The place we want is just beyond here,' Hulten said. He silently pulled the gun from his waistband and gripped it in his lap. He pulled the slide back, cocked the pistol and glanced at Georgina. Roughly 25 yards beyond the roundabout, Hulten said, 'We'll get out here.'

Heath stopped the car and leaned into the backseat to open Georgina's door with his left arm at the precise moment Hulten pulled the trigger. The muzzle flash in the car's dark interior was blinding, but overall the roar of the gun failed to live up to Georgina's Hollywood-bred expectations. 'I was surprised,' she later said, 'there was not a loud bang.' In the front seat, Heath let out a loud moan, the force of the slug spinning him toward the steering wheel. Hulten scrambled out of the backseat with the smoking gun in hand and opened the driver's door.

'Move over,' Hulten said.

Heath stayed put and moaned softly, his chin resting on his chest and blood blossoming on the front of his shirt. He lay across the front seat at a sharp angle with his right foot beneath the clutch. Hulten got in the front and tried to push Heath aside.

'Move over,' Hulten said again, 'or I'll give you another dose of the same.'

Heath tried to speak, but the words came out in a blood-choked gurgle.

Hulten pushed Heath aside and positioned himself behind the wheel. The cabbie somehow managed to prop himself against the passenger side door. In the back seat, Jones listened to each laboured breath the stricken man take catch in his throat and seemingly perish there. Hulten, the gun now resting in his lap, eased the car back on the road and told Jones to pat Heath down.

'Find his wallet,' Hulten said.

Jones leaned over the front seat, her hand momentarily hesitating over the red stain spreading across Heath's chest. She rifled through his overcoat pockets and pulled out a wallet, four pound notes, a brown fountain pen, a silver pencil, a silver cigarette case and matching lighter. From one of his trouser pockets, she took a pound in silver. In another pocket, she found an identity card, cheque book, petrol coupons and some photographs. She fell back in her seat, picked through Heath's wallet and studied the pictures. There were photos of Heath with his two children and a woman Jones presumed to be Heath's wife. It was from the identity card she learned Heath's name and shared it with Hulten.

'Well,' she said, 'I think I took everything from his pockets.'

Hulten told her to pocket the valuable items and dump the papers and photographs on the backseat. Next, he asked her to get on the floor and search for the bullet and spent shell casing. She slid off the seat, got on her hands and knees and groped in the darkness, swaying with the car's movements. She gave up after several minutes of fruitless searching, climbed back on the seat and tore down the rear window blind to make sure they weren't being followed. In the front seat, Heath's breath came and went in sporadic gasps. Hulten accelerated and took the car over a narrow bridge into the town of Staines. He turned left at the local police station and drove another mile before turning left off the main road onto a gravel driveway. Hulten drove a short distance, pulled the car of the driveway and came to a stop. He got out, looked around and saw he had parked on what appeared to be a common. In the darkness, he could see a ditch about 3 feet from the car.

He shoved the gun in the waistband of his trousers and walked round to the left side of the car with Georgina following close behind. He opened the front passenger door and grabbed Heath beneath the arms. The cabbie was no longer breathing. He pulled Heath from the car, the dead man's shoes hitting the wet grass. Jones grabbed the body by the ankles and helped Hulten carry it to the edge of the ditch. They dropped Heath down the steep embankment and watched him roll to the bottom.

'I have blood on my hands,' Hulten said, holding up his dark, glistening palms.

'Use this,' Jones replied, and passed him a handkerchief she had pulled from Heath's pocket.

Hulten wiped his hands clean and led Jones back to the car. They eased down the uneven driveway and regained the main road. Jones, now sitting in the front, retrieved Heath's papers and photographs from the backseat and tossed them and the empty wallet out the window. Making use of Heath's torch, she resumed her search for the bullet and found it on the floor near the front passenger door. She showed the bronze-coloured slug to Hulten and, on his orders, threw it out the window. They drove back to Hammersmith and parked the car in the Old Gaumont Car Park, where Hulten had kept the truck. They took their handkerchiefs and wiped down every surface they had touched, cleaning the vehicle as best they could. It was now 3.45 on the morning of Saturday, 7 October. They left the taxi and walked to the Black and White café for an early breakfast. They ate in silence and returned to the King Street flat.

'He's dead, isn't he?' Jones asked as they walked through the door.

'Yes,' Hulten said.

They spread Heath's possessions out on the bed and wondered how much they would fetch on the street. Then, exhausted from their busy night, they crawled beneath the sheets. In the darkness, Hulten listened to Georgina's breathing, felt the warm weight of her body beside him. It was hardly comforting when one considered her cold disposition. Why he felt the need to prove himself to a down-and-out stripper he couldn't say, but he had now done the unthinkable. He pictured George Heath's body lying in the ditch and wondered how long it would be before someone made the gruesome discovery. And how long after that, if at all, would police pick up his trail? Countless questions, none with answers, ran through his mind. He was still pondering the immensity of what he had done when sleep finally came over him.

Hulten left the flat shortly after waking at 11 that morning. He walked down to the café, where he hoped to find Len Bexley. He stopped at a newsstand along the way and scanned the morning papers, relieved to find no news of the murder. When he entered the Black and White, he saw Bexley sitting at a table and pulled up a chair.

'I'm broke,' Hulten said by way of greeting. He placed the fountain pen, silver pencil, cigarette lighter and case on the table and pushed them toward Bexley. 'I need some money.'

Bexley appraised each item with the care of a jeweller examining a fine stone. Liking what he saw, he slapped eight shillings down for the lot. Not bothering to stick around, Hulten hurried next door to the barbershop, where he often went for a trim. Just recently, Morris Levene, the barber, had told Hulten he was in the market for a new watch. Now, on this Saturday morning, Hulten had a leather-strapped watch he was willing to part with for £5. Levene, thinking it a good deal, handed over the cash.

'I thought he was a very decent chap,' Levene later told authorities.

Later that afternoon Hulten took Georgina to White City Stadium to watch the greyhound races. They encountered Bexley on the way and asked him to join them. The excitement of the track and the thrill of betting provided a nice distraction for Hulten, but the knowledge of what he'd done and the image of Heath's body lying in that ditch proved all but impossible to escape. Even the £7 he won did little to ease the burden. The couple parted ways with Bexley in Hammersmith Broadway after the races and walked to Victoria, where they grabbed dinner and caught a movie. Hulten opted not to spend the night with Jones and slept in the ballroom at the Eccleston Hotel.

The following evening, Sunday, 8 October, they drove around the West End in Heath's cab convinced they had pulled off the perfect crime. 'It's all right,' Hulten said, when Jones questioned whether it was wise to be driving around in the dead man's car.

'There's nothing in the papers and the police have not found the body yet.'

Hulten spoke the words not realising investigators were already on the case. The body of George Heath – discovered early the previous morning, approximately 8 hours after the shooting – now lay autopsied in Feltham Mortuary. By late afternoon Monday, Detective Inspector Tarr had identified the victim and recovered his wallet and papers alongside the Great West End Road, 4 miles from the crime scene. Armed with the deceased's name, it did not take long for police to track down Heath's associates and learn he was driving a borrowed Ford V8 saloon. Early on Monday evening, Tarr circulated a description of the grey Ford and met with a local gunsmith, hoping the man could determine the calibre of the murder weapon based on the holes in Heath's clothing.

At 6 p.m. on Monday, Hulten picked Joyce up at the bakery and drove her home. He parked the car opposite her house on Lurgan Avenue, went inside and left the Ford's headlights burning. Walking his beat 2 hours later, Police Constable William Waters passed Lurgan Avenue and noticed the car's lights. He approached the vehicle and, seeing RD 8955 on its number plate, knew it to be the 'murder car'. He ran to the nearest call box and phoned Hammersmith Police Station, relaying the information to Detective Inspector Percy Read,[1] 'F' Division. Read ordered several uniformed officers to accompany him to the scene. They drove in two cars. Read had one take position down the block on Lurgan Avenue behind the Ford and the other opposite the street on Fulham Palace Road. The cars parked and their lights dimmed, Waters joined Read in the car on Lurgan Avenue and waited.

Read, 43 years old and a 19-year veteran of the Met, took great pleasure in his work. A man of considerable strength, who was not afraid to mix things up with the occasional lowlife, Read enjoyed the physical aspects of his profession. He initially followed in the footsteps of his father – a lifelong railway worker – and took a job at the age of 14 with the Eastleigh Railway Works in Hampshire, helping build and repair locomotive carriages. It was gruelling work but appealed to Read's strenuous nature. Shortly after his 18th birthday, he joined the Royal Flying Corps and served as an observer in France in the waning days of the First World War. He returned to the railyard after the war with an awakened sense of adventure and joined the Metropolitan Police in 1924. Five years later, at the relatively young age of 28, he achieved the rank of Detective Inspector.

He said nothing as he sat in the car, waiting. It was 9 p.m. when he saw movement in the garden of a nearby house. A shadowy figure emerged from an open door, walked down the garden path and approached the parked Ford. It stopped near the driver's side door, lit a cigarette and climbed into the vehicle. Read flashed the lights of his police car and slapped Waters on the shoulder, signalling it was time to move. The two men scrambled from the car and rushed toward the Ford. As they approached, the police car, which had parked across Fulham Palace Road, roared into Lurgan Avenue with lights blazing and screeched to a halt in front of the Ford. Waters, closing in on the Ford's passenger side, yelled to distract the car's sole occupant as Read approached the driver's side door.

Read shone his torch in the car and saw a young man sitting behind the steering wheel in what appeared to be an American military uniform. The detective opened the door, grabbed the man's right arm and yanked him hard from the vehicle. Waters quickly joined Read's side and the two men wrestled the young American onto the bonnet of the car. Read pinioned the suspect's arms behind his back and slapped on a pair of handcuffs. Pulling the American upright, the officers spun him around and pinned him against a nearby wall. Read patted the man down and removed from the left trouser pocket six rounds of ammunition and a .45 Remington automatic with six rounds in the magazine and one in the breach. The hammer was back and the safety catch was off.

'Is this your car?' Read asked, pointing at the Ford and catching his breath.

'No,' the man replied.

'I'm taking you to Hammersmith Police Station for questioning,' the detective said.

The American said nothing as Read took him by the arm and pushed him into the back seat of the nearby police car. The car immediately pulled away and headed for the station at 226 Shepherds Bush Road. Read and Waters returned to their vehicle and followed in the other car's wake. At the station, in the harsh light of the interrogation room, Read noticed the gold bar of a second lieutenant on the American's tunic.

'What's your name?' Read asked.

'Richard John Allen, aged 22, No. 0/1283187, 501 Parachute Infantry, US Army,' the young man replied, rattling off his answer as though being questioned by a German interrogator. Read slid a pack of cigarettes across the table and left the room. He notified the American military police and Detective Inspectors Tarr and Tansill, lead investigators on the case. Robert De Mott, an agent from the 8th Military Police Criminal Investigation Division, arrived at the station within the hour and was debriefed on all known facts relating to the murder of George Heath. He transferred the lieutenant to American C.I.D. Headquarters in Piccadilly for questioning. The soldier again gave his name as 'Allen' and told the agent he had stolen the car from the Old Gaumont Car Park in Hammersmith earlier that afternoon. He stuck with his story and endured what he later described rather cryptically as 'American methods' of interrogation. De Mott questioned him well past midnight before returning Hulten to Hammersmith Police Station, where inspectors Tarr and Tansill waited.

It was 3.10 in the morning of Tuesday, 10 October, when Tarr and Tansill sat down to question their prime suspect. De Mott introduced the inspectors to 'Lieutenant Allen,' who, with loosened tie, bloodshot eyes and unkempt hair, appeared fatigued and depleted. De Mott informed the soldier of his rights as an American citizen.

'It is your privilege to remain silent,' he said. 'Anything you say may be used either for or against you in the event that this investigation results in a trial. Do you understand your rights?'

'I do,' Allen said, before submitting to another round of questioning. The previous interrogation, however, had taken its toll on his stamina. He soon dispensed with the phony identity and told investigators his real name was Karl Gustav Hulten, a private with the 501st Parachute Regiment. He confessed to having been 'over the hill' (absent without leave) for approximately a month and a half and said he found the car abandoned 'outside Newbury, on the edge of the wood, at 4.15 Monday afternoon'. He drove to London in it to meet his girlfriend that evening and was subsequently picked up by the police.

When asked to account for his movements over the weekend, Hulten said he had spent Friday night in Newbury, sleeping in the back of a US Army truck. The following morning, he hitched a ride into London and arrived in Hammersmith between 11 o'clock and noon. 'I slept at the Eccleston Hotel, Victoria, on Saturday night and stayed with a "commando" last night,' he said, employing the euphemism for prostitute. 'She goes by the name of Georgina Jones and lives in the beginning of the street by King Street on the same side as the cinema.'

The cobblestones on Lurgan Avenue were slick with early morning rain when Tarr arrived to examine the Ford. Several plain-clothes detectives – including Chief Superintendent Frederick Cherrill of Scotland Yard's Fingerprint Department – and a uniformed constable were already on the scene. As Cherrill went to work, dusting the vehicle's door handles, dashboard and steering wheel, Tarr opened the driver's door and examined the car's interior.

A pair of grey flannel trousers and a chauffeur's hat lay on the front floor of the car; a similar hat lay on the floor behind the passenger seat. While there was no blood inside or outside the car, two indentations in the vehicle's interior marked what Tarr believed to be the trajectory of the bullet. Having passed through Heath's body, the bullet had ricocheted off the brass trim beneath the front-passenger window, where it left a shallow dent, and bounced off the glove compartment. The two markings were 13½ inches apart. A search of the car failed to produce the bullet or spent shell casing. Thinking back to the crime scene and the spring he had found in the grass, Tarr tried the Ford's handbrake. The return mechanism was faulty, as he suspected. Once Cherrill had finished lifting prints of varying quality from the vehicle, Tarr ordered the car be towed to Hammersmith Police Station. There, the Ford was photographed inside and out before being moved again to the police garage at Barnes.

At 3.50 that afternoon, De Mott took Hulten into custody on US military charges of desertion. The following day, Wednesday, 11 October, inspectors Tarr and Tansill, along with De Mott, asked Hulten to show them the location of the prostitute's flat where he said he had spent Sunday night. Sitting handcuffed in the back of a black Austin with De Mott by his side and the two inspectors in the front, Hulten directed them from Hammersmith Police Station to King Street. Hulten told them to stop the car outside No. 311 and said the girl he knew occupied the front room on the second floor. He watched sullenly out the back window as the two inspectors walked up the front path and entered the house. The two men didn't bother knocking on Jones's door. They barged into the room, almost removing the door from its hinges, and found Jones lying in bed. She shot upright with a startled scream and pulled the sheets up under her chin.

'I am Inspector Tarr and this is Inspector Tansill,' Tarr said, approaching the bed, 'Do you know an American officer?'

'Do – do you mean Ricky Allen?' she asked, still clutching the sheets.

'Yes,' Tarr said, 'Will you tell me what nights he stayed with you here?'

'Every night since last Tuesday,' she said, 'except Saturday when he stayed at the Eccleston Hotel.'

Tarr glanced around the squalid room, with its peeling wallpaper and shabby furnishings, and pointed to an American Army officer's uniform hanging behind the door.

'That's Ricky's, and that,' she said, pointing to a duffel bag in the corner.

Tarr took possession of the uniform and the bag, as Tansill radioed for another car to transport Jones to the station. Sitting in the same room where Hulten had given his statement in the early morning hours, Jones repeated her story. She told Tarr and Tansill 'Georgina' was her stage name and that she and 'Ricky' had spent every night that past week together. Yes, she knew of George Heath's murder, but only from what she read in yesterday's morning paper. The investigators, not quite believing Jones, told her she was free to leave but would have to answer more questions in the coming days. It was 4.30 in the afternoon. She left the station, bought a paper at a nearby newsstand and walked to a dry cleaner's on Hammersmith Broadway to pick up some laundry. At the counter, she saw Henry Kimberly, a war reserve constable she had known socially two years before. Kimberly offered her a warm smile and asked what she'd been up to.

'Since you saw me last, I've turned into a bad girl,' Jones said. 'I've been drinking a lot.'

'Yes,' Kimberly said, 'you look tired.'

'I should think so,' she replied. 'I have been over to the police station for some hours regarding this murder.'

She opened the newspaper and showed Kimberly an article on the killing. Kimberly took the paper and glanced over the story. 'What have you got to worry about?' he asked. 'You had nothing to do with it, did you?'

'I know the man they have got inside,' Jones said. 'It would have been impossible for him to do it as he was with me all Friday night.'

'Well,' Kimberly said, 'you must stop this worrying and try and get some rest. You really do look worn out.'

Jones lowered her voice, cast a conspiratorial glance over her shoulder and stepped in close. 'If you had seen someone do what I had seen done,' she said, 'you would not be able to sleep at night.'

'Then you must have something on your mind,' Kimberly said. 'The best thing for you to do is to go back to the police station and tell the truth.'

'I have made a statement over there,' Jones said. 'If I have to remember what's in it, I could not repeat it.'

Jones left the cleaner's perhaps not realising the full implication of her statement. Kimberly immediately called Tansill at Hammersmith Police Station and relayed the details of the conversation. Investigators had by now inventoried the contents of the duffel bag removed from Jones's flat and discovered the bloodstained clothing. Tansill picked up Kimberly and drove to Jones's King Street address. There was no response when they knocked on her door, so the two men waited in Tansill's unmarked car. They didn't have to wait long. It was shortly after six when a lorry pulled into the street and dropped Jones off. She waved to the driver and was opening the front door when the two officers approached her. She did little to hide her displeasure, scowling at Kimberly before leading them to her room.

'I want to talk to you by yourself,' she told Kimberly, as the two officers entered her room. Tansill stepped back into the hallway; Jones closed the door. 'Why did you bring the inspector here?'

'It's because of what you told me in the cleaner's shop,' Kimberly said. 'I think you should tell him the whole truth.'

Jones offered little resistance. 'All right,' she said, 'I'll tell him.'

She opened the door and allowed Tansill back in the room. 'I'm sorry I told you lies at the police station,' she said, 'I'll tell you the truth now.'

At 7 o'clock that evening, Jones was back at Hammersmith Police Station and confessed to witnessing George Heath's murder. Although informed of her right to remain silent, she insisted on talking. She told Tansill and Tarr how she met Ricky

Allen and how he bragged of running with the mob in Chicago. On their first night together, she said, Ricky placed a gun against her head and threatened to kill her should she ever reveal his ties to organised crime. He told her his henchmen would have her under constant surveillance – whatever she did, he would know about it. She naturally agreed to anything he suggested from that point forward. It was his idea, she said, to rob a taxi.

'I was in the car when Heath was shot,' she said, 'but I didn't do it.'

She said the killing disturbed her, but Hulten dismissed her concerns and argued that people in his line of work didn't have time to contemplate their actions.

'Would you like to write down what happened?' Tarr asked, pushing a pad and pen across the table.

'Yes,' Jones said. 'Have you found the other girl yet?'

Tarr and Tansill exchanged a glance. 'What girl?' Tarr asked.

'The one that Ricky and I robbed on Thursday night by the river,' Jones said. 'There are some of her things in my room.'

The inspectors placed Jones in a holding cell and returned to her flat, where they found the other victim's suitcase stashed away in a corner. Back at Hammersmith Police Station, they called local constabularies to see if any were investigating the beating of a woman somewhere along the Thames on Thursday night. The Surrey Joint Police said they were working such a case and detailed Violet Hodge's ordeal.

At 10.30 that evening, Jones put down on paper all that had transpired from the moment she and 'Ricky' met to the time of their apprehension. When faced that same evening with Jones's statement, Hulten confessed to beating Hodge and shooting Heath, but was adamant he did not mean to kill the man. He identified his Remington automatic, serial No. 1009424, as the murder weapon. He said 'Georgie' seemed turned on by violence and desperate to play the part of a 'gangster's moll'.

'I did tell Georgina that I had broken into a pub and that I had been running around with a mob in Chicago,' Hulten said. 'This was not true; it was just a build-up for me … If it hadn't been for her, I wouldn't have shot Heath.'

The couple – who still knew one another as Ricky and Georgina – were charged with the murder of George Heath on Friday, 13 October. They were transported separately and booked at Staines Police Station. Tarr drove Jones, and as the car made its way along the Great West Road – between the Chiswick High Road and a railway bridge – Jones looked out the window and recognised Knowle Green.

'That's where he shot him,' she said.

When their trial got under way on Tuesday, 16 January 1945, Jones and Hulten were – if not exactly celebrities – at least public curiosities. The story of the American paratrooper and the British stripper had seized the media's attention and sparked the collective imagination of the public, who envisioned a couple not unlike Bonnie and Clyde. News of their deeds had managed to do what no other crime had thus far done: push the war off the front pages. The papers christened the killing 'The Cleft-Chin Murder' after one of Heath's more prominent physical features. Some publications referred to it as 'The Inky Fingers Killing' because the fingers on the victim's left hand were stained with ink.

Crowds queued outside the Old Bailey that cold Tuesday morning, hoping to get in the courtroom and catch a glimpse of the infamous couple. The press had played up the gangster-and-stripper angle, invoking in the public mind's eye dapper dons and glamorous dames. The case proved to be an international sensation. Additional seating was required to accommodate the large number of reporters – including members of the American media – covering the legal proceedings.

The couple was tried before Justice Ernest Bruce Charles in Number One Court. Hulten's lawyers, on that first day of trial, sought to render the soldier's statements to investigators as inadmissible on the grounds he was subjected to hours of 'long and gruelling questioning'. Such interrogation methods, they argued, were 'an offence against the principles of British justice'. The argument carried little weight with Charles, who allowed the statements to be read into the public record. The trial lasted five days, during which time Jones portrayed herself as a helpless victim. She admitted in the witness box to her involvement in Heath's murder, but said she took part only because a menacing Hulten threatened her if she didn't. After shooting the cabbie, she said, Hulten stuck a gun to her head and made her go through the dead man's pockets. For his part, Hulten stuck to his claim that shooting Heath had not been his intent; he had merely fired the gun to impress a young woman aroused by violence.

'When I pulled the trigger, I intended to pull the trigger and fire the pistol,' he said. 'I intended to fire it through the car, but I did not expect George Heath to raise up to open the door just as I did it.'

In the end, Hulten's intent and Jones's claims of coercion failed to sway the jury, which took little more than an hour to find the pair guilty of murder. The verdict meant only one possible sentence. Jones screamed and begged for mercy as officers led her from the courtroom to await her fate. 'The screams went on in the corridor below,' noted one reporter. 'A door banged, and then the court was silent again.'

Hulten was sent to the condemned cell at Pentonville Prison, where British law dictated he would remain at least three Sundays following the date of sentencing. The pair's day of reckoning was set for Tuesday, 8 March. No one, with the exception of his mother and young wife back in Massachusetts, disputed the fact that Hulten should hang, but public debate raged over whether Jones deserved the rope. Some viewed her as an unwilling accomplice, while others dismissed her version of events as the last-ditch lies of a desperate individual. Even George Bernard Shaw weighed in on the matter with a letter to the *Sunday Times* two days before the scheduled execution:

[Jones] has been found guilty of theft and murder; and apparently her highest ambition is to be what she calls a gun moll, meaning a woman who thinks robbery and murder are romantically delightful professions ... Clearly we have either to put such a character to death or to re-educate her. Having no technique of re-education immediately available, we have decided to put her to death. The decision is a very sensible one ...

The following day, however, Home Secretary Herbert Morrison announced Jones had been reprieved. The news caused a considerable uproar, even in Jones's hometown, where graffiti appeared on walls proclaiming, 'She should hang!' Hulten's execution, scheduled for 8 the following morning, would go forward as planned despite an appeal for clemency from the soldier's family in Boston. Massachusetts State Senator Charles Innes went so far as to ask President Franklin D. Roosevelt to intervene on Hulten's behalf, but to no avail.

'I've done everything I can – there's nothing more to be done,' Hulten's wife, Rita, told the *New York Times* the day before the hanging, which also happened to be her 21st birthday. 'After he's gone, this woman can say anything she wants and there'll be no one there to deny it.'

Back in Britain, angry readers inundated newspapers with letters and phone calls, now demanding to know why Hulten should hang when his accomplice got off. Five young women, employed by a Glasgow factory and proclaiming to speak on behalf of their many co-workers, appeared at Glasgow Sheriff Court and threatened to walk off the job should Hulten die at the end of a rope. Isolated in his cell, Hulten, having been weighed and measured for the drop, quietly awaited his rendezvous with the hangman. Prison officials reported that he appeared relatively unconcerned with his impending death and was 'sleeping and eating regularly'.

The morning of Thursday, 8 March, cold and overcast, revealed a crowd of more than two hundred people outside Pentonville

Prison. Dressed head-to-toe in black, Violet Van Der Elst – an author of ghost stories, aspiring politician and a vocal opponent of capital punishment – took up position outside the prison gates and led those present in a chorus of jeers as the hour of execution drew near. When she asked a guard to escort her to the prison's gallows, she was politely rebuffed.

'You let the girl go, but you let the man hang,' she yelled at the prison walls, 'It's a damned shame!'

Van Der Elst's protest grew increasingly desperate with each passing minute. Her request to enter the death chamber denied, she stormed across the street and climbed inside the cab of a parked dustcart. Following the orders of an enthusiastic woman, the truck's driver gunned the engine and aimed the vehicle at the prison's wooden gates. The daring plan, however, failed. Before the lumbering truck reached its target, a number of police officers on the scene were able to block its path with a truck of their own. The dustcart swerved, jumped a kerb and skidded to a stop. Constables swarmed the vehicle and dragged the grinning driver and an irate Mrs Van Der Elst from the cab.

'Don't touch me,' she yelled as bobbies led her away.

Inside the prison, a bell tolled 9 o'clock. With two American Army officers serving as official witnesses, Karl Hulten was noosed and dropped. The noise of the commotion outside didn't penetrate the stone walls of the execution cell, where the only sound now was the morbid creaking of the gallows. In Boston, the news of her son's hanging rendered Signe Hulten inconsolable with grief. 'I'd be better off dead with my boy,' she told reporters.

A second-hand car dealer – imbued with the entrepreneurial spirit – purchased Heath's car and put it on display in Oxford Street, complete with mannequins of 'Chicago Joe' and 'Blondie', as some in the press had dubbed the killers. A sign above the car, proclaimed, 'See the actual scene of the year's most sensational crime!'

Following Hulten's execution, Elizabeth Maud Jones began serving her life sentence at an institution for young women in Aylesbury in Buckinghamshire. She served nine years for the murder of George Heath before Home Secretary Herbert Morrison granted her a reprieve in 1954. Jones kept a low profile and moved to the country, where she reportedly married and raised a family. She has since passed away.

If stardom is what Jones ultimately craved, her dream somewhat came true in the end. The 1989 film 'Chicago Joe and the Showgirl,' starring Kiefer Sutherland and Emily Lloyd, brought the murderous duo's story to the silver screen.

---

1. Percy Read is the author's paternal grandfather.

9

A Body of Lies

The man who sat in the interrogation room at Putney Police Station on Tuesday, 31 March 1953, might easily have been mistaken under differing circumstances for a university professor or any well-respected gentleman of professional means. Soft in voice but well spoken, he told his story with little emotion, sharing details of a nightmarish nature with the disinterest of a man recounting his day at the office.

Detective Inspector Kelly and Chief Inspector Griffin took the man's statement, a sickening narrative of violent death and sex with corpses. The grisly remnants of John Reginald Halliday Christie's work had only recently been discovered in his squalid flat in Notting Hill. The inspectors kept their expressions blank as Christie shared with them his disturbing proclivities. He offered the two men a weak smile and ran a hand over his bald scalp.

'I have not been well for a long while,' he said, his voice registering barely above a whisper.

No. 10 Rillington Place looked no different from the other three-storey houses that lined the decrepit street in Ladbroke Grove, Notting Hill. Whatever Victorian charm the home once possessed had long since succumbed to a rubbish-strewn communal garden, musty interior and window coverings faded to a sickly yellow. The attached house was the last one in the block and abutted the wall of a converted iron foundry. Soot blackened the brickwork of not only No. 10, but all the dank housing in Rillington Place. It was here on this dead-end street, where the clatter of trains on the Metropolitan Line was an ever-constant racket, that John and Ethel Christie moved in December 1938.

The couple occupied the small, three-roomed flat on the ground floor. The front room offered a view of the run-down street and the foundry wall. A short hallway led to the bedroom, its window providing an unflattering glimpse of the claustrophobic back garden with its overgrown weeds and communal washhouse. Further back was the miniature kitchen, furnished with a gas stove, kitchen range, a small table and a sink. The staircase leading up to the building's top two floors was just past the entrance to the front room, meaning anyone who lived above them had to walk through the couple's living space to get upstairs. When the Christies moved in, the only other tenant was Charles Kitchener, a retired railway worker, who had lived in the first-floor flat for more than a decade. The top-floor flat with its bed-sitting room in the front and kitchen in the back was unoccupied.

Christie lived with Ethel in the house for fourteen years until the day he killed her. He awoke shortly after 8 on the morning of Sunday, 14 December 1952, and supposedly found his wife convulsing in bed. He sat up and saw, even in the room's dim light, Ethel's features turning blue. 'It appeared,' he told the detectives, 'too late to call for assistance.' Christie alleged his wife's health had been in decline for some time. She was prone to nervous breakdowns and scared to leave the flat, he said, because she feared the 'black people' who had recently moved in upstairs. He propped himself up and briefly watched Ethel struggle to take in a breath. When he had seen enough, he reached for one of his wife's stockings lying on the floor, wrapped it around her throat and strangled the life out of her.

Kneeling over the body, he saw on Ethel's bedside table his bottle of phenol barbitone tablets, which he took for his insomnia. The night before, the bottle had contained twenty-five pills – now, there were only two. A half-drunk glass of water sat beside the bottle. 'I knew then,' Christie claimed, 'she must have taken the remainder.' For three days he kept the body in the bed and lay beside it at night, unable to sleep and wondering what to do with the corpse. On the third day, he had an idea. In the flat's cramped front room, he pulled a small coffee table off to the side and rolled up the centre rug to reveal the wooden floorboards beneath. He pried the floorboards loose and walked back into the bedroom. He pulled his wife's wedding ring from her finger and placed a pillowcase over her head. He wrapped the body in a flannel sheet, silk nightgown and floral-print dress, and tried to lift it off the bed. When the body proved too heavy, he simply pulled it off the mattress and dragged it into the living room.

Straining, his weak back aching, he pulled the bundled mass to the edge of the hole in the floor and pushed it in. He covered the body with what loose earth there was, put the floorboards back in place and repositioned the rug and small coffee table. 'I thought,' he said, 'that was the best way to lay her to rest.' Two days after the killing, he pawned his wife's wedding ring for 37s to a jeweller in Shepherd's Bush so he could buy food. To avoid arousing the suspicions of Ethel's family, with whom she kept in regular contact, he penned several letters to her sister in Sheffield and explained he was doing the writing because Ethel's rheumatism was acting up. In one letter, he presented himself as the doting husband. 'Don't worry, she is OK,' he wrote. 'I shall cook Xmas dinner.' He also sent Christmas cards, signing them, 'From Ethel and Reg.'

'I was in a state and didn't know what to do,' he said when looking back on events. 'After Christmas, I sold all my furniture. I made a bed on some bedding on the floor in the back room; I had about four blankets there. I kept my kitchen table, two chairs, some crockery and cutlery. These were just enough for my immediate needs because I was going away. I wasn't working and had a meagre existence.'

For the flat's furnishings, which he had sold shortly after New Year's, Christie pocketed £11. No. 10 Rillington Place, squalid at the best of times, was now dank and barren. By early January, the body beneath the floorboards was beginning to ripen, prompting Christie to sprinkle Jeyes fluid about the premises to nullify the stench. One evening in early January, he left the flat to get some fresh air and a meal of fish and chips at a cheap café on Ladbroke Grove. Walking home, he was propositioned by a drunken woman lounging in a doorway. Christie waved her off and kept walking, but the woman gave chase.

'Give me a pound and take me around the corner,' she slurred.

'I am not interested,' Christie replied, still moving, 'and I haven't got money to throw away.'

In the days after his wife's murder, he forged her signature and stole £10 15s 2d from her bank account. Out of work, his only source of regular income was the weekly payment of £2 14s he received from the unemployment exchange. Money was a constant worry. He scurried along with the woman still following close behind, now yelling at his back. She demanded he pay her 30s, threatening to scream and accuse him of assault if he didn't. Christie, having long suffered from impotency, had never fared well in the bedroom; it had been two years since he last had sex. He was intimidated by women and terrified of domineering females – and so he kept walking. The woman, however, had latched onto her target and followed him back to Rillington Place.

'She wouldn't go, and she came right to the door, still demanding 30s,' Christie said. 'When I opened the door, she forced her way in … she was still on about the 30s.'

Ignoring Christie's demands that she leave immediately, the woman followed him into the kitchen, where she supposedly grabbed a frying pan from the clutter on the small counter and lunged at him, wielding the pan like a club. Christie grabbed the woman's wrist and tried to wrestle the weapon away. He forced her back toward the kitchen table and one of the chairs he had kept – a deck chair made of rope. He twisted the pan free of her grip with one hand and shoved her hard with the other. The woman stumbled backwards, lost her balance and fell against the chair.

'I don't remember what happened, but I must have gone haywire,' Christie said. 'The next thing I remember she was lying in the chair with rope round her neck.'

Christie stared momentarily at the body then turned toward the kitchen counter and brewed himself a cup of tea. He drank it in the front room, where he had buried his wife weeks before. It had occurred to him long ago that he felt more comfortable around dead women than he did live ones. He sat on the floor with his back against the wall and pondered the slightly sagging floorboards in the centre of the room. When he finished his drink, he put the tea and saucer in the kitchen sink and went to bed.

'I got up in the morning, went to the kitchen and washed and shaved,' he said. 'She was still in the chair. I believe I made some tea then.'

He sat at the table with the corpse and drank his morning brew, eyeing the body over the rim of his cup and wondering how to dispose of it. Burying it in the garden was out, lest he risk being seen by a neighbour, and there was only so much crawl space beneath the front room. Peeling up the linoleum in the kitchen would most likely be too time consuming and hell on his problematic back. As he put down his cup, his eyes settled on the small cupboard in the corner beside the sink. A water pipe in the wall behind the cupboard had frozen and burst the previous winter, prompting Christie to call a plumber. The repairman had pulled the cupboard away from the wall to reveal a hollow alcove through which the flat's piping ran. Christie now got up and pulled the cupboard toward him; it moved with little effort. He stripped the dead woman down to her bra, underwear and stockings, and dragged the body across the kitchen floor. He shoved it in the alcove and positioned the body on its knees with its back facing out toward the kitchen.

'Sometime after this, I suppose it was in February,' Christie said, 'I went into a café at Notting Hill Gate for a cup of tea and a sandwich. The café was pretty full, and there wasn't much space. Two girls sat at a table, and I sat opposite at the same table. They were talking about rooms, where they had been looking to get accommodations.'

Christie told the two young women he would soon be leaving his flat and was looking to sub-lease it. They accepted his invitation to come and view it later that evening, but at the agreed upon hour, only one of the women showed up. In relating what happened next, Christie again portrayed his victim as the initial aggressor and claimed she offered him sex in exchange for him putting in a kind word with the building's landlord. When he refused, she turned violent and attacked him. 'I am very quiet and avoid fighting,' he said. 'I know there was something – it's in the back of my mind. I must have put her in the alcove right away.'

A putrid, sweet odour – one not so easily nullified by disinfectant – now permeated the dingy flat. Christie, when home, shuffled from one dark room to another, ever fearful his crimes might be discovered. He wandered the streets of Notting Hill to clear his mind and stopped in the occasional pub and cheap café. It was in such a dining establishment in Hammersmith that he met his next victim in early March. She was a young Scottish woman with whom Christie somehow managed to strike up a conversation. When she told him she and her boyfriend had recently been evicted from their flat, Christie was more than willing to help. 'I told her that if they hadn't found anywhere, I could put them up for a few days,' Christie said.

The couple arrived at Rillington Place that evening and stayed with Christie for the next three days. If they noticed the off-putting stench, they never said anything – at least not to their host. Christie, despite opening his home to the couple, found the situation discomforting. He worried they might stumble across the bodies and cared little for the woman's boyfriend, an out-of-work lorry driver with a temper. On the third day, Christie kicked the couple out.

'I told them they would have to go, as he was being very unpleasant,' Christie later explained.

The woman returned alone later that evening and said she and her boyfriend had each gone off in search of a place to live. Could she spend the night at Rillington Place in case he came by looking for her? When Christie said no, the woman forced her way into the house, ignoring his protestations. He followed her into the kitchen, grabbed her by the arm and tried to pull her toward the front door. 'She started struggling like anything and some of her clothing got torn,' he said. 'She then sort of fell limp as I had hold of her. She sank to the ground, and I think some of her clothing must have got caught round her neck in the struggle.'

Unable to detect a pulse, he dragged the body to the corner of the kitchen and once more pulled the cupboard away from the wall. 'I must have put her in there,' he said, claiming his memory of the event had grown hazy.

Detective Inspector Kelly and Chief Inspector Griffin knew the rest of the story.

Desperate to flee the flat, Christie sublet it to a couple named Reilly who paid him £7 in advance rent. On the afternoon of 19 March 1953, with his few scant belongings packed into a single suitcase, Christie left No. 10 Rillington Place for good. That same evening, Charles Brown – the landlord and building owner – stopped by the address to collect back rent Christie owed him. Knocking on the door, he was surprised to find a new couple living in the flat. He told the Reillys it had not been within Christie's rights to sublease the property and informed the couple they would have to leave by morning. Once the couple were gone, Brown allowed upstairs tenant Beresford Brown (no relation), a Jamaican immigrant, to move into the larger, ground-floor residence.

The first thing Brown noticed when he moved in on the afternoon of Tuesday, 24 March, was the foul smell, which seemed to originate in the kitchen. He immediately set about clearing out the rubbish Christie had let accumulate, believing the scattered empty tins, yellowing newspapers and smeared food wrappings were to blame. Sweeping the refuse into the garden, he decided to hang a bracket for his wall-mounted wireless. He tapped a spot on the wall, searching for a beam to support the weight of the radio, and realised the wall was hollow. Curious, he pulled away a loose piece of grimy wallpaper and discovered what appeared to be some sort of closet or alcove, its opening partially covered by a wallpapered piece of plasterboard.

Brown cleared the opening and shone his torch into the dark space beyond. He leaned forward, peered in and wrinkled his nose against the awful stench. The beam of his torch cut through swirling clouds of dust and settled on something large and ghostly white. He staggered backwards, unsure at what he'd just seen, but another tentative glance confirmed what his mind could not grasp: a naked woman sitting slumped amidst the rubble, her head bent forward, her back facing out toward the kitchen.

Chief Superintendent Peter Beveridge arrived at Rillington Place with several officers and a divisional police surgeon shortly after five that evening. Police photographer Percy Law documented the ghastly find before investigators did anything to disturb the scene. Detectives removed the woman's body and laid it out in the front room. She wore suspenders and stockings; her bra, black sweater and white jacket were pulled up around her neck. A cursory examination by the surgeon revealed ligature marks around the throat. The victim's wrists were bound in front of her with a handkerchief tied in a square knot.

The removal of the body revealed a large, blanket-wrapped bundle pushed further back in the alcove. Upon closer inspection, police discovered this to also be a body. The corpse lay with its legs vertical to the wall and its head, wrapped in a pillowcase with a sock tied around the neck, against the ground. Another corpse, wrapped in a blanket, lay beyond this one, its ankles secured with an electrical cord. In all three cases, manual strangulation seemed to be the cause of death. The bodies were removed to Kensington Mortuary for autopsy – but another gruesome discovery lay in store when detectives noticed several loose floorboards in the front room. Prying the boards up and clearing away a layer of loose gravel, they were startled to find yet another body.

News of the gruesome discoveries in what the press quickly dubbed 'the Notting Hill house of murder' turned No. 10 Rillington Place into the most notorious address in Britain. Uniformed constables stood sentry at the front door day and night to dissuade morbid souvenir seekers and to keep the curious at bay. Behind the curtained front window and the guarded door, detectives launched a painstaking search of the premises, tapping on the walls in search of more hidden crypts and pulling up every floorboard in the flat. 'Detectives,' noted one press account, 'are prepared to take it apart brick by brick and board by board if they find evidence that more bodies are concealed within it.'

Four days after the initial discoveries were made, officers from Scotland Yard – under the supervision of Chief Detective Superintendent Tom Barratt – discovered in the garden, beneath a rockery bordered with blooming forsythia, a large rubbish bin containing what appeared to be charred human bones. Dr Francis Camps, Home Office pathologist, jarred samples of the soil from the forsythia roots and bagged a scrap of clothing found with the remains. On hands and knees, investigators continued combing the shabby garden, sifting through grass and soil, determined – in the words of one reporter – 'to wrest from it all its grim secrets'.

As the house continued surrendering one morbid find after another, Britain's most wanted man wandered aimlessly about London. With only his shaving gear, a few letters, and some pencils packed in his suitcase, he was ill-prepared for a life on the run. He made his way to King's Cross and checked into Rowton House, a cheap hotel for single men, on Friday, 20 March. Not bothering to use an alias, he initially planned on staying a week but left four days later. By then, the police had released a photograph of Christie to the media and issued a general alarm, which urged 'persons letting rooms, café proprietors, or any other persons' to keep their eyes open for the former Rillington Place tenant.

The picture appearing in London's newspapers showed a dapper gentleman in suit and tie, hat in one hand, and a handkerchief folded neatly in the breast pocket of his jacket. The façade of respectability, the press declared, disguised a monstrous nature. A mad man was now on the loose. Would he dare strike again? The conceived notion that Christie was stalking the streets, planning his next kill, was far removed from reality. Desperate and out of money, Christie was living the life of a vagrant, sleeping on park benches and seeking shelter in the occasional cinema. He traded his raincoat for an overcoat in a meagre attempt at disguise and wandered about the capital with nowhere to go.

A man who relished being in control of all things, Christie grew increasingly desperate. He had always pictured himself in his misguided mind as a model citizen, morally superior to all who crossed his path. It was the only way he could live with himself. Now, however, he had become nothing more than a hunted animal – a vulgar creature whose grotesque secrets had been exposed to everyone. Hoping not to draw attention to himself, he began spending his days wandering along the Thames embankment.

On the morning of Tuesday, 31 March, Police Constable Thomas Ledger was patrolling the river's edge near Putney Bridge. He saw, leaning against a railing and staring into the grey waters, a gentleman who looked down-and-out in his shabby raincoat and worn clothing. He appeared in need of a shave and in want of a good night's sleep. The man wore a hat, its brim pulled down low, but there was something familiar about the tall, lanky figure and the horn-rimmed spectacles.

'What are you doing?' Ledger asked. 'Looking for work?'

'Yes,' Christie replied, 'but my unemployment cards haven't come through.'

'What's your name and address?'

'John Waddington,' Christie replied, assuming his brother-in-law's name, '35 Westbourne Grove.'

'Have you anything to prove your identity?'

'No,' Christie said, quietly, 'Nothing at all.'

'Will you remove your hat?'

Taking off his hat, there was no disguising the bald scalp and its defeated fringe of ginger hair.

'You are Christie, aren't you?' Ledger asked.

Christie nodded.

'Will you come with me, please,' Ledger said.

On a rather anti-climactic note, Christie went along peacefully, ending a weeklong manhunt without so much as a word of protest. Searched at Putney Police Station, he was found to be in possession of an identity card, ration book and a union card – all in his name. News of Christie's apprehension hit the airwaves that afternoon and caused considerable excitement. Crowds, including children in their school uniforms, gathered outside the station to catch a glimpse of the Rillington Place strangler. Oblivious to the excitement outside, Christie detailed his crimes for Kelly and Griffin. He claimed to tell them all he could remember, but did not refer once to the bones in the garden. Only when he finished his statement did he imply he had more to tell.

'I know there's something,' he said. 'I keep picturing something, but it's not very clear. If I could remember anymore, I'd tell you. Perhaps it will come back to me; I will tell you right away.'

It had just gone five in the evening when Kelly bundled Christie into a van and transferred him to Notting Hill Police Station, where he was charged with Ethel's murder. He appeared at West London Magistrates' Court the following morning and entered a plea of not guilty before being remanded to Brixton Prison to await trial.

Going on the evidence already gathered, Kelly and Griffin knew Christie had withheld details – but there would be time to question him again. Although Christie passed off Ethel's murder as a mercy killing, saying she had tried to kill herself by overdosing on a bottle of pills, a post mortem revealed no evidence of drugs in her system. Most likely, the detectives believed, he simply wanted Ethel out the way so he could go trolling for victims. For now, they would simply play along. While Christie had not mentioned names in his statement, police had already identified the victims found buried in the kitchen alcove.

The first body retrieved from the wall was that of 26-year-old Hectorina Maclennan, a prostitute. She had moved from Scotland in 1948 with her parents, who had since returned and taken Maclennan's two illegitimate children with them. It was Maclennan who had spent three nights at Rillington Place with her boyfriend. The body found stashed behind Maclennan's was identified as Kathleen Maloney, a 26-year-old prostitute and mother to five illegitimate children. Raised as an orphan in a convent, Maloney escaped the nuns at 19 when she ran away. The third body was that of Rita Nelson, a blonde prostitute from Belfast who, by her early twenties, had already accrued a record for various petty crimes.

Autopsies confirmed all three women had died of manual strangulation, but also revealed evidence of carbon monoxide poisoning. Interior body tissues and organs, including the heart cavities of the victims and the bronchial membranes of their lungs, were cherry red in colour. Drops of blood from each victim were placed in test tubes and mixed with equal amounts of sodium hydroxide. Had carbon monoxide not been present, the blood would have turned a greenish-brown. The fact the blood maintained its red hue indicated the victims had been gassed.

In revealing the details of his post-Ethel murders to Kelly and Griffin, Christie sought to present himself as a quiet man harassed by demanding women. Kathleen Maloney, he said, tried to strong-arm money out of him as he walked home from a fish-and-chip shop. Police learned he actually picked her up at the Westminster Arms in Paddington, as she sat having drinks with another working girl. Christie had previously met Maloney three weeks before Christmas, when he paid her and another prostitute to pose for some nude photographs. On the night of the slaying, he brought her back to Rillington Place, gassed her and had sex with her lifeless body. He placed a cloth between her legs when done, wrapped her in a towel and shoved her body in the kitchen alcove.

Police found no eyewitnesses to Christie's encounter with his next victim, Rita Nelson. As he had done with Maloney, he gassed her and had sex with the body, wrapping a makeshift nappy between Nelson's legs before putting her in the wall. The autopsy revealed Nelson to be 24 weeks pregnant. In the course of their investigation, detectives learned she had been referred to the Samaritan Hospital for Women but never showed up for her appointment. It's unlikely Nelson tried to force sex upon Christie in exchange for room and board, as he subsequently claimed. A more plausible scenario is he presented himself as a medical expert upon their first meeting and offered to help her with an abortion. Accepting his assistance out of desperation, Nelson unwittingly went to her death.

When Christie met Hectorina Maclennan one month later, his desire to kill had become a rabid compulsion. He initially told authorities Maclennan's death was accidental, the result of a struggle to try and get her out of the house. An autopsy, however, revealed he gassed her before once again satisfying his grotesque fantasies and disposing of the body in the alcove.

Now, as Christie sat in his cell, awaiting his day in court, investigators continued piecing together the horrific details of what exactly happened inside No. 10 Rillington Place.

10

The Killer Inside

John Christie's fascination with death began at a young age. His maternal grandfather, a strict figure who instilled the young boy with dread, died when Christie was eight. At the wake, his family urged him to view the body and bid a final farewell. He approached the open casket with an overwhelming reluctance, terrified at what he might see in its satin-lined interior. When he peered in, he found himself not repulsed as anticipated, but instead strangely fascinated. The man who had frightened and intimidated, now lay pale and still. The human body as an empty shell immediately struck Christie as a strange and enthralling concept. Seeing his grandfather flat on his back, lifeless, and realising the old man could do nothing more to scare him, imbued the boy with a wonderful sense of power. For Christie, it was the start of a life-long attraction to the macabre.

After the funeral, the Christie family returned to their home in Chester Road in the Boothtown district of Halifax. From the house, one could view All Souls Cemetery and the intricate church steeple that loomed over the burial grounds. Here, he could now indulge his gruesome fascination and escape, if only temporarily, a difficult home environment. He enjoyed roaming the cemetery, traversing the graves and reading the faded inscriptions on moss-covered tombstones. He strolled the cemetery's wooded paths beneath the leaden Yorkshire sky and conjured in his mind the contents of caskets underground. Of particular interest to him was a vault where children lay interred. A crack in the stone wall allowed the boy to eye the small caskets lining the vault's shelves. Christie was repeatedly drawn to this spot to satisfy his increasingly morbid curiosity.

John Reginald Halliday Christie's life began ordinarily enough on 8 April 1898 on the West Yorkshire moors in Black Boy House, a home dominated by females. Four of his five siblings – Florence, Winnie, Effie and Dolly – were sisters, meaning Reggie (as he was known) and eldest brother Percy were hopelessly outnumbered. The Christie sisters teased their youngest brother mercilessly and often sent him crying into the arms of his mother, Mary, who coddled and pampered the boy. Her domineering and overprotective nature, coupled with his sisters' bullying, stripped the young Christie of his burgeoning masculinity and reduced him to a shy, frail child easily intimidated by women. His father's influence did little to improve matters. Carpet designer Ernest John Christie took great pleasure in doling out harsh punishment and routinely thrashed his children on a whim.

A founding member of the Halifax Conservative Party, Ernest Christie was well known and admired throughout the community. He sought to instil in his children discipline and a toughness of character he believed were necessary to succeed in life. A favourite Sunday pastime of the father's was taking his children on five-mile hikes across the West Yorkshire moors. He barked commands like a drill sergeant and insisted his children march the whole way like guards on parade, their backs and shoulders ramrod straight, their arms swinging high.

The father lived by a strict moral code that forbade even the slightest transgression. Anything from the raising of a voice to John perhaps sitting too close to one of his sisters were grounds for a beating. And so it was, suffocated by his mother and terrified of his father, John Christie retreated inside himself, untrusting of men and scared of women. The family left Black Boy House when

Christie was still young and moved into the house at 67 Chester Road, across the street from All Souls Cemetery. It was while living here Christie found school to be a relief from the torment at home.

Christie's penchant for numbers earned him a scholarship to Halifax Secondary School when he was 11. He excelled at maths and found an outlet in the choir at All Souls Church, where he eventually joined the church's scout troop. For one so emasculated, he felt a sense of empowerment whenever he donned his scouting uniform. In these special clothes, he was no mere boy, but someone of importance. He took great pleasure in various scouting activities and worked his way up to assistant scoutmaster, delighting in the sense of authority the title bestowed. He sought to maintain that sense of power in his everyday life and often went about his daily routines in his scout uniform. At school, he was something of a nonentity – not popular, but not picked on, a solitary figure who, although he enjoyed playing games, did not establish any close friendships. The other children he did play with were merely acquaintances who found something strange in Christie's desire to hang about the local graveyard. His attraction to the macabre was coupled, when he was 10, to conflicting thoughts on sex after visiting his married sister at her home in Barkisland, Halifax.

After hosting her younger brother for several days, the sister in question was preparing to take him home and placed her foot on a table to do up a shoelace. In doing so, she revealed her knee and a good portion of leg. Christie caught a glimpse of his sister's bare flesh and turned a dark shade of crimson. Noticing the change in colour, his sister scoffed at Christie's reaction and told him he would likely see many more knees in his lifetime. For Christie, there was something oddly stimulating and simultaneously repulsive about his sister's exposed leg. The experience aroused only a greater ambivalence towards women and confusing thoughts on the nature of sexual attraction.

His dark take on sex worsened after he left school at the age of 15. He took a job as a projectionist's assistant at a local cinema and continued his involvement with All Souls Church. Following one Sunday evening service, he ventured with a group of young people to the local lovers lane and found himself in the company of a more experienced girl. Their attempt at sex was thwarted by a horrified Christie's inability to perform. The girl, out of amusement, or simply insulted by Christie's lack of response, shared the boy's failure with the rest of the group. Word of Christie's miserable sexual prowess quickly made the rounds, resulting in open taunts and the unfortunate nicknames 'Can't-do-it-Christie' and 'No-Dick Reggie'. The experience left him deeply humiliated and only reinforced his burgeoning disdain for the opposite sex.

Following his 18th birthday, Christie enlisted in the army and was called to service in April 1917. He trained as a signalman with the 52nd Nottinghamshire and Derby Regiment. It was during this time that he began frequenting prostitutes. While it's not uncommon for young men facing the prospect of war to engage in various delights while time allows, Christie appreciated purchased sex for more psychologically complex reasons. His frequent inability to perform was not an issue when the woman lying next to him was, in a certain sense, under his employ. They did not laugh at his inadequacies and were there to do whatever he so desired. For the time a few pounds allotted, he had power over a woman, an entity he usually felt powerless against – but the experiences hardly left him satisfied. Scurrying from a back alley or leaving a dingy flat in the wake of these sordid trysts, he felt only shame at having to resort to such behaviour.

In April 1918, his orders came through and sent him across the Channel to France, where he was seconded to the Duke of Wellington's (West Riding) Regiment. He served three months with the unit behind the front lines. What action he saw was unintended when, on 27 June, a mustard-gas shell overshot its frontline target and exploded in the rear flanks. The blast knocked Christie unconscious and resulted in seven weeks hospitalisation. Christie often feigned illness – or exaggerated legitimate symptoms – to garner attention and the sympathies of others. Later in life, he would claim the gas attack left him blinded for three months and unable to speak for three years. In reality, he was mute for several weeks. Doctors diagnosed his condition as functional aphonia most likely brought on by the shock of the attack. He returned to active duty in August but was hospitalised in March 1919 when his voice left him again, resulting in the same diagnosis as before. Nearly a week of treatment in Newcastle followed before he returned to his regiment and finished his tour of duty. He received his honorary discharge at the end of 1919 and returned to Halifax. Although he bore no physical scars from the gas attack, his voice was permanently altered. For the remainder of his life, he hardly spoke above a whisper.

Back home, Christie took a clerical position at the wool mill in Sutcliffe. Making an attempt at what he hoped would be a normal life, he struck up a courtship with Ethel Waddington, whose family lived near the Christie home. Like her shy suitor, there was nothing outwardly extraordinary about Ethel. Squat in appearance and quiet by nature, she had never been one to turn heads. She harboured few opinions, avoided confrontation and most likely struck Christie as someone with whom he could exist on an equal plane. The same age as Christie, she did not seem sexually adventurous and was therefore less likely to make an issue of his problems in the bedroom. They married on 10 May 1920 at the Halifax Register Office and established their home in a small house on Brunswick Street. Behind this façade of normality, Christie remained a troubled individual. The marital bed was cold for some time, and rare were the occasions when Christie was able to perform. Ethel shrugged off her husband's impotence and sought to assure him in his moments of doubt, but her emotional support did nothing to soothe his inner turmoil.

Not long after the couple settled in their new home, Christie left his clerical job and became a postman. Wearing the postal uniform gave him a sense of pride and reminded him of his scouting days, but he still struggled to find fulfilment in what he did. Seeking a satisfaction that always seemed just out of reach, Christie once again began fraternising with prostitutes – an expensive pastime, which might explain why, after only a few months on the job, he was caught stealing postal orders from work.

One month shy of his first wedding anniversary, Christie was found guilty of petty theft and sent to prison for three months. Ethel, always supportive, promised to wait for him. After serving his time, Christie rejoined his wife but failed to control his dark impulses. In 1923, he appeared before the local magistrate on charges of obtaining money by false pretences and violent conduct. Put on twelve months probation, his reputation about town was forever sullied. His family no longer wanted anything to do with him, and acquaintances – having heard rumours of his back alley encounters – kept their distance.

When Ethel suggested a new start in Sheffield, it seemed like a good idea – but the marriage, strained by Christie's behaviour and a lack of physical intimacy, did not survive the move. The couple argued frequently, and Christie – feeling confined – left Ethel for London in the early months of 1924. Moving to the city did little to improve Christie's circumstances. He had no fixed address, or prospects for meaningful employment, and spent his time lounging about low-class cafés and public houses. He worked odd jobs during the day and most likely squandered what money he made on cheap sex.

In London, where no one knew him, Christie could indulge his needs and remain anonymous, a nameless face in the bustling crowds. He impressed the ladies with whom he associated, offering medical advice and pretending to be a doctor. To them, he looked the part with his spectacles and dark-coloured suits. By 1929, he had moved into the Battersea home of one such woman. The relationship proved less than harmonious and was often punctuated by bitter rows. During one confrontation in May, Christie's long-gestating animosity towards women got the better of him. Enraged by some perceived slight, he picked up a cricket bat and beat her about the head with it, opening a 5-inch gash in her skull. He was taken into custody and sentenced to six months of hard labour.

Life behind bars did little to put Christie straight. Upon his release, he befriended a Roman Catholic priest, who saw in Christie a soul in need of guidance. Christie, in turn, stole the priest's car – a crime for which he was sentenced in 1933 to three months in prison. In the cramped confines of his cell, Christie fell into a depression, overcome by the increasingly turbulent path his life had taken. He wrote a letter to Ethel out of desperation and pleaded with her to join him in London once he had served his sentence. Nine years had now passed since their initial separation. The letter found Ethel in Sheffield living a lonely life, working as a typist and socialising primarily with her family. For someone as shy and quiet as Ethel, now in her mid-thirties, life in London seemed a daunting proposition, but it also meant escaping the banality of her current life and re-establishing a relationship with her husband. She travelled south by train to visit Christie in prison. He apologised for the trouble he had caused and said their reunion would be a new start for them both – a chance to live happily ever after. Ethel, touched by Christie's apparent sincerity, agreed to join him.

The couple moved shortly thereafter into Rillington Place, and Christie found a clerical job to pay the bills. Whether he truly believed Ethel's presence would offer some sort of stability is suspect – but even with his wife back at his side, he found it impossible to control his prurient interests. Sex with Ethel remained occasional at best, yet he still trolled for prostitutes when opportunity allowed. Ethel's frequent visits to her family in Sheffield gave Christie the freedom to roam the streets and acquaint himself with the local streetwalkers. It was a routine he'd stick with until the very end.

Christie's clerical job did not last long, and he continued to bounce from one dead-end job to another. The growing threat of war, however, opened an unexpected door. As more men were called up for military service, the Metropolitan Police Department sought to bolster the ranks of its Emergency Reserve. Christie, who had always relished positions of power, applied and in September 1939 was duly sworn in as a full-time constable in the War Reserve. Police officials, overwhelmed by the number of applicants, never checked Christie's criminal record. Serving in a policeman's uniform was a chance for Christie to be the man he had always wanted to be. He was assigned to the Harrow Road Police Station and went about his duties with admirable enthusiasm, earning a first aid certificate and two commendations for his tackling of neighbourhood crime. Despite his performance on the job, Christie's crisp, blue uniform camouflaged only so much of the man beneath it.

Enforcing the law, he could also take advantage of it, agreeing not to arrest streetwalkers who were willing to show their appreciation. In many ways, Christie was once again that young boy in the Church scout troop, enthralled with a sense of purpose and relishing any opportunity to be seen in his uniform. He became known about the neighbourhood for his officiousness and took great pleasure in bossing others. He assisted in various recovery efforts during the Blitz and helped pull the dead from bomb-ravaged homes. The morbid work appealed to his affinity for the macabre, and he enjoyed viewing the bodies, just as he had the graves at All Souls Cemetery as a child.

Police work bolstered not only Christie's sense of self worth, but his long-suppressed masculinity. In the summer of 1943, he developed a liking for a younger woman who worked at the Harrow Road Police Station. With her husband fighting overseas, she began spending time with Christie after work, which eventually led to the occasional encounter in her bedroom. It's open to speculation whether Christie fully consummated the affair, but that was of no concern to the woman's husband who unexpectedly returned from war one evening and caught Christie in bed with his wife. Enraged, he dragged Christie from the bedroom, beat him mercilessly and kicked him out of the house. The humiliating episode reduced Christie once more to the weak and emasculated wretch he had always been, igniting a long-suppressed rage he was now powerless to control.

Going by Christie's subsequent statements to police, he either met her in a grimy café on the corner of Lancaster Road and Ladbroke Grove in August 1943 while investigating a local theft, or made her acquaintance walking the beat. Attractive, with dark skin and brunette hair that fell about her shoulders, 21-year-old Ruth Fuerst worked as a part-time prostitute to supplement the wages she made at a munitions factory in Davies Street. Originally from Austria, she had moved to England at the outbreak of war and took a small flat in Oxford Gardens, a short distance from Rillington Place. How Christie made his introduction is not known, but he later told investigators the relationship developed over time, with Ruth visiting Rillington Place on several occasions while Ethel was away in Sheffield. It's unlikely Christie would have allowed an attractive woman like Ruth to survive more than one visit to his home.

Whatever developed between the two, Christie – perhaps offering money for sex – managed to lure Ruth back to his flat one afternoon. She wore a leopard-print coat over her dress and in her heels stood nearly as tall as Christie's 5 feet 9 inches. Not long after Christie invited Ruth in, a telegram from Ethel arrived at Rillington Place, saying she was on her way back from Sheffield. Whatever Christie had in mind, he would have to do it quickly. The two made their way to the back bedroom. Ruth slipped out of her clothes and beckoned Christie onto the bed. He undressed and joined her beneath the sheets, pleased to find he was able to perform. He slipped himself inside her, and as he felt her body beneath his, he wrapped a rope around her throat and strangled her to death. 'I remember urine and excreta coming away from her,' he later recalled. 'She was completely naked.' With little time to admire what he'd done, he climbed off the bed and gathered Ruth's clothes. He wrapped the body in the leopard-print coat and dragged the girl into the front room. 'I put her under the floorboards,' he said. 'I had to do that because of my wife coming back.'

He bundled up Ruth's clothes and shoved them down beside her before putting the floorboards back in place. In the bedroom, he stripped the mattress and put clean sheets on the bed. He moved with a sense of exhilaration, enthralled by what he had done. Intimidated by women all his life, he had just delivered what he thought to be a damning blow against the years of sexual oppression that had caused him so much misery. He got dressed and waited for Ethel, who returned home late that afternoon with her brother, Henry, much to Christie's chagrin. He and Ethel slept that night in the murder bed; Henry slept in the front room, mere inches from a cooling corpse.

The following afternoon, Henry returned to Sheffield and Ethel went to her job at Osram's. Christie, alone in the flat, retrieved the body from beneath the floor and dragged it into the small back garden. He stashed the body in the communal washhouse, grabbed a spade and dug a hole near the back of the garden alongside the rockery. As Christie dug, a neighbour in the adjoining building peered out an upper-floor window and waved. Christie offered a smile in return and kept digging. Done, he leaned the spade against the garden's sagging fence and went inside.

Ethel came home later that evening, and the two of them sat in the front room and listened to the wireless. It was about 10 p.m. when Christie said he had to run outside to use the lavatory. In the garden, he stared up at Mr Kitchener's flat and eyed the windows in the buildings next door, making sure the blackout curtains were drawn. He hauled the body under the cover of darkness from the washhouse and pulled it to the edge of the hole he had dug. He pushed the body, along with the girl's clothing, into the shallow grave and moved quickly as he shovelled in the earth. He dragged his sleeve across his forehead and returned to the front room, where Ethel still sat listening to the radio.

Early the next morning, he returned to the garden and dug up the clothes. He raked over the grave to level it out and put the clothes in a trash bin he frequently used to burn garbage. He struck a match and incinerated Ruth's dress, stockings, blouse and shoes. Next, he dug a hole about 18-inches deep near the base of the rockery and partially buried the bin, leaving the opening exposed so he could still burn rubbish. It struck him, as he went about his work, how easy it had been to kill the girl and dispose of her and her belongings. 'My wife,' Christie later said, 'never knew.' To him, the girl's murder was of no concern – of greater worry was being able to still burn refuse.

He returned to work that evening, donning his police uniform and walking the beat – but something had changed. In killing Ruth Fuerst, he had nullified any sense of moral superiority he felt on the job. He was no better than the lowlifes he was charged with bringing to justice. He resigned from the police force in December 1943 to take a job with Ultra Radio Works in Acton, filling various low-level positions within the company and dined each afternoon in the factory canteen. Muriel Eady, a 31-year-old assembly line worker, took lunch the same time as Christie and often engaged him in casual conversation.

Over one particular lunch, Muriel, a short, heavy-set woman who lived with her aunt in Putney, mentioned a young man she had recently started dating. Christie, for his part, spoke proudly of his time as a police constable. The two eventually developed what Muriel believed to be a friendship – but for Christie, their acquaintance was merely one of opportunity. He decided almost immediately that Muriel would be his next victim. He had crossed a line when he killed Ruth Fuerst and had no intention of stepping back.

He planned Muriel's death while cultivating the relationship and invited Muriel and her boyfriend over on several occasions for tea. Ethel enjoyed the younger couple's company and encouraged Christie to invite them one evening to the cinema. The more time they spent together, the more Christie and Muriel got to know one another. It was this familiarity that allowed Christie to lure Muriel by herself to Rillington Place one fateful evening in October 1944. During one afternoon of idle conversation, Muriel mentioned she suffered from chronic catarrh, a severe swelling of the mucous membranes in the head. Christie, who had earned a first aid certification as a constable and enjoyed posing as a medical expert, said he owned a device that would cure her condition. She was more than welcome to come over and give it a try.

Muriel readily accepted and stopped by the flat one evening after work. Christie let her in and explained that Ethel had gone off several days before to visit her brother in Sheffield. He led Muriel into the kitchen and sat her in a chair with its back to the window. From a nearby shelf he retrieved what he claimed to be a medical inhalant. In actuality, the device was nothing more than a glass jar filled with a liquid mixture of Friar's Balsam. Christie had punched two holes in its metal screw-top lid and fed a length of rubber tubing through one of the holes. At the other end of the tube, he affixed a facemask, made from cardboard and a handkerchief, and told Muriel to place it over her mouth and breathe deeply.

She leant back in the chair and inhaled. Christie put the jar back on the shelf, out of Muriel's line of sight, and fed another length of hose through the lid. This tube, submerged in the jar's liquid contents, was connected to a wall-mounted gas valve near the kitchen window. As Muriel continued breathing in, Christie released a clip from the gas tube, filling the jar with lethal fumes. All Muriel could smell, however, was the Friar's Balsam. 'The idea,' Christie told detectives, 'was to stop what was coming out from smelling like gas. She inhaled the stuff from the tube. I did it to make her dopey. She became sort of unconscious, and I have a vague recollection of getting a stocking and tying it around her neck.'

Christie scooped her out of the chair and dragged her into the bedroom. He managed to get her on the bed and pulled off her underwear. He removed his clothes, climbed on top of her and tightened the stocking, choking her to death as he violated her prostrate form. When he finished, he rolled off the body and sat on the edge of the mattress, admiring what he had done. He took his time getting dressed and temporarily stored the body in the washhouse. Disposing of Muriel was much easier than getting rid of Ruth, for he wasn't rushed. He dug a grave on the right-hand side of the garden and rolled Muriel into the ground. 'She was still wearing her clothing,' he said. 'Several years afterwards, I was digging the garden and came across a bone, which was broke in half.'

He bent down and picked up the broken shard, later determined to be a femur, and stuck it in the ground to support a sagging section of fence. Christie didn't worry about the police coming around and asking questions. More than a year had passed since he killed Ruth Fuerst, who, by the very nature of her work, moved in undesirable circles. Would anyone care that a prostitute was missing? Certainly, in the case of Muriel Eady, her aunt and boyfriend would notify authorities. So what? Who would believe a man like Christie, with his balding head, thick glasses and quiet manner, to be capable of such monstrous behaviour? Not his wife. Ethel returned from Sheffield none the wiser.

Killing Muriel seemed to quell Christie's violent impulses, though it did nothing to ease his sexual torment. He still purchased sex when circumstances allowed and loitered in seedy cafés to make idle conversation with the working girls. He resigned from Ultra Radio Works and took a job once more at the Post Office, where officials – desperate to fill vacancies in wartime – skipped the background check. His criminal past, however, caught up with him after four years of employment and resulted in his dismissal. The firing stoked his penchant for feigning illnesses. He made frequent visits to his doctor, claiming to suffer from various maladies, and was soon living off unemployment. He padded around Rillington Place in his tattered slippers and worked in the shabby garden. Detectives who later went through the house said they found evidence of chronic masturbation. He slept nightly in the bed where he had strangled two women, penetrating them as they died, but he hardly touched his wife. The marriage was one of comfort and convenience with Ethel providing Christie at least some modicum of stability. His existence was an ugly and depressing one. Life in Rillington Place meandered through its joyless routine day-in and day-out. But things were about to change.

Estate agents Martin East of Soho handled the property and, in early 1948, put a 'FOR LET' notice in the top-floor window. Shortly before Easter, Eileen Evans, riding the eastbound train on the Metropolitan Line, looked out the window as her carriage rattled past the north end of Rillington Place and saw the sign. It just so happened that her brother, Tim, and his young wife, Beryl, were looking for a place of their own. They were currently living with Tim's mother in St Mark's Street. Eileen told Tim of the available flat and suggested he take a look. He and Beryl liked what they saw and decided to take it, moving in shortly thereafter. As Tim scribbled his signature on the rental agreement, he had no idea he was signing away not only his life but that of his young family.

Things had never been easy for Timothy Evans. He was born in the Welsh mining town of Merthyr Vale on 20 November 1924, his coal miner father having deserted the family before the birth. Tim's mother, Thomasina, abandoned with a new baby and 3-year-old Eileen to care for, eventually married Penry Probert, also a coal miner, in 1929. Not long thereafter, daughter Maureen joined the family. Life in Wales was far from idyllic. The coal-mining industry was in a slump and work for Penry was sporadic at best. For young Timothy, life presented its own challenges – particularly when it came to schooling. He was slow to develop, and by five still had problems verbally expressing himself. He could hardly pronounce his own name when his mother enrolled him in a local school. Over the next three years, he struggled through his lessons with minimal success.

The town of Merthyr Vale, then surrounded by blackened hills scarred by mining, sits on the eastern bank of the River Taff. One afternoon, while splashing around in the river, Tim sliced his left foot open on a piece of broken glass. An infection soon developed and prevented the wound from fully healing. The injury interrupted his schooling and would result in repeated hospital stays for years to come.

By now, Penry had focused his search for a steady job in London and moved the family there in 1935 after finding work as a painter and decorator. They soon settled in Notting Hill, where a nine-month hospital stay thwarted Timothy's resumed efforts at school. The recurring infections took a heavy toll on his younger years. Unlike other boys his age, he could not rough-house or kick a football around, resulting in a lonely childhood. He almost spent more time in bed than on his feet, with the infection sometimes running up to his groin and making the whole leg swell.

In 1937, after repeatedly asking his mother, Timothy returned to Merthyr Vale to live with his grandmother. Thomasina hoped the familiarity of their one-time home would go a long way to improve Tim's health. Back in the country, Tim's condition did take a slight turn for the better. He began venturing into the hills to hunt rats and enjoyed exploring abandoned coal shafts, imagining he was some great adventurer on a dangerous quest. His grandmother enrolled him in school, but Tim – who could neither read nor write – was beyond all hope in the classroom.

At 15, Tim left school permanently and entered the mines to work. The year was 1939. His life appeared to be heading in a new direction when the pain in his foot returned and forced him into Merthyr Tydfil General Hospital. His mother brought him back to London several months later and checked him into the Moorland Clinic for Tubercular Children at Alton in Hampshire. He remained hospitalised for a year before rejoining his family in Notting Hill. Britain was by now at war, and the world he returned to was one of blackouts, bombardments, sandbags, rationing and barbed wire.

Physically unfit for military service and limited mentally in what he could do, Evans bounced from one job to another. He found pleasure leaning against the bars in his two favourite pubs, the Kensington Park Hotel and the Elgin, both in Ladbroke Grove. Well known in both establishments for a mostly cheerful demeanour, it took little to spark his temper. Although not angry by nature, his lack of mental prowess left him easily confused by things beyond his comprehension and resulted in the occasional outburst. What others might have perceived to be a harmless joke uttered in the tradition of good pub conversation, Evans might have perceived as a slight. Nevertheless, his fellow bar patrons enjoyed his company.

Although he might have been simple, Evans had a knack for lying. He often told outlandish tales that cast various members of his family in positions of wealth and power. He routinely made such claims between pints of ale, much to the amusement of his drinking companions, who were always eager to hear his latest story. He did not limit his lying to the pub. He would sometimes stay out for nights at a time and tell his mother upon returning home that he couldn't remember where he had been. His lies were seen by those who knew him as his way of countering feelings of inadequacy. All too aware of his physical limitations and lack of mental acumen, he sought to impress in other ways. The one person he never dared subject to his wild stories was older sister Eileen, whom he loved dearly. He continued floundering along until 1946, when he and his mother both went to work in a London toy factory. It was also the year his family moved into No. 11 St Mark's Road, a short walk from Rillington Place.

Not long thereafter, Evans met 18-year-old Beryl Thorley, a telephone operator at Grosvenor House in Mayfair. The two met by chance when the girl Evans was dating at the time invited Beryl to join them one evening at the cinema. Evans, immediately smitten with the dark-haired girl, had no qualms about pursuing her. She lived not far from St Mark's Road in Cambridge Gardens, allowing Evans to walk round and visit her in the evenings. He took her out with what little money he had and doted on her to the best of his ability. Beryl – her mother dead and father living in Brighton – enjoyed being the centre of such loving attention. The two were engaged within weeks. The infatuated groom-to-be routinely brought Beryl around to see his mother who, in turn, became something of a surrogate mother to the young girl. The couple married on 20 September 1947 at the Kensington Register Office and promptly moved into the house on St Mark's Road. Under one roof now lived Thomasina and Penry, the newlyweds, and Eileen and Maureen. Fortunately, the house was spacious and able to accommodate the large brood.

Beryl took quickly to her new surroundings. It was the first time in a long while she felt as though she belonged. In Mrs Probert she found a strong, nurturing influence, while Eileen and Maureen lavished her with the affection befitting a younger sister. Everyone contributed to the household. Evans, by now, had left his job at the toy factory and found work as a delivery driver for Lancaster Food Products. He enjoyed married life and its accompanying sense of normality. He no longer felt like a social outcast and was thrilled in early 1948 when Beryl told him he would soon be a father. And so the young couple, eager to make it on their own, came to live at No. 10 Rillington Place.

11

The Man Downstairs

Timothy and Beryl liked the Christies and saw something parental in the older couple downstairs. They were a comforting presence for the young people striking out on their own. The two-room flat upstairs, with only a kitchen and small bedroom, suited Timothy and Beryl just fine but was in dire need of redecorating. The wallpaper had yellowed and started to peel; the painted door and window trims were flaking. With the help of Maureen and Eileen, the couple started fixing the place up.

Christie – as the building's senior tenant and self-appointed landlord – took a keen interest in his new neighbours and paid frequent, uninvited visits to their flat. Eileen found the man exceedingly creepy from the outset. His thick glasses seemed to magnify his already large, gazing eyes, and the soft timbre of his voice leant itself to something smarmy. What unnerved Eileen the most, however, was Christie's off-putting ability to appear seemingly out of nowhere. She spent many hours in the upstairs flat, helping her brother and Beryl with the decorating. On numerous occasions, she would turn around and find Christie standing behind her with a cup of tea, not having heard him approach up the stairs. Eileen tried to avoid contact with him whenever possible and felt sorry for his wife, who seemed submissive in Christie's presence.

The wallpapering and painting complete, Timothy rented some furniture on his mother's credit and settled in with his wife. In October, Beryl entered Queen Charlotte's Hospital and gave birth to a daughter they named Geraldine. Fatherhood instilled in Evans a sense of pride he had never felt before. He saw in Geraldine a creation of absolute beauty and took great pleasure in showing her off to anyone he could. He worked long hours – leaving before sunrise and returning after dark – to put food on the table and clothe the baby.

On Wednesday nights, he and Beryl would drop Geraldine off with his mother and enjoy an evening out at the cinema. He spent Saturday nights at the pub and went round to St Mark's Road every Sunday morning to help his mother with the household chores. Life in Rillington Place, however, was far from pleasant. Their flat was too small for a family of three. When the couple asked Christie if they could sometimes take Geraldine into the back garden, he refused for reasons obvious only to him. Beryl's casual approach to housecleaning contributed to the flat's claustrophobic atmosphere.

Evans often returned home from work in the evening to find the place a mess. Clothes lay scattered about the floor and dirty dishes sat unattended in the sink. Much to Evans's frustration, his wife seemed oblivious to the squalor – or simply didn't care. Whenever he broached the issue, an argument ensued. Rare, too, was the occasion when a meal sat waiting for him on the kitchen table. Beryl, an increasingly angry Evans thought, was shirking her matrimonial duties. He did his part by bringing home the money, the least she could do was clean the place and cook dinner. Beryl thought nothing of leaving Evans to fix his own meals after work, which only caused more grief between the two.

The financial pressure of having to buy food and clothes for the baby, on top of everything else, exacerbated the strain. There was simply too much for the young couple to handle. Evans's mother and sisters helped clean the place whenever they paid a visit, scrubbing crockery and folding clothes. On Saturdays, Eileen began picking up Geraldine and bringing her back to the house on St Mark's Road to bathe and change her. The family intervention did little to placate the unhappy couple, who by now screamed at one another most nights. Neighbours often saw the two of them, cast in silhouette behind drawn curtains, going at one another. The fights grew increasingly loud and violent, with threats and inanimate objects being thrown back and forth. Their angry voices carried down Rillington Place and drifted across the garden to the neighbours in the back. On some occasions, one would lash out and strike the other. The arguments generally ended with Evans storming out.

In their sitting room on the ground floor, Christie and Ethel would listen to the ruckus above them but never intervened. Ferocious as the fights were, Timothy and Beryl remained fond of one another and sought to put aside their differences when tempers allowed – but their recurring truces proved fragile. When Beryl's friend Lucy Endicott, a pretty blonde of 17, came to stay late in the summer of 1949, the yelling and screaming started anew. Beryl and Lucy shared the bed and made Evans sleep on the kitchen floor. Evans soon tired of the new arrangement and let his disapproval be known. The resulting confrontation was the loudest one yet.

'In August 1949,' Christie recalled, 'there was a terrific row upstairs on the top floor between Mr and Mrs Evans and a blonde who was living with them. My wife told me afterwards that a woman who lives in Lancaster Road, overlooking the back of 10 Rillington Place, had told her that she had seen Mr and Mrs Evans fighting at their open kitchen window and that Mr Evans appeared to be trying to push his wife out of the window.'

Evans's mother arrived at the flat mid-argument and ordered Lucy to pack her things and clear out, further enraging Beryl, who accused Evans of lusting after her friend. Not denying the accusation, Evans threatened to leave Rillington Place with Lucy. 'That evening,' Christie remembered, 'Evans went out with the blonde, and he was carrying a suitcase.' Evans's life with Lucy did not last long, and he returned to the flat the following day. He came home and found a note from Beryl waiting for him. Unable to read, he took the letter to a friend and was shocked to learn Beryl wanted him out. He blamed Lucy for the miserable turn of events and stamped about for several days, threatening to do her harm. Evans, however, had always been an excitable chap and soon settled down. He and Beryl apologised to one another and settled back in together, but her announcement towards the end of summer that she was pregnant again put the couple on a tragic trajectory.

Both agreed they were in no position to care for another child. Evans's paltry salary of £7 a week barely covered what bills they had. Beryl, not yet 20, found it hard enough to cope with Geraldine and told Evans she wanted an abortion. Although opposed to the idea, he soon began asking around in the hopes of finding someone who might be able to help. Beryl also did her own investigating and told Evans's sisters she heard about a man in Edgware Road who would do the procedure on the cheap. Within the cramped confines of Rillington Place, it was hard to keep secrets from the ever-snooping Christie. He had taken an immediate liking to the young, vibrant Beryl and often kept her under surveillance. He stood, listening at the base of the stairs, and routinely sneaked up to the top floor, his slippered feet silent on the bare floorboards. He had waited patiently, since the young couple moved in, for the right moment and found circumstances were now aligning themselves in his favour.

Mr Kitchener, the retired railway worker who had lived on the first floor since before the Christie's moved in, checked himself into the Western Ophthalmic Hospital in Marylebone Road on 3 October 1949 for an operation on his failing eyes. He was away from Rillington Place for more than a month, which meant Christie had one less person in the house to worry about. Fully aware of the young couple's predicament, Christie made his move in early November and invited Evans one evening into his sitting room for a friendly chat. He assumed the tone of a concerned father and said he knew Beryl was seeking an abortion. He moved to the small fireplace and stood beneath the framed first-aid certificate he'd received as a war reserve constable. It just so happened, he told Evans, he possessed some medical knowledge that might prove useful.

Christie pulled an old first-aid manual from his bookshelf and passed it to Evans, saying it was a medical text. As the younger man flipped through the pages, Christie gently chastised Evans for not seeking his help first. Evans looked up from the book and said he never realised Christie had a medical background. Christie dismissed the excuse with a shrug of the shoulders and claimed he had performed abortions before. Should Beryl and Evans so wish, he would be more than willing to offer his services and help them out. There was, he said, the slightest chance of the patient dying during the procedure. Evans shook his head and handed the book back to Christie. When he went upstairs and repeated the conversation to Beryl, telling her he had refused Christie's help, she scolded him for making a decision on her behalf. She fully intended, she said, to abort the foetus and would do so with Christie's help. Timothy Evans, 24, with the intelligence quotient of a 14-year-old, found himself in a no-win situation and completely out of his depth.

Evans woke up before dawn as he normally did on Tuesday, 8 November 1949, and got ready for work. He sat at the small kitchen table, nursing a cup of tea and a cigarette. He stared out the window and watched the sky above the rooftops opposite slowly lighten to a dark shade of grey. He took one last drag on his smoke, threw back the contents of his cup and got up to leave. Beryl followed Evans to the door and told him to let Christie know she wanted the procedure done that day. Christie, who undoubtedly heard the conversation, met Evans in the downstairs hallway and asked him if everything was all right. Evans, resigned to his wife's wishes, relayed Beryl's message. Christie nodded and watched him walk out the front door, knowing Evans would never see his wife alive again.

What transpired later that morning in the top flat of Rillington Place remains shrouded in mystery. Christie, who never gave a straight account of the day's events, told police in one statement Beryl had sought his help to commit suicide. 'She begged of me to help her go through with it,' he said. 'She said she would do anything if I would help her. I think she was referring to letting me be intimate with her.'

When Christie went upstairs that afternoon, he found Beryl waiting for him in a light-blue woollen jacket worn over a spotted cotton blouse and black skirt. She brought a quilt from the sitting room and placed it in front of the small fireplace in the kitchen. She smiled nervously, as Christie assured her everything would be okay. 'She lay on the quilt,' Christie recalled. 'She was fully dressed.' He knew better than to try anything without first immobilising the girl and produced a strip of rubber tubing, which he attached to a gas valve near the fireplace. He turned the valve on and placed the end of the tube near her face. The fumes, he said, would help minimise the pain. 'The gas wasn't on very long,' he explained. 'Not much over a minute, I think – perhaps, 1 or 2 minutes.' He encouraged her to take deep breaths and felt a sexual charge surge through him as her body relaxed. Young and beautiful, she symbolised the type of girl that always remained beyond his reach. Now, she lay helpless before him.

He ran his eyes up the length of her legs to her parted thighs and could no longer control himself. In one version of events, he told police Beryl was unconscious when he did his thing: 'I turned the tap off. I was going to try … to have intercourse with her, but it was impossible. I couldn't bend over. I think that's when I strangled her. I think it was with a stocking I found in the room.'

In his subsequent statements, Christie claimed to be unsure of certain details and often contradicted himself, frustrating investigators and leaving a convoluted record of the goings-on in Rillington Place. The accepted scenario of what happened to Beryl Evans is that she remained conscious and realised at the last minute what Christie was up to. She smacked the hissing gas tube away and fought to free herself from Christie's grasp. Panicked and sexually frustrated, he punched her repeatedly in the face and beat her to the brink of unconsciousness before choking her to death. Tense, he loomed over the body and listened, wondering if his wife two floors below had heard the commotion. Outside in the garden, two workmen – hired by the building's owner – busied themselves repairing the roof on the washhouse. They had arrived earlier that morning and heard nothing over the noise of their own labour.

Christie got up and stared at the body but had little time to enjoy his work. Downstairs, Joan Vincent – a childhood friend of Beryl's – had stopped by for an unannounced visit. She entered the street-level door and ascended the stairs. The sound of her high-heeled shoes on the bare wood alerted Christie and threw him into a panic. Was it Ethel? He had no way of knowing. Unable to hide the body, he did the only thing he could and pushed himself against the flat's door. He fought to maintain his composure when he heard the knock and the young voice on the other side call out Beryl's name. The sound of his own breath seemed to roar in his ears and only got louder when the obtrusive girl knocked again and tried the doorknob.

On the landing, Joan couldn't understand why the door only opened partway. It was, she mused, as though someone was placing their weight against it on the other side. She called out Beryl's name one last time and waited. Insulted by her friend's lack of response, she turned, retreated down the stairs and left the building.

Christie listened for the sound of the building's front door opening and closing before he relaxed his guard. He returned to the body and, with considerable effort, dragged it into the bedroom. His back ached as he heaved the body onto the bed and bent down to straighten Beryl's clothing. He turned up her collar and buttoned the cardigan to hide the dark bruising around her neck. He passed Geraldine in her crib and drew the bedroom curtains before leaving the flat and joining his wife downstairs.

Evans returned home from work at 5.30 that evening eager to see Beryl and Geraldine. Christie had anxiously been waiting for Evans and heard him approaching in the street. He stepped into the passageway and met Evans as he walked through the front door. Immediately, Evans asked how the procedure went. Christie, his face sombre, told Evans to go upstairs and followed close behind. The two men entered the darkened kitchen and waited while Evans lit the gas lamp, bathing the room in a weak, yellow glow. Evans looked at Christie expectantly, desperate for some word on his wife's condition. The older man took a step forward and shook his head. 'It's bad news,' Christie said. 'It didn't work.'

Evans, as though gut-punched, felt the air leave his lungs in a violent rush. He simply looked at Christie, hoping for some clarification. 'Where,' Evans whispered, 'where is she?'

'Laying on the bed in the bedroom,' Christie said.

'What about the baby?' Evans asked.

'The baby's in the cot.'

Evans stared through the kitchen doorway; the darkened bedroom beyond seemed unnaturally still. He moved quickly toward the bed and fumbled with the gas to get some light in the room. Looking about the place, he noticed the curtains were drawn across the window and saw the shapeless form on the bed, beneath the eiderdown. He cast a furtive glance at Christie, who stood watching intently from the kitchen doorway.

Evans slowly grabbed a corner of the sheet and braced himself before pulling it off the mattress. Beryl's pale face, still bearing the evidence of her violent death, stared up at him. 'I could see that she was dead and that she had been bleeding from the mouth and nose,' Evans later said, 'and that she had been bleeding from the bottom part.' It didn't occur to Evans to ask Christie why his wife had bled from the nose and mouth. He staggered backwards, his eyes wet, and moved toward the cot, where baby Geraldine lay oblivious to the tragedy. Evans picked her up, wrapped her in a blanket and brought her into the kitchen. Christie moved to the grate and lit the fire.

'I'll speak to you after you feed the baby,' Christie said.

His mind and body numb, Evans fed Geraldine a hard-boiled egg and changed her nappy. He spread her blanket in front of the grate and placed her on it before turning to Christie.

'How long has she been dead?'

'Since about 3 o'clock,' Christie said, telling Evans his wife's stomach had been 'septic-poisoned'. It was just a matter of time, he continued, before the infection would have resulted in Beryl's hospitalisation. Evans, stunned by the tragic turn of events and not smart enough to know any better, took Christie at his word. The older man took full advantage of the situation. 'I told Evans that no doubt he would be suspected of having done it because of the rows and fights he had had with his wife,' Christie subsequently told police. 'He seemed to think the same.'

Christie said the best course of action would be to dispose of the body and told Evans to stay in the kitchen with Geraldine and keep the door closed. Evans did as instructed and sat with the baby for several minutes before hearing what sounded like Christie struggling with something heavy on the stairs. He opened the kitchen door and saw Christie standing over the body in the stairwell. Out of breath, Christie said he needed help and asked Evans to grab the body by the legs. Believing Christie to be on his side, Evans picked his dead wife up by the ankles and assisted in carrying her into Mr Kitchener's empty flat. Christie, holding the body under the arms, told Evans to lay her down on the kitchen floor. The two men worked quietly so as not to disturb Ethel one floor below.

'What are you going to do with her?' Evans asked.

'I'll dispose of it down one of the drains,' Christie said. 'You'd better go to bed and leave the rest to me. Get up and go to work as usual in the morning.'

Evans looked down at his wife – his under-developed mind failing to notice Christie's reference to the body as 'it' – and wondered what would become of Geraldine. Who would keep an eye on her while he worked during the day? Sharing his concern with Christie, Evans suggested he take Geraldine to his mother's house in St Mark's Road. Christie shook his head and told Evans that doing so would raise the alarm. The family would want to know what had happened to Beryl, and what would Evans say then? The best thing for all involved, Christie said, was to wait until morning when both he and Evans could think more clearly. Evans, overwhelmed by it all, nodded and slowly climbed the stairs.

Despite the soft cooing of Geraldine in the kitchen, a lonely silence permeated the small flat. Evans picked his daughter up and held her close before laying her gently in the crib. He pulled the bloodstained eiderdown off the bed and stashed it in the bedroom cupboard. Unable to sleep on what he believed to be his wife's deathbed, he spread a blanket on the bedroom floor and settled into an uneasy sleep beside Geraldine's crib.

He awoke the next morning, fed and changed the baby, and got ready for work. In his sitting room, Christie heard Evans moving about and went into the passageway when Evans came down the stairs. In whispered tones, he told Evans he would look after Geraldine for the day and that he knew a couple in East Acton who were willing to take the baby. Although loath to give up his daughter, Evans was now under Christie's complete control and surrendered to his scheme. He went off to work and left Geraldine in the care of his wife's killer.

Throughout the day, Christie went upstairs to check on the baby and feed her as needed until Evans arrived home shortly before 6 that evening. One can only speculate how much Ethel Christie knew of the goings-on in Rillington Place. It's unlikely she knew her husband was a murderer, but she must have known – living in such close quarters – that something was amiss with the young couple upstairs.

When Evans walked through the door, Christie stood waiting for him in the passageway. He told Evans he had paid a visit to the East Acton couple and arranged everything. Evans nodded and went upstairs to spend one last evening with his child. Nothing made sense to him any more; the simple world he knew had descended chaotically into something far beyond his grasp. In the bedroom, Evans found Geraldine sitting in her crib. He took her into the kitchen, lit the grate and sat with her in front of the fire. He prepared her hard-boiled egg and brewed himself a cup of tea, drinking half the cup before giving the rest to Geraldine. He was playing with her in the kitchen when Christie came upstairs and told him the East Acton couple would be stopping by in the morning to collect the baby.

'In the morning when you get up, feed the baby and dress her, then put her in the cot,' Christie said. 'The people will be here just after nine in the morning to fetch her. I've told them to knock three times and I'll let them in.'

Evans agreed with Christie that should anyone ask, Beryl had simply gone off on holiday. The next morning, Evans fed and changed his daughter for the last time. He packed Geraldine's clothes into a small case and gave it to Christie on his way out the door. Shortly after Evans's departure, Christie went up the stairs and approached Geraldine's crib with a necktie in his hand. He could hear the workmen, who had returned that morning to continue their repairs on the washhouse, as he wrapped the tie around Geraldine's throat and pulled hard. Although it's not known for sure what he did with the body when done, it's more than likely he carried the lifeless Geraldine down the stairs into Mr Kitchener's flat and placed her next to Beryl. He returned to his own flat and carried on with the morning. When Evans returned home later that night, Christie followed him up the stairs and said the couple had taken the baby away. Although expected news, it was another jolt for Evans in what had been a rough day.

It was common practice for Evans to ask his employer for an advance on his wages. He and Beryl had never been on stable financial ground, and their poor money-management skills meant they were always just barely hanging on. When, that afternoon, he asked for money to send to his wife – whom he said was holidaying in Brighton – Evans's exasperated boss responded by firing him. In the course of three bewildering days, Evans had lost everything. Rillington Place no longer felt like home; everywhere he looked harboured a memory. Standing in the kitchen, with Christie beside him, Evans gazed into the bedroom at the empty crib and wondered when he'd see his daughter again. Christie was still talking, saying he would take the remaining baby items – the crib, pram and high chair – to the East Acton couple at his earliest convenience. All Evans could do was go along with what Christie said.

Bending Evans to his will gave Christie a perverse sense of power. The younger man's subservience was essential to Christie's plan, which now involved getting Evans out of the house. Saying Beryl had gone off on holiday with the baby would only placate friends and family for so long. Just that afternoon, Joan Vincent had returned to Rillington Place wanting to see Beryl. No sooner had she set foot on the stairs than Christie charged from the front room and told her that Beryl and the baby had left town. From her vantage point, Joan could see over Christie's shoulder and noticed Geraldine's pram and high chair in his sitting room. When she asked what they were doing there, Christie became irate and banished her from the premises. Joan, angry and more than slightly confused, left Rillington Place and never returned.

Christie realised at that moment he would never be free of such interruptions while Evans continued living upstairs. Orchestrating another murder was not a viable option; he had more than enough bodies to deal with. Convincing Evans to move, however, would prove an easy proposition for there was no longer anything to keep him in his squalid flat. And so that evening, as the two men stood in Evans's kitchen, Christie suggested a permanent change of scenery might do Evans good.

'Now the best thing you can do,' Christie said, 'is to sell your furniture and get out of London somewhere.'

'All right,' Evans sighed.

The next day, Friday, 11 November, at Christie's behest, Evans sold his rented furnishings to Robert Hookway, a furniture dealer in Portobello Road for £40. He used some of the money to purchase a nice camelhair overcoat for himself and spent the weekend downing pints in various pubs, going to the cinema and sleeping. He missed Geraldine and thought often of Beryl, believing Christie had disposed of her body down one of the building's drains. Had Evans taken it upon himself to visit Mr Kitchener's flat one last time, he would have discovered the truth.

Three days had now passed since Beryl's murder, and the ripening bodies upstairs were becoming an ever-increasing concern for Christie. By Friday afternoon, the workmen had finished their repairs to the washhouse, which Christie deemed a suitable location to stash the bodies until he could settle on a more permanent solution. 'The washhouse was a communal one but, actually, it was only used for keeping rubbish and junk in,' Christie later said, explaining his decision. 'There was no key to it, and the lock was rusted and broken and not usable. It could be opened and shut by turning the handle but could not be locked. The washhouse was only used for getting water to rinse down pails or put down the lavatory.'

He knew there was minimal chance of Ethel wandering out to the dilapidated shack and didn't have to worry about Evans, who had never been allowed access to the garden. It's most likely Christie moved the bodies – having wrapped them in blankets and tablecloths, and securing them with cording – either late Friday night or early morning Saturday. In the washhouse, the bodies would remain undisturbed until their eventual discovery by police.

'On Sunday afternoon,' Evans recalled, 'I went to see a rag dealer. I met him outside a café in Ladbroke Grove – that's where he lives. I told him that if he came down to my place on the Monday there was quite a lot of rags he could have. I got up at 6 o'clock on the Monday morning and ripped up all my wife's clothes and the eiderdown, and cut up the blanket. The man came round just after 9 o'clock and he took two sacks full, and I didn't take nothing off him for them.'

Later that afternoon, Hookway stopped by Rillington Place in his van to collect the furniture from the flat. Evans stood in the kitchen after Hookway's departure and had one last look around. The place had once been the symbol of a new life for Evans and his wife. Now, it was merely a macabre reminder of all that had gone wrong. 'The only thing left in the house then,' he said, 'was vases, a clock, some dishes, saucepans and a bucket, and the case with the baby's clothes, her pram and small chair. Christie had all that stuff. He asked me where I was going to go, and I told him I didn't know.'

With that Evans left Rillington Place, intent on never returning. He made his way to Paddington Station and checked in his case before whiling away several hours at the cinemas and a local pub. He returned to the station at 12.30 a.m. and caught the 12.55 train to Cardiff. He gazed sullenly out the window, his own reflection staring back at him as the train made its way through the night. At Cardiff Station, he changed trains and arrived in Merthyr Vale shortly after 6.30 on the morning of Tuesday, 16 November.

12

An Innocent Man

In his new camelhair coat, Evans knocked on the door of the small house at 93 Mount Pleasant, where his aunt and uncle – the Lynches – lived. The couple, not expecting a visit, was surprised by their nephew's sudden appearance. Evans said he and his boss were on a tour of the West Country to scout out new business opportunities. Their car, however, had broken down in Cardiff and would take several days to repair. The Lynches said Evans could stay with them while waiting for the repair work to be done – but what about Beryl and the baby? They were visiting Beryl's father in Bristol, Evans said.

He spent the next six days enjoying the familiarity and comfort of his hometown. His aunt fed him well and his uncle took him for drinks at the village pub, where Evans regaled the locals with stories of life in London and sang songs at the piano. In the afternoons, he wandered about the surrounding hills – the playground of his youth – and found some solace in more pleasant memories, but his wife and daughter continued to weigh heavily on his mind. It never occurred to him he would not see his daughter again. He often spoke affectionately of Geraldine and purchased a doll for her while out shopping one day.

In the parlour of the Lynch home, a framed photograph of Geraldine hung from the wall. On more than one occasion,

Evans's aunt caught him talking quietly to the picture. Privately, he wondered how the couple in East Acton was treating her. Would she remember him when they reunited? When did Christie plan on putting him in touch with her caregivers? The questions nagged at him. On the sixth day, he knew he had to act – he could not sit by while his daughter languished in the care of strangers. He told his aunt and uncle he was returning to London to collect his pay and left early that morning.

It's unlikely Christie expected to see Timothy Evans again, so it must have been a shock when he found the man standing on his doorstep on the afternoon of 23 November. Evans wasted no time stating the purpose of his visit and demanded to see his daughter. Christie, not wanting to let Evans in the house, grabbed a coat and said he was just leaving for a doctor's appointment. An undeterred Evans walked with him and insisted on seeing Geraldine. Christie told Evans it would not be wise to visit the baby just yet, as she needed several more weeks to settle into her new environment. The two men boarded a bus and got off at different stops. Christie had no particular place to be that day, he simply wanted Evans as far from Rillington Place as possible. Evans returned to Merthyr Vale with no definitive answers and the weight of his many lies wearing him down.

When his aunt and uncle asked if Beryl and the baby were back from their holiday, Evans came up with yet another story. He said he arrived home to find Beryl had walked out on him and left Geraldine unattended in her cot. He'd had no choice, he said, but to leave her in the care of a couple he knew in Newport. Knowing Evans's penchant for bending the truth, and concerned for Beryl and Geraldine's wellbeing, Evans's aunt wrote an urgent letter to his mother. Mrs Probert received the letter on Monday, 28 November, and replied immediately, writing that a month had passed since she last saw Beryl and the baby. Family pressure to reveal the true whereabouts of his wife and child now came at Evans from all directions and proved too much for him to bear.

On the afternoon of Wednesday, 30 November, he wandered into the Merthyr Vale Police Station.

'I want to give myself up,' he said to on-duty Detective Constable Gwnfryn Howell Evans, 'I put her down the drain.'

When the detective constable cautioned Evans not to incriminate himself, Evans brushed the warning aside. 'I know what I'm saying,' he said, 'I can't sleep, and I want to get it off my chest.'

Cautioned again of his rights, Evans was taken to the CID in Merthyr Vale, where he gave a statement to detectives. He said his wife had been pregnant and wanted an abortion. When he opposed the idea, he said Beryl threatened to kill herself and Geraldine. Evans resigned himself to his wife's wishes and shared his troubles one afternoon with a man he met in a café 'between Ipswich and Colchester'. The man told Evans not to worry and gave him a bottle of pills that he said would terminate the pregnancy. Evans returned from work that evening and gave the pills to Beryl, who took them with fatal results. He waited until the early morning hours – between 1 and 2 – before dragging his wife's body down the stairs and into the street. He opened the manhole cover in front of the house and 'pushed her body head first into the drain'. Throughout his statement, Evans made sure he never mentioned Christie's name, for he still believed his one-time neighbour had been trying to help him.

Detective Constable Howell Evans passed the information along to the Notting Hill Police Station. Officers went at once to Rillington Place, where it took the strength of three men to remove the heavy manhole cover outside No. 10's front door. Expecting to see something gruesome when they shone their torches down the shaft, detectives were surprised to find it empty. Back in Merthyr Vale, Howell Evans received the news shortly before 9 that evening and shared it with Tim Evans, who stuck by his story. When the detective told Evans it took three men to lift the drain's cover, Evans shrugged. 'I did it myself,' he insisted. The detective, unconvinced, hammered away until Evans relented.

He had lied only to protect Christie but now saw no reason to cover for the man. He launched into another statement, explaining how Christie had volunteered to abort the baby and how Beryl died in the process. Christie, he said, had promised to put the body down a drain and leave Geraldine in the care of an East Acton couple. An emotionally drained Evans finished talking at midnight. Welsh police again notified investigators at Notting Hill and informed them of Evans's revised story.

Evans spent the night at the Merthyr Vale Police Station and answered more questions on the morning of 1 December. He told detectives the last time he saw his wife's body was when he helped Christie carry it down the stairs into Mr Kitchener's flat. In response to Evans's accusations, Notting Hill detectives paid a visit that evening to Rillington Place and brought Christie back to the station, where they grilled him from 11 p.m. until 5 the following morning.

When told of Evans's statement, Christie reacted with disgust. Never, he said, had he attempted to abort Mrs Evans's pregnancy – nor had he ever claimed to be an expert in medical matters. Why Evans would say such a thing was not only puzzling, but hurtful. While he knew Beryl had been pregnant and trying to abort the baby herself, he had advised her in his wife's presence not to pursue such a dangerous course of action. He told his interrogators he had done all he could to make the young couple feel at home in Rillington Place, despite the constant arguing that occurred in the upstairs flat.

On multiple occasions, he said, Beryl had come downstairs and said she feared for her life. Evans, he told police, had a violent temper. He told investigators he last saw Beryl and the baby the first week of November. Shortly after that, Evans said his wife and daughter had gone to Bristol on a holiday. The following week, Christie said, Evans sold his belongings and left.

Sitting there, watching the police scribble in their notepads, Christie knew all too well the potential consequence of his statement. The police would no doubt return to Rillington Place and conduct a thorough search of the premises. In the washhouse, they'd discover the two bodies and charge Evans with the murder of his wife and child. Life, for Christie, would regain some sense of normality. The Evans dilemma had caused him considerable stress over the previous weeks – but now the perfect solution had presented itself.

It was still dark when he left the station. He walked home and found a uniformed officer standing guard in front of the building. Inside, a concerned Ethel sat waiting for him in the sitting room. She told Christie as he entered that detectives had taken her statement late the night before. Christie, expecting an eventuality such as this, had coached his wife shortly after Beryl's disappearance on what to say. The couple now waited for the inevitable knock on the door. It came the next day after investigators, checking in Bristol, learned Beryl and Geraldine had never holidayed there. They searched the building top to bottom and found nothing before turning their attention to the garden.

Ethel and a nervous Christie followed them into the back. Evans would take the fall for the bodies in the washhouse, but what of those buried by the rockery? Only recently, the garden had revealed one of its secrets. 'It was about this time,' Christie said, 'that my day had been spent digging in the garden, and I found the skull from the body of the woman Eady that I had buried in the nearest corner of the garden. I just covered it up with earth and, later in the evening when it was dark, I put my raincoat on. I went into the garden and got the skull, and put it under my raincoat. I went out and put it in a bombed house, the last standing bombed house next to the tennis courts in St Mark's Road. There was corrugated iron covering some bay windows, and I dropped the skull through the window where the iron had been bent back. I heard it drop with a dull thud.'

The investigators – Chief Detective Inspector George Jennings, Chief Superintendent Tom Barratt, and a police biologist from Scotland Yard – moved slowly through the garden. To Christie's immense relief, they saw no signs of digging and failed to notice Muriel Eady's femur propping up the sagging section of fence. Not seeing anything unusual, the detectives examined the washhouse. They swung open the door, shined a torch inside and noticed a stack of lumber leaning against the sink. Christie had just recently put the wood in place to better conceal the bodies. One of the detectives bent down, ran his hand behind the wood and felt something. He aimed his torch behind the wood and saw an object wrapped in a green tablecloth and tied with a length of cord. Christie later detailed what happened next:

> They asked my wife to go to the washhouse ... They pointed to a bundle and asked her if she knew anything about it. She said she did not, and they asked her to touch it to see if she knew what it was.

Ethel crouched on her haunches and touched what appeared to be a large package. She shook her head and said, truthfully, she had no idea what it was or who put it there. The detectives cleared the lumber out of the way and dragged the object into the garden. When they untied the length of cord, the green tablecloth parted and revealed Beryl Evans's feet. Under another pile of wood behind the washhouse door, the detectives found Geraldine's body with the necktie still knotted around her throat. The bodies were removed to Kensington Mortuary and arrangements were made to bring Evans back to London.

Evans, escorted by two London detectives, arrived in the capital by train later that night. On the platform at Paddington Station, a tipped-off news photographer stepped from the milling crowds and snapped the beleaguered man's picture. The image captured Evans in a bewildered state: tired, scared and wedged between two men nearly double his size. Indeed, nothing made sense to him. Until several hours ago, he believed his wife's body to be languishing in a drainpipe – not stashed in the washhouse behind Rillington Place. A police car was waiting to take him to Notting Hill Police Station, where Chief Inspector Jennings told Evans that not only his wife – but his daughter – had been strangled to death. Shown the clothing both bodies had been found in – and the tie used to strangle Geraldine – Evans broke down.

Throughout the night and well into the early morning hours of 3 December, Jennings and Detective Inspector Black grilled the emotionally shattered Evans, who signed two questionable confessions. In his first statement, Evans claimed Beryl's uncontrollable spending habits made him snap and strangle her with a piece of rope, and the baby with a necktie. In the second statement, he said he and his wife got into an argument the night of Monday, 7 November, after he returned late from the pub. He ignored Beryl and went to bed. 'I got up Tuesday morning and went straight to work,' the statement reads. 'I came home at night about 6.30 p.m., my wife started to argue again, so I hit her across the face with my flat hand. She then hit me back with her hand. In a fit of temper, I grabbed a piece of rope from a chair which I had brought home off my van and strangled her with it.'

He continues in the statement, saying he murdered Geraldine two days later and put both bodies in the washhouse. 'I then locked the washhouse door behind me and came in closing the back door behind me. I then slipped back upstairs and laid on the bed all night, fully clothed.'

So determined were police to believe that Evans had committed the murders, they never stopped to consider the actual facts of the case. Evans's claim that he locked the washhouse was not true because the door had a broken lock. His assertion that both bodies were in the washhouse by the night of 10 November also fails to hold water. The workmen who repaired the washhouse roof the week of the killings cleared their tools and rubbish out of it on the morning of 11 November and would have seen two bodies lying there. Such discrepancies beg the question: why would Evans confess to a crime he didn't commit? Questioned for hours without legal representation and shocked by news of the murders, Evans didn't know what else to do. The following morning, Sunday, 4 December, Jennings charged Evans with Beryl and Geraldine's murder.

Remanded to Brixton Prison to await trial, Evans began asserting his innocence and told his family that Christie was the killer. His statements to police, however, all but guaranteed a rendezvous with the hangman. His trial commenced in No. 1 Court at the Old Bailey on the morning of Wednesday, 11 January 1950. Although charged with two murders, he was tried solely on the death of his daughter.

Christie played the role of star witness for the prosecution. On the stand, he again told tales of Evans's stormy marriage and the defendant's hasty departure from Rillington Place shortly after Beryl and the baby had gone off 'on holiday'. He managed to incorporate into his testimony his military service on the Western Front and his time as a war reserve constable, thus establishing the nature of his character for the jury. It was a pre-emptive strike against the defence, for Christie knew he would soon have to dispute Evans's allegations against him. Indeed, Evans's attorney, Malcolm Morris, put Christie on the defensive by suggesting it was Christie who had killed Beryl and Geraldine. Christie balked at such a 'ridiculous' notion and fell back on his poor physical health as an alibi. 'At that time this fibrositis in my back was so bad ... that I could scarcely bend,' he lied under oath. 'I had to crawl out of my bed, and if I wanted to pick anything off the floor, I had to get on my hands and knees. Physically impossible.'

Morris next sought to undermine Christie's character by bringing up his past convictions, but the prosecution countered on redirect examination. 'The last time you were in trouble with the police for any offence was in 1933, was it?' asked Christmas Humphreys, barrister for the Crown.

'Yes,' Christie said.

Having established that nearly twenty years had passed since Christie last committed a crime, Humphreys excused his chief witness from the stand. If Christie came across to the jury as an upstanding citizen, Timothy Evans made the opposite impression. His statements to police, read in as evidence, severely handicapped the defence. Questioned by Morris, Evans said he confessed to the murders because he feared the police would severely beat him otherwise. 'I was upset pretty bad, sir,' he said. 'I had been believing my daughter was still alive.'

Through no fault of his own, Evans, when cross-examined by Humphreys, struck those in the courtroom as an uneducated simpleton. He could offer no possible motive for Christie killing Beryl and Geraldine, and was easily confused by Humphreys' questions regarding his multiple statements to investigators. All this brought into doubt the sincerity of his grief. There was little Evans could do but flounder through each question and try and stick to what he knew to be true, but the prosecution played up Evans's reputation as a liar. Through his questioning, Humphreys succeeded in portraying Evans as a man who couldn't get his story straight. By the time Evans left the stand, the hangman's noose was all but tied around his neck.

Both sides having rested their cases, the judge presented his summation to the jury on 13 January 1950. He spoke highly of Christie's character, reminding jurors once again of the man's military and civil service. A man such as Christie would never stoop so low as to murder a mother and child; an individual like Evans, however, was something else entirely. The defendant, through his own actions, proved he was incapable of telling the truth. He made statements to the police he later claimed were false and told lies – such as accusing Christie of the crimes – to suit his own benefit.

The judge's summation all but convicted Evans of murder. He now placed the decision upon the jurors, who left the courtroom at 2.10 p.m. and returned 40 minutes later with a guilty verdict. Standing alone in the dock, a terrified Evans listened to the judge pass sentence.

From the public gallery, Christie watched a court officer lead Evans away. That another man would suffer for the crimes he committed relieved Christie of an incredible burden. He felt an overwhelming sense of emotion course through him and, in the heavy silence of the courtroom, hanged his head and wept tears of relief.

Timothy Evans was hanged at Pentonville Prison on Thursday, 9 March 1950. He maintained his innocence up until the end, insisting his wife and child had died at Christie's hands.

The trial and Evans's execution were watershed moments for Christie. Life at Rillington Place had forever been altered. Thoughts of his past crimes and fear of eventual discovery now plagued Christie almost constantly, sending him to the doctor on multiple occasions for the treatment of depression. At the time of the trial, he had been holding down a job at a local post office. The revelations of his past crimes, however, had brought his employment to an abrupt end and exacerbated his already fragile condition.

He and Ethel were living alone at No. 10 by the summer of 1950, Mr Kitchener having moved out after becoming too feeble to care for himself. The solitude suited Christie just fine, but it didn't last long. The owners, in a decision that caused Christie considerable stress, decided to put the building up for sale that summer.

A new owner would more than likely renovate the place and discover the bodies buried in the back garden. Christie did his best to dissuade one potential buyer, a Mr Ernest McNeil, by telling him two bodies had been discovered the previous year out in the washhouse. McNeil, a one-time undertaker, shrugged off the story and commissioned a surveyor's report on the property. An inspector went through the house and concluded the place was filthy and infested with bed bugs. While McNeil ultimately decided not to purchase the building, No. 10's advanced state of decay did not deter Jamaican immigrant Charles Brown.

Brown disrupted the Christies' insular world by moving black tenants into the two empty flats. The Christies were less than pleased to have West Indians – whom they considered to be an inferior species – living upstairs and sharing the building's single lavatory. Ethel feared for her safety, while Christie worried the new inhabitants would prove meddlesome and somehow stumble across the bodies. He found something of a distraction when he started a new job that August as a clerk with British Road Services. He enjoyed being out of the house during the day but dreaded returning in the evenings. Tensions between the Christies and their neighbours ran high and resulted in frequent arguments. On at least one occasion, Ethel claimed to have been assaulted by one of the black tenants.

As the Christies struggled to cope with the changes around them, their marriage began showing signs of deterioration. What little sex the couple enjoyed had ceased in the wake of Evans's execution, prompting Ethel to make the occasional snide comment regarding her husband's impotency. Her gentle ribbing riled Christie, who kept hoping Ethel would go and visit her family in Sheffield and allow him some time alone. Much to his chagrin, she stayed put.

Christie's nerves grew increasingly frail over the next two years. He lived in constant fear that someone would discover his past deeds. He had always considered himself an upstanding citizen, a man of strong moral standing, and spent his life trying to perpetuate that image. The revelation he was a killer would forever shatter a façade he had worked tirelessly to maintain. In March 1952, the ongoing stress sent him to St Charles's Hospital for a three-week convalescent stay. He saw a psychiatrist at Springfield Mental Hospital in July who believed Christie – with his effeminate voice – to be a closet homosexual.

Christie, who refused long-term psychiatric care, was now visiting his physician on a weekly basis for the treatment of various nervous ailments. His decline proved rapid and, on 6 December, he quit his job. He told his employer a better opportunity had presented itself in Sheffield. Six days later, Ethel dropped her dirty linens off at a Laundromat on Walmer Road. It was the last time anyone outside Rillington Place saw her alive.

Waiting in Brixton Prison for his trial to begin, Christie bragged about his crimes. His ultimate goal, he told fellow inmates, had been to kill a dozen women. The psychiatrists charged with discerning his mental state found him to be a pathological liar, a raging egotist, and privately noted the repulsion they felt when sitting in close proximity to him.

It was during a psychiatric examination with Dr J.A. Hobson on 27 April 1953 that Christie confessed to killing Beryl Evans. Three more confessions – all differing in various ways – followed, but not once did he admit to killing Geraldine. He found something righteous in the death of his adult victims. Harassed by women all his life, he had merely stood up for himself. Confessing to the child's murder, however, would negate the moral certainty of his actions.

Christie's trial commenced at the Old Bailey on Monday, 22 June, in the same courtroom where Timothy Evans had stood trial three years before. For a man who kept a picture of himself in his prison cell, Christie must have marvelled that so many people took an interest in his case. The public benches were packed with spectators curious to glimpse the Rillington Place killer. Aligned against a formidable mountain of evidence, Christie's attorneys pursued an insanity defence, arguing their client had no concept of right or wrong.

Christie testified on the second day and spent 3 hours in the witness box, answering questions in a voice that barely registered above a whisper. Those expecting to hear the ramblings of a madman were disappointed. The only time he showed any emotion was when testifying about his wife's death. He told prosecuting barrister Sir Lionel Heald that he buried Ethel beneath the floorboards of his front room because he couldn't bear to part with her. When not on the stand, he stood in the prisoner's dock and nervously rubbed his bald scalp. The psychiatrists who had thus far interviewed him testified, describing Christie as sexually immature and conceited, a man prone to fits of hysterics and who feigned illness when life threw challenges his way. One doctor could not help but point out Christie's 'remarkable capacity for dismissing the unpleasant from his mind'.

The case went to the jury on Thursday, 25 June, following a nearly 3-hour summation by Mr Justice Finnemore. Jurors took 85 minutes to reach their verdict and filed back into the courtroom shortly before 5.30 that afternoon. Christie looked on, betraying not the slightest emotion. Despite efforts by the defence, there was never any doubt as to Christie's fate. Just like Evans before him, Christie stood in the dock and watched the court clerk place the black cloth upon the judge's head. A visibly distraught Finnemore, perhaps disturbed by Christie's sad and pathetic existence, passed the only sentence the law allowed.

Christie spent his remaining days at Pentonville Prison in the same condemned cell once occupied by Evans. He apologised to no one and ignored a plea from Evans's mother to reveal what really happened the day Beryl died. In the wake of Christie's conviction, public outcry over the hanging of Timothy Evans prompted the government to create a board of inquiry and look into whether British justice had killed an innocent man. Court transcripts were studied and witnesses, including Christie, were questioned.

With only one week remaining until his own death, Christie – always a small, contemptible human being – still sought to cast himself in a positive light and denied murdering Geraldine. Despite telling his prison psychiatrist in April that he was responsible for Beryl's murder, he now told the Crown's board of inquiry he had no memory of committing the crime. The board's findings, however, maintained that Evans had indeed killed his wife and daughter. The public and the press blasted the government's conclusions with claims of a cover-up.

The hangman came for Christie as the prison clock struck 9 on the morning of Wednesday, 15 July 1953. His arms pinioned behind him, he was led onto the same trap door through which Evans had dropped into the afterlife. A white hood was pulled over his head and the noose properly positioned beneath the angle of the left jaw. Minutes later, John Reginald Halliday Christie ceased to exist.

In 1965, the British government launched another inquiry into the Evans case. The findings this time concluded that Evans did not kill his daughter, but most likely murdered his wife. Because he hanged for strangling Geraldine, he received a posthumous pardon on 18 October 1966. His remains were disinterred from the graveyard at Pentonville Prison and reburied in consecrated ground at St Patrick's Cemetery, Leytonstone.

13

The Vanishing

For nine years, Mrs Constance Lane had called the Onslow Court Hotel in Kensington home. The surroundings were elegant and suited Mrs Lane's sense of style, much as it did her friend and fellow hotel resident Mrs Olive Durand-Deacon. The two women were of the upper-crust variety and enjoyed their leisurely existence. They took great pride in their appearance, bedecking themselves in jewels and furs for casual meals in the hotel's well-appointed dining room. And so it was, on the evening of Friday, 18 February 1949, that Mrs Lane noticed the table where Mrs Durand-Deacon regularly ate dinner was unoccupied.

This struck her as being somewhat odd as Olive routinely took her evening meal at the same hour every day. At breakfast the next morning, Olive's table again sat empty. As Constance sipped her morning cup of tea and eyed her friend's vacant chair, John Haigh – a fellow guest she knew only as 'a nodding acquaintance' – entered the dining room. He glanced momentarily at Olive's table before casting his gaze about the room. He was well dressed in a dark suit, which seemed to be his preferred choice of clothing. A pencil-thin moustache followed the curve of his upper lip; his black hair was slicked with a sharp parting down the right.

He seemed to be looking for Olive and smiled when he caught Constance eyeing him over the rim of her cup. He strolled across the room and bid her a good morning.

'Do you know anything about Mrs Durand-Deacon?' he asked, 'Is she ill?'

'No,' Constance said, putting down her cup, 'I haven't seen her.'

The last time Constance had in fact seen her friend was early the previous afternoon. The two women had chatted only briefly, during which time Olive had said Mr Haigh was keen to show her his engineering workshop in Crawley.

'Do you not know where she is?' Constance asked, 'I understood that you were going to take her to your factory.'

'Yes,' Haigh replied, 'but I was not ready. I had not had my lunch, and she said she wanted to go to the Army & Navy store. She asked me to pick her up there.'

Haigh continued, explaining that after his lunch the previous day, he drove to the store in Victoria Street shortly before 2 o'clock to pick Olive up. He waited for more than an hour, but she never appeared. Deciding the woman had simply changed her mind about viewing his factory, Haigh had driven off.

'Well,' Constance said, 'I must do something about it.'

She excused herself from the table and tracked down the hotel's chambermaid, who said from the look of Olive's bed, the missing woman had not spent the night in her room. Constance, although alarmed by the news, convinced herself there was a reasonable explanation for her friend's absence. She would most likely find Olive sitting at her regular table when dinner rolled around that evening. But when Olive still failed to make an appearance at the prescribed hour, Constance's sense of bafflement took on an edge of panic. It was not until the next day, Sunday, 20 February, that she took action. As she sat and ate her breakfast, debating whether or not to call the police, Haigh entered the dining room and approached her table.

'Any news of Mrs Durand-Deacon?' he asked.

'No,' Constance said, 'I have not had any news – and I'm going to the Chelsea Police Station after lunch to ask them to take up the matter at once.'

Haigh nodded and offered no further comment on the subject. He wished Constance a good day and left the dining room. Constance finished her breakfast and considered her friend's possible whereabouts. At 69, Olive was not one for gallivanting around town, nor was she likely to have run off with a male suitor. What options did that leave? None of the possibilities she considered were appealing. She got up from her table and went in search of Haigh. She found him reading a newspaper in the Tudor lounge and was happy when he suggested they not wait until after lunch to inform police.

'I will drive you there,' he said.

The two drove to Chelsea Police Station and reported Olive Durand-Deacon missing. Police Sergeant Alexandra Lambourne launched her inquiry the next day – Monday, 21 February – at the Onslow Court Hotel. Questioning various guests and employees, she learned the missing woman was widowed and financially well off. For the past six years, she had lived in room 115 and always informed hotel management of her plans to leave for extended periods of time, which were exceedingly rare. She was, according to manager Alicia Robbie, a woman 'of very regular habits'.

Lambourne, sitting in Robbie's office and scribbling the details in her notebook, turned her thoughts to Haigh. From the outset, the man who brought Mrs Lane to the police station had struck her as smarmy. He seemed almost too eager to help. While Mrs Lane fretted nervously about her friend, her male companion carried himself with a jovial air – hardly the demeanour of one concerned about a missing acquaintance. Going with her instincts, she casually asked Robbie about the gentleman staying in room 404.

The manager shifted slightly in her seat and said Haigh had been living in the hotel for the past five years. Asked if he ever caused problems for the staff, Robbie said there were recent issues with his weekly bill. He had been slow to pay.

'He kept us waiting and, after a fortnight, of course, we pressed him,' Robbie said. 'About 3 February he was owing us thirty-two odd, and we had asked him for payment two or three times … I sent up my head bookkeeper to his room for the money, and he said he was not well and was unable to collect the money for us, but would settle in a few days' time. We wrote to him that we must have the money, or else he must vacate his room.'

By 18 February, the day Constance first noticed Olive's absence, Haigh had paid his bill in full. An intrigued Lambourne returned to the Chelsea Police Station and shared her findings with Divisional Detective Inspector Shelley Symes, who ran Haigh's name through Scotland Yard's Criminal Records Office. In less than an hour, it emerged that John George Haigh, 39, had a shady past, having been convicted multiple times for fraud. Symes – a large, round-faced man – and Detective Inspector Albert Webb paid a visit to the Onslow Court Hotel. They ventured up to the fourth floor and knocked on Haigh's door. He answered, cigarette in hand, and smiled when the detectives introduced themselves.

'I am making enquiries with respect to a lady who is missing from this hotel,' Symes said.

'Yes,' Haigh replied, 'I thought you would see me as I went with her friend, Mrs Lane, to the police station to report her missing. I will tell you all about it.'

Haigh invited the detectives in and, responding to their questions, said he was director of Hurstlea Products Ltd, an engineering firm based in Crawley, Sussex. He drove down to his factory once or twice a week to check on the 'various inventions' his engineers were working on. In regard to the missing woman, he said the two often took their meals in the dining room at adjacent tables and developed a casual friendship. On a recent afternoon, Mrs Durand-Deacon – aware of Haigh's engineering background – told him of an idea she had to produce a new kind of artificial fingernail. 'She showed me some she had made of paper and had glued to her nails.

She asked me if I could make something similar which could be sold,' Haigh said. 'On the following Tuesday or Wednesday, I told Mrs Durand-Deacon that I thought I could do something about the fingernails and suggested that she come down to the factory at Crawley to show us what she wanted.'

The story Haigh told the detectives was no different from the statement he gave at Chelsea Police Station the day before. He said he saw Mrs Durand-Deacon at lunch on Friday, 18 February, and arranged to meet her at 2.30 that afternoon and take her down to the factory. She said she wanted to stop first at the Army & Navy Stores on Victoria Street to pick up samples of current artificial nails on the market. Haigh said he would have his lunch at the hotel while she ran her errand and would pick her up outside the store at the agreed upon time. 'She got up and went out into the street,' he said:

> She was dressed in a black cloth hat and a black Astrakhan coat. She was carrying a small, red, plastic handbag, about nine inches by five. She was wearing a brass crucifix about five inches long on a chain around her neck. This was the last time I saw her. I went to the Army & Navy Stores, reaching there approximately five-and-twenty to three. I had to take the car round the back to park it … I walked round to the front but could not see anything of Mrs Durand-Deacon. I waited until nearly half-past three and as she did not arrive, I went on alone to Crawley.

Haigh lit another cigarette and said he arrived at his factory at about 4.30.

'I attended to some business with some small fans we are making,' he continued:

> I had my dinner in the Ancient Prior's Café and left there just before seven and returned to the hotel at about 8 o'clock. I went straight up to my room … The following morning, when I came down to breakfast, the waitress asked me if Mrs Durand-Deacon was ill as she had not been down to

dinner on the previous night. I said I did not know. I then went round to Mrs Lane to ask her what she knew about Mrs Durand-Deacon.

Haigh detailed Mrs Lane's efforts to find her friend before deciding to report her missing. The detectives thanked Haigh for his time and left, not entirely convinced by the man's story. Once alone, Haigh retrieved a wrapped bundle from his bedside table and slipped it into his coat pocket. He checked the hallway outside his room to ensure the detectives weren't hanging about, walked down to his car and drove to a jewellery shop he knew in Horsham. The man behind the counter smiled when Haigh entered and placed the wrapped item on the glass countertop between them.

Haigh unwrapped the package to reveal a large, awkward-shaped stone and said he wished to have it appraised for probate purposes. The jeweller, a man named Horace Bull, held the stone up to a light in the ceiling.

'This is a curious piece of jewellery,' Bull said, 'how did the lady wear it?'

'She wore it with a piece of wire twisted into the setting to make a ring,' Haigh said.

Bull nodded, put a jeweller's loop to his left eye and examined the stone. 'I'd assess this piece at £131,' he said, putting the jewel back on the counter. 'I'll give you £100 for it.'

Haigh smiled. He needed the money.

The police, with no solid leads to go on, pushed forward with their investigation. While there was no physical evidence suggesting Haigh's involvement in Mrs Durand-Deacon's disappearance, the dapper man had nevertheless become the primary focus of their inquiry. Symes, curious to learn more about Haigh's supposed company, Hurstlea Products Ltd in Crawley, called the West Sussex Constabulary and asked them to investigate the firm.

On Wednesday, 23 February, Detective Sergeant Patrick Heslin paid a visit to 15 West Street, Crawley – the company's listed address – and spoke with Edward Jones, who identified himself as the firm's managing director. Jones told Heslin the company had moved into its current premises two years earlier. Before that, the firm occupied a small warehouse in Leopold Road, which, until recently, was used to store steel and other materials. When asked if he knew Haigh, Jones answered in the affirmative and said Haigh had approached him in 1947 with the idea of building a small gadget that automatically threaded needles. Enthusiastic about the idea, Jones spent a considerable amount of time with Haigh trying to make the product a reality. Their efforts, however, ultimately failed. The venture had cost Haigh £200 of his own money.

'I offered him a directorship as security against the money he put down,' Jones said. 'He said he would like the opportunity, but the matter was dropped. Of recent years, he has been associated with us inasmuch as he has been our London representative more or less, because I cannot leave Crawley too often.'

When in Crawley, Jones said, Haigh never worked out of the small West Street office, preferring instead to use the warehouse on Leopold Road. 'On one occasion he used it, I asked him what he was doing there,' Jones said. 'He said it was a conversion job, but I could not get anything more from him than that.'

The warehouse keys had been kept in the West Street office until Haigh took full-time possession of them, said Jones, who realised the detective had not once mentioned the reason for his interest in Haigh. On his way back to the West Sussex Constabulary, Heslin drove past the warehouse to have a look. It was really more of a shed, a small two-storey structure in Giles Yard built of dirty red brick and surrounded by a 6-foot-high fence. There seemed to be nothing extraordinary about the place from the outside – in fact, it looked quite run down, as though it hadn't been used in a while. Heslin drove on, determined to have a look inside.

Jones, feeling uneasy, returned to his work in the wake of Heslin's departure. His business was on the level, but Haigh's activities in the warehouse were obviously something of a crooked nature. What else would explain the detective's visit? The last thing Jones wanted was for his business to be tainted by association. It would be best, he decided, to confront Haigh and get whatever secrets the man harboured out into the open. He had last seen Haigh the previous day, but there was nothing in the man's behaviour to suggest he was up to anything illegal. In fact, Haigh had repaid £36 of a £50 loan with a promise to pay the remainder in the coming days.

The sound of someone entering the premises derailed Jones's thoughts. He looked at the clock and saw it was coming up on the lunch hour – an odd time for a business call. When Haigh entered the office, he did so with a cheerful greeting. The man always seemed to be in a good mood. He reached into his pocket, pulled out a wad of cash and began counting the bills. It occurred to Jones that the usually broke Haigh seemed to have come into quite a bit of money. Jones spoke when Haigh handed him the cash.

'I've been interviewed by the police,' he said. 'Have you been up to anything? I hope you're not in trouble.'

'No,' Haigh said.

'If there is any trouble,' Jones persisted, 'I prefer you not to come to the works. I prefer you to stay away if there is any trouble.'

Haigh simply laughed. He offered Jones no other reply and left the office, his laugh continuing down the hall.

Mrs Durand-Deacon's disappearance found its way onto the front pages within days. Eager reporters, fascinated by the tale of a wealthy widow gone missing, flocked to the Onslow Court Hotel. The story had all the makings of an Agatha Christie yarn. Reporters staked out the hotel's lobby and bar, anxious to chat with the handsome gentleman last seen in Mrs Durand-Deacon's company. The man in question seemed happy to field their queries. John Haigh was not a subtle individual and relished the spotlight, holding court amidst the blinding flash of camera bulbs and the eager shouts of newspapermen. When one well-informed reporter asked Haigh about his criminal record, Haigh dismissed the question with a grin. 'Let us skip that,' he said, 'we are talking of Mrs Durand-Deacon.'

On the afternoon of Thursday, 24 February, Inspector Symes and Sergeant Webb returned to the Onslow Court Hotel to question Haigh once more. Having learned from Detective Heslin that Haigh had lied in regard to being director of a large engineering firm, Symes was curious to see what else Haigh had lied about. As with their previous encounter, Symes and Webb met with Haigh in his hotel room. He seemed neither surprised nor put out when they again knocked on his door. Haigh stuck to the story he had told from the beginning. He had carefully scripted the tale out in his head and did not deviate from the plot.

'I draw no wages from Hurstlea Products although I am a director,' Haigh said when asked by Symes about his job. 'I buy and sell engineering machinery and tools.' When asked how he managed to repay Jones the £50 and cover hotel expenses without drawing a wage, Haigh had his answer at the ready. 'I also back dogs and horses,' he said. 'I won £50 over Cavalary Major at White City on Saturday and £300 over Black Tarquin last year.'

Still lacking sufficient cause to take Haigh into custody, Symes and Webb again left the hotel empty handed. In Crawley, Sergeant Heslin met once more with Edward Jones on Saturday, 26 February, and drove to the warehouse on Leopold Road. Two padlocks secured the door to the shed. Jones had the key to one lock, but Heslin had to force the other with a crowbar. The detective pushed the door open and peered inside, not sure what he expected to see.

A large L-shaped workbench was pushed against the white-washed walls in one corner of the shed. Three acid carboys sat in the centre of the floor, while in another corner Heslin spotted a rubber apron, rubber gloves, a mackintosh and a stirrup pump. A pair of goggles hung from a hook in the wall. Heslin entered the cramped space and approached a large, leather case that sat atop the workbench. He peered inside and found a holstered .38

Webley and eight rounds of ammunition. Near the gun was a receipt from a cleaner's in Reigate for a Persian lamb coat. Heslin seized the items, booked them as evidence and notified Symes in London of his findings.

The two men rendezvoused the following day and paid a visit to Cottage Cleaners in Reigate's High Street. They presented the receipt found in Haigh's workshop to Mabel Marriot, the woman behind the counter. She made note of the laundry number and rummaged through the racks of clothes behind her, retrieving a black fur coat. She told detectives a man had dropped the coat off a week ago Saturday, 19 February. Symes held the coat up in front of him and noticed what appeared to be fresh patchwork on the coat's left sleeve and along the bottom trim.

He returned the following morning to the Onslow Court Hotel and asked the manageress to let him into Mrs Durand-Deacon's room. The bed was made and the makeup and brushes on the bureau neatly arranged. Symes knew the revolver was enough reason to arrest Haigh, but what he sought to eliminate any doubt was physical evidence tying Haigh to the victim. Symes opened the bureau drawers, not knowing what he was looking for. Finding nothing, he cast his gaze about the room and noticed a workbasket tucked away in a corner. He looked inside and found a bag of sewing supplies and fabrics, among which were several swatches of cloth that looked familiar.

Later that day, Symes turned the coat and fabric samples over to Dr Henry Holden, director of the Metropolitan Police Laboratory at New Scotland Yard. A microscopic analysis of the fabric discovered in Mrs Durand-Deacon's room found it to be an exact match to the patchwork fabric on the coat. Symes, not wanting to waste any more time, ordered Detective Inspector Webb to bring Haigh in for questioning. The detective pulled up in front of the Onslow Court Hotel at 4.15 p.m. and saw Haigh sitting in his parked Alvis motor car, registration BOV 463. Webb approached the driver's door and knocked on the window. Haigh looked up and smiled.

'I want you to come to the Chelsea Police Station at once and see Superintendent Barratt and Detective Inspector Symes,' Webb said.

'Certainly,' Haigh replied, stepping out of the vehicle, 'I will do anything to help you, as you know.'

At the station, Webb ushered Haigh into the office of the Divisional Detective Inspector and told him to have a seat. The suspect's demeanour remained upbeat and his mannerisms relaxed. He sat himself down, lit a cigarette and helped himself to a newspaper, idly flipping through the pages and stealing the occasional glance at his watch. If Haigh harboured any curiosity as to why police had brought him in, he made no mention of it. Instead, he expressed his gratitude when an officer brought him a cup of tea just after 6 o'clock. He finished the drink, had another smoke and, to Webb's considerable surprise, dozed off as the minutes ticked slowly by. All the while, Symes busied himself pursuing a last-minute lead.

Reading the newspaper that afternoon, jeweller Horace Bull skimmed a story concerning the disappearance of Mrs Durand-Deacon. Along with a general description of the missing woman, the article listed various items of jewellery she was believed to have been wearing the day she vanished. Among them were a pair of pearl earrings, an emerald-and-diamond clasp, a sapphire-and-diamond engagement ring, and other assorted valuables that Bull now realised were sitting in his display case. He put the paper down and phoned the Chelsea Police Station. Detective Inspector Symes took the call and immediately left for Horsham.

In the store, Bull arranged the jewels on his countertop for Symes's inspection. He described the man who had pawned the items, detailing Haigh down to his rakish smile and styled hair. The man, Bull said, had been in the shop on three or four occasions. Symes took possession of the jewels and brought them back to London to show Durand-Deacon's sister, who confirmed they belonged to the missing woman. When Symes finally returned to the police station and took a seat opposite Haigh, the wall clock said 7.15.

'I have continued my enquiries into the disappearance of Mrs Durand-Deacon, and I want you to answer some more questions,' Symes said.

'I am quite willing to answer anything I can,' Haigh replied, 'and to help you all I can.'

Symes, getting straight to the point, asked Haigh how many trips to Horsham he had made in recent days.

'I used to go to Horsham a lot,' Haigh said, 'but lately I have gone there once in the evening, to the pictures.'

'You have been there in the morning recently on no less than four occasions,' Symes shot back, revealing what he knew about Haigh's visit to the cleaner's and jewellery shop. 'I want you to tell me about that.'

Haigh smiled. 'I can see you know what you are talking about,' he said. 'I will admit that the coat belonged to Mrs Durand-Deacon and that I sold her jewellery to Bull's, the jewellers in Horsham, as you know.'

Symes turned and nodded to a uniformed officer who stood watch against the wall behind him. The officer handed Symes a box from which he retrieved the laundry receipt found in Haigh's workshop and six pieces of jewellery taken from Bull's.

'How did you come by this property?' Symes asked, 'Where is Mrs Durand-Deacon?'

Haigh leaned forward in his chair and lit a cigarette. 'It is a long story,' he said. 'It is one of blackmail, and I shall have to implicate many others. How do I stand about that?'

'What you have to say is entirely a matter for you.'

A knock on the door halted the conversation. An officer stuck his head in the room, apologised and explained Symes was needed momentarily on another matter. The detective inspector excused himself and left Haigh alone with Webb. Several minutes passed in silence before Haigh asked if it was ever possible, once committed, to be released from the insane asylum at Broadmoor.

'I cannot discuss that sort of thing with you,' Webb said.

'Well, if I told you the truth, you would not believe me,' Haigh teased. 'It sounds too fantastic for belief.'

Webb cautioned Haigh of his right not to incriminate himself.

'I understand all that,' Haigh said, 'I will tell you all about it. Mrs Durand-Deacon no longer exists. She has disappeared completely, and no trace of her will ever be found again.'

'What has happened to her?'

'I have destroyed her with acid,' Haigh said in the casual manner of one discussing the weather. 'You will find the sludge that remains at Leopold Road – every trace has gone. How can you prove murder if there is no body?'

When Symes re-entered the room, Webb repeated the exchange.

'That is perfectly true,' Haigh said, a measure of pride in his voice. 'It is a very long story and will take hours to tell.'

'I am prepared to listen,' Symes said.

'I have been worried about the matter and fenced about it, in the hope that you would not find out about it,' Haigh confessed. 'The truth is, however, that we left the hotel together and went to Crawley together in my car. She was inveigled into going to Crawley by me in view of her interest in artificial fingernails.'

Haigh leaned back and settled into his story.

He drove Mrs Durand-Deacon to his workshop in Leopold Road and invited her inside. Haigh pointed to a roll of construction paper on his workbench and said it would be used in the manufacturing of the fingernails. Intrigued, Mrs Durand-Deacon stepped forward to have a closer look. Haigh moved quickly to the other end of the workbench, where he kept his revolver concealed in a leather hatbox. Keeping his eye on Mrs Durand-Deacon's back, he freed the weapon from its holster and took aim. There was no need to check the chamber; he had taken all the necessary precautions several days before. 'I shot her in the back of the head,' he said, lighting another cigarette, 'then I went out to the car and fetched in a drinking glass and made an incision, I think with a penknife, in the side of the throat, and collected a glass of blood, which I then drank.'

Haigh took another drag on his cigarette, his eyes fixed on Symes in dull appraisal. As there was no corpse to autopsy, Haigh knew police had no way of verifying his story. Symes, wondering if Haigh was simply aiming for an insanity plea to escape the hangman, urged him to continue.

'Following that,' Haigh said, 'I removed the coat she was wearing – a Persian lamb – and the jewellery, rings, necklace, earrings and crucifix, and put her in a 45-gallon drum. I then filled the tank up with sulphuric acid, by means of a stirrup pump, from a carboy. I then left it to react. I should have said that in between having her in the tank and pumping in the acid, I went round to the Ancient Prior's for a cup of tea. Having left the tank to react, I brought the jewellery and revolver into the car and left the coat on the bench. I went to the George for dinner.'

Haigh said he went back to his warehouse to drop off the gun before returning to the Onslow Court Hotel at 10.30 p.m. The next morning, Saturday, 19 February, he ate breakfast in the downstairs dining room and feigned concern when Mrs Durand-Deacon failed to make an appearance. Driving back to Crawley that afternoon, he stopped off in Putney and pawned the dead woman's watch for £10 at a jewellery shop in the High Street. When he eventually reached his workshop, he checked on the tank. He found the acid had thickened into sludge, but the body was only partially dissolved. Deciding the process 'was not satisfactorily completed', Haigh returned to his car with the Persian lamb coat and drove to Horsham.

'I called at Bull's, the jewellers, for a valuation of the jewellery, but Mr Bull was not in.,' Haigh said. 'I returned to town, and on the way dropped in the coat at the Cottage Cleaners in Reigate. On Monday, I returned to Crawley to find the reaction almost complete, but a piece of fat and bone was still floating on the sludge. I emptied off the sludge with a bucket and tipped it on the ground opposite the shed, and pumped a further quantity of acid into the tank to decompose the remaining fat and bone. I then left that to work until the following day. From there, I went to Horsham again and had the jewellery valued, ostensibly for probate. It was valued at just over £130. I called back at the West Street factory and eventually returned to town.'

It was that Monday afternoon at the Onslow Court Hotel that Symes and Webb first interviewed Haigh in regard to Mrs Durand-Deacon's disappearance. Satisfied the police were unaware of his involvement, he returned on Tuesday, 22 February, to his warehouse – stopping off in Horsham along the way to sell some of the jewellery – and found the body had almost completely dissolved. He slipped his hands into a pair of long rubber gloves, put on a body-length rubber apron and pulled a gasmask over his face. Using his stirrup pump, he emptied what acid he could back into the carboy and dumped the remaining sludge and liquid in the shed's small courtyard.

'I found that the only thing which the acid had not attacked was the plastic handbag, and I tipped this out with the sludge,' Haigh said. 'On the Tuesday when I completely emptied the tank, I left it outside … Before I put the handbag in the tank, I took from it cash – about thirty shillings – and her fountain pen and kept these, and tipped the rest into the tank with the bag. The fountain pen is still in my room.'

On his way back to London, shortly before 2 that Tuesday afternoon, Haigh stopped off at Hurstlea Product's West Street office to partially repay a £50-loan from Edward Jones. With money he had received that morning from the jeweller's, Haigh gave Jones £36 and promised to pay the rest off shortly thereafter. The following morning, he made his fourth visit in five days to Bull's jewellery shop to collect another £40 for the dead woman's jewellery.

He arrived in Crawley just before the lunch hour and made good on his promise to Jones, who mentioned the police had stopped by that morning with questions about Haigh. Three days after Haigh's last visit to Jones, Sergeant Heslin forced entry into the Leopold Road warehouse and discovered the gun, laundry receipt and acid carboys. From there, the pieces had quickly fallen into place – but Haigh's story was far from over. Having confessed to murdering Olive Durand-Deacon, he had more nightmarish tales to share.

14

Acid and Blood

There was nothing to suggest while growing up that the young boy Haigh harboured a murderous disposition. There was no strange fascination with the dead or cruelty to small animals. He was born on 24 July 1909, at Stamford in Yorkshire, to a devoutly religious couple, who belonged to a sect called the Peculiar People. They adhered to a strict interpretation of the Bible, which frowned upon frivolity and any pursuit that did not ultimately serve the Almighty.

'Though my parents were kind and loving, I had none of the joys, or the companionship, which small children usually have,' Haigh wrote in later years. 'Their religious beliefs were to them more important than anything else in life. They lived by precepts, and they talked in parables. It is true to say that I was nurtured on Bible stories, mostly concerned with sacrifice. If by some mischance I did, or said, anything, which my father regarded as improper, he would say: "Do not grieve the Lord by behaving so." And if I suggested that I wanted to go somewhere, or to meet somebody, he would say: "It will not please the Lord."'

The family moved to Outwood when the boy was young and settled in a small home, a 'monastic' environment of wall-mounted crucifixes and religious texts on the bookshelves. The Haigh clan kept to themselves and preferred the company of scripture over people. His father, to encourage the family's isolation, built a large brick wall around their garden to keep outside evil at bay and prevent passers-by from looking in. Although they maintained their distance from others, Haigh's parents sought to create a close, familial bond with their son. 'My parents loved me deeply, and they devoted themselves to moulding my life,' he wrote. 'Their hopes were high, and to me they remained all that is noble.'

To Haigh's father, the greatest nobility lay in death. To be content in the world of the living was a sin, for only in the afterlife would one find true salvation and happiness in the presence of God. Often Haigh's father would talk of 'Heavenly places' and refer to the 'worms that will destroy this body'. As an adult, looking back on his childhood, Haigh would write, 'It was inevitable that I should develop an early inhibition regarding death'.

The father encouraged his son to ponder the world beyond the physical and warned against the evils of temptation. One afternoon, Haigh's father sat him down and pointed to a bluish scar shaped like a lop-sided cross on his forehead. 'This is the brand of Satan,' the father said. 'I have sinned and Satan has punished me. If you ever sin, Satan will mark you with a blue pencil likewise.'

Haigh leaned in close and stared at the mark, touching it lightly with a finger. 'Well,' Haigh said, almost in awe, 'Mother isn't marked.'

'No, she is an angel.'

Haigh, still young enough to believe that all things his parents said were true, took the words to heart. He shared his father's story with the other children at his grammar school and took pride in believing he was the only child 'of an angel and the one man who had sinned'. His schoolmates naturally dismissed the story with derision and mocked Haigh's gullibility. Nevertheless, on the days he misbehaved, he lay in bed at night and ran his finger across his forehead, fearful of Satan's branding. Only after he convinced himself he was free of Satan's mark was he able to fall asleep. 'Years later,' he wrote, 'after I knew that my father's 'brand' had been caused by a piece of flying coal in the mine, I [still] found myself looking at the foreheads of passers-by to see if they carried Satan's mark of sin.'

The strange tales about his home life – and his parents' belief that socialising angered God – rendered Haigh an outcast among other children. Although a kind and gentle boy, others his age viewed him as something of a curiosity. An only child, Haigh had no one with whom he could relate. Perhaps, out of an overwhelming sense of loneliness, he developed a strong affection for animals. Rabbits were his pet of choice, and it was not uncommon for him to venture out in his neighbourhood in search of stray dogs to feed.

On the very rare occasions when he did play with other children, he showed the same generosity and willingly offered his toys to others. More often than not, however, his parents forbade such interaction out of fear it might somehow corrupt their son. For the young Haigh, relief came in visits to his maternal aunt, who viewed the world in more accepting terms. 'At her house I used to enjoy reading the comic strip in a newspaper,' he wrote. 'When I asked my father why we didn't have a newspaper at our house, I was told "It is a thing of the world: there is not time enough to read the Bible."'

He began school when he was 7. When one of Haigh's teachers at Wakefield Grammar School assigned *Treasure Island* as mandatory reading, Haigh's father complained to the headmaster. A book about pirates, he said, who murder and craved riches was hardly suitable reading for children. Haigh, raised on daily Bible readings, dismissed his father's opinion as being ludicrous when he considered the savagery depicted in the Old Testament. When he told his father what he thought, the older Haigh simply smiled and reminded his son 'that the Lord was Jehovah, and, therefore, totally different'. Haigh, not yet a teenager, could only shake his head at the hypocrisy of such an argument.

When other families on the street began putting wireless sets in their homes, Haigh's father frowned at the suggestion he do the same. A wireless, he said, would bring outside influence into the home. 'From my earliest years,' Haigh later complained, 'my recollection is of my father saying "Do not" or "Thou shalt not" … there was always condemnation and prohibition.'

Everything in the Haigh household was done for the greater glory of God. Although he felt increasingly disconnected from the real world, Haigh did nothing to act out or give vent to his frustration. His teachers considered him an intelligent student who failed to apply himself. Unlike other young boys, whose general rough-housing resulted in scuffed knees and scruffy clothing, Haigh took great care to maintain his appearance. His most troublesome trait was his penchant for telling lies – the product, he later said, of simply lying to his parents about certain things to avoid lengthy lectures about God.

Immaculate appearance and lying aside, Haigh also stood out for his refusal to participate in school sports. Music became his true passion, and he insisted on taking piano lessons. He took quickly to the instrument and soon became a proficient player. Through music, he could express himself without upsetting his parents; it was like the opening of a pressure valve. Before long, he was playing the organ at Wakefield Cathedral and singing in the church choir – much to the delight of his mother and father. While in church, he would often stare at the large cross hanging above the altar and the Christ figure nailed upon it. He sometimes dreamed of the crucifixion at night, the blood dripping from Christ's hands and his speared side glowing a vibrant red.

He subsequently developed a grim fascination with blood. When he misbehaved, his mother would sometimes smack the back of his hand with her hairbrush. The bristles drew beads of blood to his skin, which he studied closely before going somewhere private to lick the blood from his hand. Something about the copper taste appealed to him, he alleged in later years, leading him to frequently slice his own finger and suck the wound.

Haigh remained at Wakefield Grammar School until he turned 17. The proceeding years for Haigh passed without much direction. He still lived at home with his parents and worked a variety of random jobs before launching, at the age of 21, his own advertising and insurance firm. He possessed a natural talent for business and instinctively knew the art of the deal. Despite being older and a successful businessman, his parents still required that he live his life by their strict standards. 'The atmosphere in my home,' he wrote, 'did not belong to the outside world.' And it was to the outside world that Haigh yearned to escape.

Sexually, Haigh was a late bloomer and never seemed pre-occupied with the subject. He showed no real interest in girls throughout adolescence, preferring instead the company of books and his musical pursuits. He lost his virginity when he was 20 and found it to be an unspectacular event. Sex, he believed, was overrated. Why other men his age spent so much time lusting after it mystified him. Perhaps his strict religious upbringing accounted for such an attitude, though he saw nothing sinful in the activity. If sex served any benefit, other than short-term gratification, it offered an escape from the claustrophobic confines of his parents' house.

On 6 July 1934, at the age of 24, Haigh married Beatrice Hammer, three years his junior and pregnant with his child. The two moved into their own small house and tried to settle down for the long haul. Charming and a smooth talker, Haigh believed his talents were better suited for something other than advertising and insurance. He had never entertained thoughts of criminality while growing up, nor did his behaviour ever suggest a delinquent streak. The responsibility of marriage and family, however, brought with it new pressures, while the legitimate nature of his work struck him as increasingly dull.

His entire life had been one of restrictions with the threat of eternal damnation for committing the slightest sin. Just as his curiosity about sex had been late to bloom, so too was his desire to rebel against the system he'd been raised in. The seeds were planted one morning while reading the newspaper. On an inside page, he read the story of a con artist who had recently made a tidy fortune selling cars he had acquired on hire-purchase. 'When I first discovered there were easier ways to make a living than to work long hours in an office, I did not ask myself whether I was doing right or wrong,' he recalled some years later. 'That seemed to me to be irrelevant. I merely said: "This is what I wish to do." And as the means lay within my power, that was what I decided.'

He hatched a similar scheme, believing he had found a way to make good money with minimal effort. The crooked venture lined his pockets for several months until his arrest in November 1934. He appeared in Leeds Assizes on the 22nd and was sentenced to fifteen months in prison on multiple charges of 'conspiring to defraud; aiding and abetting the forgery of a document and obtaining money by false pretences'.

Shortly after his arrest, his wife gave birth to a baby girl. Not wanting to raise the child on her own, and unwilling to spend the remainder of her years with a convicted felon, Beatrice gave the child up for adoption and left Haigh. The sour turning of events came as a blow to his parents, who viewed their son as nothing less than angelic. Sitting in his prison cell, Haigh wrote a letter to his parents and begged them for their forgiveness. 'May God give me time to redeem the past,' he wrote, 'and to make you happy in your later years.'

He served his time and was released on 8 December 1935. Keeping in mind the promise he had made to his mother and father, he sought a more legitimate line of work. He settled on the dry-cleaning business. 'Dry cleaning is dry cleaning all the world over,' he wrote, 'but persuading the public that you can do it better than the rest, or that they will get something better, is quite different. That is an art.'

He opened a chain of laundries in Leeds, Bradford and Sheffield, and was soon cleaning more than 2,000 garments a week. Thrilled with his initial success, Haigh began planning the expansion of his business when tragedy struck: his investment partner died in a car accident. The man's wife pulled out of the venture and forced Haigh to liquidate his half of the business to meet his various loans. It was a shocking setback that convinced him once and for all that legitimate business pursuits were a waste of time. Pondering his next move, he decided to relocate south to London and try his luck in the capital. He took a small flat and worked briefly as a secretary and chauffeur for 26-year-old William Donald McSwan, the up-and-coming owner of an amusement arcade. He excelled at the job but had no plans of making it permanent, and all the while kept his eyes and ears open for the next scam.

Before long, he was posing as an attorney with a reputable law firm overseeing the sales of discounted shares in a public company. He opened an office, smothered on the charm and told prospective investors they could buy their way in with a 25 per cent deposit. The money was soon coming in faster than he could spend it. With success came the realization he would have to relocate the scheme elsewhere before wronged investors began asking questions. He left London and set up shop in Guildford, where his activities were finally exposed – but not before making more than £3,000. On 24 November 1937, he was sentenced to four years' imprisonment after pleading guilty 'to seven cases of obtaining bankers' cheques by false pretences, with twenty-two other similar offences taken into consideration'.

Released from prison in August 1940, he returned to London, now a city at war. In 1916, when he was 7, Haigh had joined his parents on a holiday in Goole and witnessed a Zeppelin raid. The massive bulk moved slowly across the darkening sky as several houses below went up in columns of flame. The experience traumatised the boy and, for several weeks afterwards, his nerves remained in a delicate state. So it seems odd that upon arriving in London that wartime summer, he took a job as a firewatcher in the civil defence. He kept a nightly vigil near St George's Drive in Victoria, the city blacked out beneath the sweeping search-lights. When the bombers eventually arrived, the devastation they wrought made him question his own faith. Witnessing an entire city block go up in flames one night left him feeling 'shocked in both mind and spirit'.

One evening, as Haigh sat talking with a nurse at the warden's post, the air-raid sirens began to howl. With the drone of bombers passing overhead and the anti-aircraft guns letting loose their thunderous barrage, Haigh ducked for cover in a doorway. A bomb detonated nearby, vaporising windows and knocking Haigh off his feet. 'I staggered up, bruised and bewildered; a head rolled against my feet. The nurse who, but a few minutes before, had been gay, full of life, high ideals and sense of duty, had in one instant been swept into eternity,' he wrote after the event. 'I was shocked beyond all belief. How could God allow it to happen?' His belief in a benevolent God was forever corrupted.

In June 1941, Haigh received a twenty-one-month prison sentence for breaking and entering. Confined once more to a dank cell, he swore he would never languish behind bars again. He passed the time at Lincoln Prison working in the tinsmith shop, where he first witnessed the corrosive power of sulphuric acid. Intrigued, he paid prisoners who worked the land outside the prison to fetch him rodents for experimental purposes. He quickly discovered a mouse, fully submerged in the liquid, dissolved and turned to sludge in approximately ½ hour.

He continued his strange work, experimenting with different volumes of acid and making note of the decomposition times. Hunched over boiling vats, watching acid eat away animal flesh and bone, Haigh made up his mind he would no longer waste his time with petty theft and fraud. He shared his plans with a fellow inmate. 'If you are going to go wrong, go wrong in a big way, like me,' he said. 'Go after women – rich, old women who like a bit of flattery. That's your market if you're after big money.'

Upon his release in September 1943, he moved in temporarily with his parents before heading south a month later and taking a commission-based sales job with an engineering firm in Crawley. Things seemed to be going moderately well for Haigh until the evening of 26 March 1944, when, shortly after 10 o'clock, he crashed his car. He suffered a 2-inch gash to the left side of his head and required stitches.

Following his arrest for murder in 1949, Haigh claimed that in the immediate wake of the accident, he sat dazed behind the wheel. Blood from the head wound poured in a thick cascade down his face and into his mouth, rekindling the bloodlust he had first experienced as a child. He supposedly had a dream that night in which he found himself in a 'forest of crucifixes'. As he wandered through the strange landscape, the crucifixes slowly morphed into trees. 'At first,' he recalled, 'there appeared to be dew, or rain, dripping from the branches, but as I approached I realised it was blood. Suddenly, the whole forest began to writhe and the trees, stark and erect, to ooze blood … A man went to each tree catching the blood … When the cup was full he approached me … "Drink," he said, but I was unable to move. The dream faded.'

It was purely by chance that John Haigh reconnected with William Donald McSwan, who had hired Haigh in 1936 as his chauffeur and secretary. Their fateful reunion occurred one late summer evening in 1944 at the Goat Tavern in Kensington High Street. Sitting at the bar, with a pint in hand, Haigh spotted the tall, lanky McSwan in the crowd. What the two men said to one another is not known – and McSwan's initial reaction to seeing the former employee who vacated his job under suspicious circumstances can only be guessed. But over several pints, Haigh re-established his friendship with McSwan and ultimately put in motion a savage chain of events.

McSwan and Haigh began meeting on a regular basis for drinks and dinner. They were two young men enjoying what pleasures wartime London had to offer while they still could. Haigh, called-up for military service in October 1943, had simply ignored the summons. McSwan, over a pint, told Haigh he planned to go underground to avoid conscription. Shortly thereafter, on the evening of 9 September 1944, McSwan brought a broken pin-table to Haigh's rented flat at 79 Gloucester Road – opposite the tube station – in hopes of having it repaired. There, in the small flat, Haigh made the sudden decision to kill his friend. He waited for McSwan to turn his back before lashing out. 'I hit him on the head with a cosh, withdrew a glass of blood and drank it,' Haigh said. 'He was dead within 5 minutes or so.' Staring at McSwan's bleeding corpse, Haigh realised he had no way of getting rid of the body. Not yet experienced at the art of disposal, he remembered his Lincoln Prison experiments with mice and acid. It just so happened he had in his apartment 'acid and sheet metal for pickling'.

At an abandoned worksite near his flat, Haigh found a large water cask and managed to wheel it back to his address without raising suspicion. He removed a ring from McSwan's finger and took his watch. He retrieved McSwan's identity card from an inside coat pocket and placed the body in the water cask. Using a bucket, he filled the cask with acid and, once the body had turned to sludge, poured the mess down a manhole in his basement-flat floor. His next concern was explaining McSwan's disappearance to the man's family. Mr and Mrs McSwan, who lived at No. 45 Claverton Street, had always liked Haigh and were happy when he and their son reconnected. 'I had known this McSwan and his mother and father for some time,' Haigh told investigators, 'and on seeing his mother and father, explained that he had gone off to avoid his "Call-up".'

His past criminal escapades had prepared him well for the task ahead. His various financial scams and other fraudulent activities had required that he master the art of forging. He became adept at reproducing the handwriting and signatures of others and now put the skill to use. 'I wrote a number of letters to his mother and father purporting to come from him and posted in, I think, Glasgow and Edinburgh …' Haigh explained. 'In the following year, I took separately to the basement the father, Donald, and the mother, Amy, disposing of them in exactly the same way as the son.'

The McSwans – murdered the first week of July 1945 – had made considerable money in the property business, a fact that most likely doomed them to the acid bath. On 18 July, Haigh walked into a solicitor's office in Glasgow, presented papers identifying himself as William Donald McSwan and seized power of attorney over the McSwans' holdings. He soon sold the properties, raided the family's accounts and sold the McSwans' household possessions, lining his pockets with more than £5,000.

Because the McSwans did not move in large social circles, no one seemed to notice they were gone with the exception of Mrs Lucy Phillipe, an elderly neighbour who lived in the basement flat of the McSwans' Pimlico building. She had noticed the small, smart-dressed man who had recently begun paying regular visits to the couple upstairs. 'The McSwans never said they were leaving, though I sometimes went up to see them,' she later recalled. 'The day after they left, their friend let himself in – he apparently had Mr McSwan's key – and told the landlady he had power of attorney to dispose of Mr McSwan's goods.'

Every day for nearly two weeks after the McSwans had gone away, she saw the young man pull up to the house in his small, black car and load it with items from the McSwan home. At one point, she went upstairs to see what he was up to and found the couple's living room in total disarray. 'I helped him to tidy the room … things were thrown all over the place as if the McSwans had just gone out for a night.'

To show Mrs Phillipe his appreciation for the help cleaning up, Haigh sold her some of the McSwans' belongings for £11. 'I demanded a receipt in case the McSwans returned,' she said. 'I even paid for the 2-penny stamp on the receipt.'

After the McSwan killings, Haigh, flush with cash, moved into the Onslow Court Hotel. His taste for the high life, however, and his bad luck at the track did not bode well for his financial situation. By August 1947, he was nearly broke and went in search of new prey.

'I met the Hendersons by answering an advertisement offering for sale their property at 22 Ladbroke Square,' Haigh told investigators. Dr Archibald Henderson – a veteran invalided out of the Royal Army Medical Corps – and his wife, Rosalie, were a childless couple who doted on their Red Irish Setter, Pat. Haigh called the couple and arranged a viewing of their house, located less than a mile from Rillington Place, where other dark deeds were happening behind the walls of number 10. Haigh claimed to be an interested buyer and made a generous offer on the house – but when he proved unable to raise the money, the deal fell through. It hardly mattered, the doctor and his wife had taken to the young man.

Haigh took his time planning the Henderson murders and, over a period of four months, went through the motions of being their friend. By now, he was employed with Hurstlea Products in Crawley and was using the small shed on Leopold Road as a workshop. Three days before Christmas, he purchased three carboys of sulphuric acid from Union Group Engineering – a firm with offices in Crawley and Croydon – and two 40-gallon barrels.

On Tuesday, 10 February 1948, the Hendersons – having eventually sold their house in Notting Hill and purchased a new one at 16 Dawes Road, Fulham – checked in with their dog at the Hotel Metropole in Brighton. Two days later, Haigh paid the couple a visit and talked the 51-year-old Dr Henderson into coming to view his private workspace. 'I took Dr Henderson to Crawley and disposed of him in the storeroom at Leopold Road by shooting him in the head with his own revolver, which I had taken from his property at Dawes Road,' Haigh confessed:

I put him in a tank of acid, as in the other cases. This was in the morning, and I went back to Brighton and brought up Mrs Henderson on the pretext that her husband was ill. I shot her in the storeroom and put her in another tank and disposed of her with acid. In each of the last four cases, I had my glass of blood as before. In the case of Dr Henderson, I removed his gold cigarette case, his gold pocket watch and chain and, from his wife, her wedding ring and diamond ring and disposed of all this to Bull's at Horsham for about £300.

Haigh returned to the Hotel Metropole on 16 February and retrieved the Hendersons's luggage and dog. He settled the couple's hotel bill and drove to their house in Fulham. To avoid rousing suspicion, Haigh wrote letters in Rosalie Henderson's handwriting to the couple's housekeeper and the dead woman's brother, saying they had left England to spend time in South Africa. Over the proceeding months, he busied himself selling the Hendersons's belongings – including their car – and forging the necessary documents to assume possession of the Dawes Road house before he sold it in July.

Haigh kept the Hendersons's dog, Pat, and lived with the animal for some time at the Onslow Court Hotel before turning it in at a kennel because of its bad eyesight. The Henderson murders proved to be a profitable venture for Haigh, netting him nearly £8,000. The success wrought in Haigh a sense of invincibility. 'I felt convinced,' he later remarked, 'there was an overseeing hand which would protect me.'

Whatever providence Haigh relied on, it did little to ensure financial stability. The money had run its course by the end of 1948, having been squandered once more on gambling and various luxuries. With his bank account overdrawn, his hotel bill past due and numerous debts piling up, Haigh set out to find another victim. He found her in Olive Durand-Deacon. Wealthy and widowed, she presented the perfect mark. Police knew the rest.

It was well past midnight when Haigh signed his confession at the Chelsea Police Station and was taken into custody. Later that morning, Tuesday, 1 March 1949, police arrived at the Onslow Court Hotel and searched room 404. Packed in boxes, they found ration books, property deeds, and other business and personal papers that once belonged to the McSwans and Hendersons. Chief Inspector Guy Mahon of Scotland Yard assumed command of the investigation by the end of the morning and travelled with Dr Keith Simpson, the Home Office pathologist, to Haigh's workshop in Crawley.

The workshop's yard was a cluttered tangle of weeds, rubbish and rocky soil. Standing at the gate, Simpson held out little hope of finding anything substantial but focused his attention on the far end of the yard, where a layer of thick, yellowy sludge saturated the ground. He trod slowly across the sodden area, carefully examining the numerous pebbles at his feet. He knew women of Mrs Durand-Deacon's age and rather plump physicality were susceptible to a certain medical condition, and this knowledge guided his search. Almost immediately – and much to his surprise – Simpson spotted a cherry-sized stone in the sludge, its polished facets differentiating it from the other pebbles in the yard. It was a gallstone; probably swaddled in body fat when Haigh dumped Mrs Durand-Deacon's body in the tank, it had survived its immersion in acid.

Minutes later, in a nearby clump of what appeared to be burnt grease, Simpson discovered a dense mass of partially corroded bones. Ten yards from the shed's front door, near the base of a dead tree trunk, Mahon spotted a battered, red plastic handbag like the one Mrs Durand-Deacon had last been seen carrying. A green 40-gallon drum sat in the mud a few feet away. The chief inspector and pathologist carefully removed the tank's lid, peered inside and saw a woman's hairpin resting in thick, yellowish sludge at the bottom.

Simpson told Mahon he wanted the tank, handbag and sludge-soaked soil – which covered an area of 6 feet by 4 feet – shipped to the forensic laboratory at Scotland Yard. A small army of uniformed officers and plain-clothed detectives began the arduous task of lifting the soil to a depth of 3 inches and boxing it in large, wooden crates for transport.

While others dug, Simpson and Mahon turned their attention to the workshop's interior. To the right of the doorway inside, on the chipped whitewashed wall – between the shed's two windows and Haigh's workbench – Simpson saw what looked like faint bloodstains. The splatter pattern appeared consistent with someone being shot in the back of the head while standing at the bench between the two windows. The splotches were photographed, and the splattered area of wall removed for forensic analysis. On the bench, sat Haigh's gas mask, his elbow-length rubber gloves, a stained rubber apron, his mackintosh and the stirrup pump. Near the bench on the floor sat three 10-gallon carboys, two of which were still partially filled with acid.

On the morning of Wednesday, 2 March 1949, police charged John George Haigh at Horsham Police Station with the murder of Olive Durand-Deacon. He appeared at the local magistrates' court on the charge that same morning and was remanded into custody. Arriving at Lewes Prison that afternoon, he told the reception officer that financial gain had nothing to do with his crimes. 'The thing I am really conscious of is the cup of blood, which is constantly before me,' he said. 'I shot some of my victims, but I couldn't say if I shot them in the head, if the hole was not there to show afterwards. But I can say I made a small cut, usually in the right side of the neck, and drank the blood for 3 to 5 minutes, and that afterwards I felt better.'

The self-professed vampire would prove to be a model prisoner.

15

Body of Evidence

Police eventually hauled 47 yards of greasy dirt from the crime scene. Dr Keith Simpson spent three days at the Metropolitan Police Laboratory in Scotland Yard, sifting through the 475 pounds of muck, which had been arranged for analysis on dozens of steel trays. Helping him with the grim search was Dr Henry Smith Holden, the lab's director. Together, the two men probed one pile of sludge after the other, retrieving eighteen bone fragments, three gall stones, a set of dentures, a lipstick container, a partial left foot and the handle to Mrs Durand-Deacon's red, plastic handbag. 'We eventually extracted a mass of about 28 pounds of a yellow greasy substance that looked like "melted" body fat,' Simpson noted, 'and when it was examined chemically it was proved to consist of animal fat.'

To glean a better understanding of how the victim's body melted, Simpson and Holden conducted their own experiments by submerging human limbs and animal tissue in vats of sulphuric acid. The pathologists found that the skin's natural moisture caused a chemical reaction that spiked the acid's temperature and hastened the body's erosion. The acid would bubble and turn black as the body melted away. Fat tissue, however, did not dissolve but instead turned into a thick, gelatinous slime. The recovered bone fragments were soaked clean, X-rayed and examined under a microscope.

Signs of osteoporosis suggested the bones were those of an elderly woman. Simpson and Holden were able to assemble a partial skeleton with the eighteen bone fragments. 'A groove in part of a pelvic (hip-girdle) bone showed it was female,' Simpson wrote, 'and sex was confirmed by a handle of a red plastic handbag and the metal cap of a lipstick case.' The remains were positively identified as those of Mrs Durand-Deacon by comparing the dentures found in the sludge with the dead woman's dental records.

Haigh, who believed a case against him would prove impossible without a body, had been thwarted by science.

On Friday, 4 March, the same day Simpson identified Olive Durand-Deacon's body, a sensational article ran on the front page of the *Daily Mirror*:

VAMPIRE—A MAN HELD

The Vampire Killer will never strike again. He is safely behind bars, powerless to lure victims to a hideous death.

This is the assurance which the *Daily Mirror* can give today. It is the considered conclusion of the finest detective brains in the country.

The full tally of the Vampire's crimes is still not known.

It may take squads of police many weeks to piece together full details of the murderer and his ghastly practices.

The article detailed the murders of the McSwans and Hendersons, information the police had not yet made public. Although it didn't mention Haigh by name, the report characterised the killer:

Hour after hour, before relays of detectives and shorthand writers crowded the buff-painted interrogation room of a London police station, the Vampire has been questioned.

Drinking mug after mug of strong police tea—but never forgetting to crook his little finger genteelly away from the coarse china—the Vampire has shown himself a man of easy manners.

He wears a quiet suit of immaculate cut, with a discreet tie. His hair is sleekly brushed, his nails well-kept.

In Lewes Prison, awaiting trial, Haigh sought to capitalise on the publicity and cement his insanity defence. On the same day the *Mirror* ran its article, Haigh summoned Inspector Webb to the prison and confessed to killing three more people.

'About two months or more after the young McSwan, I met a woman of about 35 years of age, 5 feet 7 inches, slim build, dark hair, no hat, wearing a dark cloth coat, and carrying a dark envelope-type blackish handbag in Hammersmith, somewhere between Broadway and Hammersmith Bridge,' Haigh said.

He detailed the killing as Webb took notes. Haigh said he had never seen the girl before but, taken by her appearance, struck up a conversation. They stood on the bridge, watched the river pass below them and spoke for nearly ½ hour. He asked the girl if she would accompany him back to Kensington and was pleased when she said yes. The two walked as far as Kensington High Street before catching the Underground and getting off at Gloucester Road. Haigh invited the girl to his flat across the street and, once inside, promptly killed her. 'I duly tapped her on the head with a cosh and tapped her for blood,' he said. 'She had next to nothing in her handbag, and I disposed of her body in the same manner as in the other cases. Similarly, there was a case of a youngish man, about autumn the same year.'

The man's name, as far as Haigh could recall, was Max. The two met one evening in the Goat Tavern, the same pub in which Haigh had rekindled his friendship with McSwan. 'On the present occasion,' Haigh explained, 'we had a drink or two and a snack in the snack bar. I talked to him about pin-tables and asked him to come down to the basement at 79 Gloucester Road, which, on this occasion, I described as a workshop. He came with me and the same thing happened as before.'

Haigh claimed his final victim to be a young girl named Mary, whom he met 'between the late summer and early autumn' of 1948 while holidaying in Eastbourne. The two crossed paths outside the Mansion Hotel and started talking. She spoke with a Welsh accent, wore a white and green summer dress, white beach shoes and carried a beige handbag. Haigh took her to dinner that evening in Hastings and treated her to a meal at a seaside café in the old part of town. 'I later took her back to Crawley in my car,' he said. 'We went to the shed at Leopold Road, where I hit her on the head with the cosh, tapped for blood, and put her in a tub, but left her there until the following morning. The tub was one of those I used for the Hendersons ... The following morning, I returned to Crawley, where I pumped sulphuric acid into the tub containing the woman's body. I tipped the sludge out the following morning into the yard.'

Over the next several days, police reviewed missing-persons reports and again went over the documents taken from Haigh's hotel room. They found no evidence supporting his claims and dismissed his confession as a desperate ploy to escape a death sentence. Haigh, however, was not the only individual in trouble. Silvester Bolam, editor of the *Daily Mirror,* came under fire for printing the 'Vampire Killer' article. Fearing the story would jeopardise his chance of receiving a fair trial, Haigh filed a complaint against the paper. Although Haigh wasn't named in the story, his counsel charged 'there were many ways in which he could be identified as the vampire killer'.

On 21 March, Bolam appeared before the Lord Chief Justice of England and found to be in contempt of court. Bolam, voicing his apologies and seeking leniency, conceded he 'was guilty of a grave error'. The Lord Chief Justice, however, was not in a forgiving mood. 'It is not an error of judgment,' he said. 'No one can say that this is an error in judgment. These things are the most horrible things that one can possibly read.'

The *Daily Mirror* was fined £100,000 and Bolam sentenced to three months in Brixton Prison.

Haigh's trial got under way on Monday, 18 July 1949, at the County Hall in Lewes. Crowds lined the High Street, hoping to catch a glimpse of the 'Acid Bath Murderer'. Haigh, his wrist handcuffed to a uniformed officer's, smiled as police escorted him into the building. On arraignment, the Court Clerk read the single charge of murder. 'How say you upon this indictment, are you guilty or not guilty?'

'I plead not guilty,' Haigh said, appearing not the least bit concerned.

A jury was immediately empanelled and opening statements began. Sir Hartley Shawcross, Attorney General, led the Crown prosecution. In his opening statement, he detailed the murder of Olive Durand-Deacon and urged jurors not to get sidetracked by stories of bloodletting and vampirism. While the manner in which Haigh disposed of his victim might be unique, his motive remained the oldest in the book. 'Whether you are satisfied that the prisoner had this morbid appetite for blood,' Shawcross said, 'you may think that it does nothing to detract from what the Prosecution suggest was the primary motive for this murder, namely, financial gain.'

The prosecution called thirty-three witnesses, of which only four were cross-examined by Haigh's attorneys. Key to the defence, led by future Lord Chancellor Sir David Maxwell Fyfe, was convincing the jury that Haigh suffered a mental imbalance and failed to understand the nature of his actions. There was little, to that effect, Fyfe could do with the prosecution's witnesses. It took one day for the prosecution to present its case and lay out the damning evidence. At the end of the first day, Fyfe commenced his case with an opening statement to the jury. He recounted Haigh's younger years and his strict religious upbringing, and detailed the defendant's dreams of bleeding trees and crucifixes.

'The human mind is so infinite in its difficulties and its inability to understand these matters is so great, even in the most normal cases, that I ask you to weigh very carefully these appearances in the prisoner's early years,' he said. 'I shall try to collate for your consideration that the mind and the reason have been so affected that the accused did not know that he was doing what was wrong.'

On the second day of trial, Tuesday, 19 July 1949, the defence called its only witness, Dr Henry Yellowlees, to the stand. His pedigree was impressive, replete with diplomas and fellowships at multiple hospitals in England and Scotland. Asked by Fyfe as to the mental state of the accused, Yellowlees testified that Haigh had a 'paranoid constitution', most likely the result of growing up in an overbearing household where 'the wrath and vengeance of God was over his head for every trifling misdemeanour'. Any child growing up in such an environment, Yellowlees explained, would likely suffer some form of mental trauma. Haigh's lack of childhood friends at school meant he had nothing to ground him in the realities outside his home. Consequently, he lived within a fantasy world of his own making.

'He said to me that he had no special interest in rights or wrongs, or in the laws of the country, or in his victims because he says that this is his destiny,' Yellowlees said. 'He says he believes that the killings are the third revelation, and his is not quite clear yet, but thinks that they may have to do with the question of eternal life, but he does not know how.'

Fyfe sought to shore up his defence. 'You have told us the beliefs that he expressed to you, but taking the last question of the legal test, would it be right to say at once that you are not prepared to express an opinion on whether he knew what he was doing was wrong?'

'That is so.'

On cross-examination, Shawcross dismantled the defence's case. 'Have you ever had or read in literature of a case where the drinking of blood has been an indication of insanity or a motive for murder?'

'No,' Yellowlees replied, 'I have not.'

'Why do you think he procured sulphuric acid in order to destroy this body, and procured it in advance?'

'You have answered the question, have you not? In order to destroy the body.'

'Why,' Shawcross asked, 'do you think it necessary to destroy the body?'

'Because I presume he wished to escape detection.'

'Why do think he wished to escape detection?'

'Because,' Yellowlees said, realising he'd been backed into a corner, 'he did not wish to be punished.'

'I am asking you,' Shawcross said, clearly satisfied, 'to look at the facts and tell the jury whether there is any doubt that he must have known that according to English law he was preparing to do and subsequently had done something which was wrong?'

'I would say "Yes" to that if you say "punishable by law" instead of "wrong".'

'Punishable by law and, therefore, wrong by the law of this country?'

'Yes, I think he knew that.'

The jury retired to consider their verdict at 4.23 p.m. and returned to the courtroom 17 minutes later. The quick deliberation time did not bode well for the defence, and the jurors avoided making eye contact with Haigh as they filed back into the room.

'Members of the jury, are you agreed upon the verdict?' asked the court clerk.

The foreman answered in the affirmative.

'Do you find the prisoner, John George Haigh, guilty or not guilty of murdering Mrs Durand-Deacon, or do you find him guilty but insane?'

'Guilty,' said the foreman, 'of murdering Mrs Durand-Deacon.'

Asked by the clerk if he had anything to say before the mandatory sentence of death was passed, Haigh replied with a cheerful, 'Nothing at all.' He showed no emotion when the judge decreed his fate. He was led away and transferred to Wandsworth Prison to await the hangman.

In the same condemned cell in which Gordon Frederick Cummins, the 'Blackout Ripper', had spent his remaining days, Haigh calmly awaited his hour of reckoning. He passed the time with visits from his distraught parents and penned letters to various acquaintances.

He found comfort comparing himself to notable figures in history. Writing to Dr Henry Yellowlees, he thanked the psychiatrist for testifying on his behalf. 'All the outstanding personalities throughout history have been considered odd,' he wrote. 'Confucius, Jesus Christ, Julius Caesar, Mahomet, Napoleon and even Hitler all possessed a greater perception of the infinite and a more lucid understanding of the omniscient mind. I am happy to inform you that my mother, writing to me during last week, was able to confirm that my headmistress at the High School and my headmaster at the Grammar School both reported that I was not at all a normal boy. How could it be otherwise in the product of an angel and one of the few men who ever sinned?'

Two prison psychiatrists examined Haigh prior to his execution but found nothing to suggest any mental instability. The night before his hanging, he asked the warden if a practice run might be possible, thus ensuring everything went smoothly at the fateful hour. The warden denied Haigh's request, but the condemned need not have worried, for everything went as it should. At 9 o'clock on the morning of Tuesday, 9 August 1949, as crowds gathered outside the prison to await the official notice of execution, Haigh fell through the trap door and found everlasting notoriety at the end of a rope.

Afterthought

The crime-story enthusiast must wonder what George Orwell would think of today's class of criminal. The perfect killing, he wrote in his *Decline of the English Murder,* should have 'dramatic and even tragic qualities, which make it memorable and excite pity for both victim and murderer'. He considered the killing of cabbie George Heath at the hands of Karl Hulten and Elizabeth Jones dull because there was 'no depth of feeling in it'. Orwell would likely hold in utter contempt today's breed of killer: the young thug who lashes out on impulse, murdering over a perceived slight or for the simple thrill of it. Perhaps he would argue that today's crime boasts little imaginative flair. Whether we would agree, it's an undeniable fact that murder fascinates.

What is it about the likes of Haigh and Christie that hold our attention? Londoners, despite the ravages of war and years of deprivation, were still shocked by these men: stunned and fascinated by their sick fantasies and propensity for violence. Having just emerged bruised and battered from history's most destructive conflict, it's surprising that Londoners – indeed, the British nation – took such interest in acts of criminality seemingly minor in the face of war's atrocities. Perhaps the sensational headlines and gruesome details behind the murders were a distraction from the bleak realities of wartime and the conflict's depressing aftermath. Or, maybe the public's curiosity about such things speaks to something else: a disbelief that – despite enduring six years of war – people were still capable of committing such random acts of cruelty. Why is the idea of war easier to comprehend than the man who wakes up one morning and kills an individual?

Rillington Place has been demolished and renamed, its once grimy tenements replaced with tidy brick housing. Haigh's workshop in Crawley is now a small-business office. In a building where the Blackout Ripper enjoyed the company of an unwitting prostitute, one will find Ronnie Scott's Jazz Club. The chapel under which Harry Dobkin buried his wife's remains is long since gone. Time has marched on, but the crimes continue to intrigue. Londoners can rightfully look back on the war years with a sense of pride, but the sinister actions of these few will continue to linger in history's dark, bloodstained corners.

Bibliography and Sources

Police files archived at the British National Archives in Kew were the primary source material for *Dark City*. Unless otherwise noted, all quoted material in the book comes from those files. They are catalogued as follows:

Murder of Rachel Dobkin (as detailed in Chapters 1 and 2):
MEPO 3/2235
HO 144/21853

Gordon Cummins, the 'Blackout Ripper', (as detailed in Chapters 3 to 5):
MEPO 3/2206
CRIM 1/1397

Karl Hulten and Elizabeth Jones (as detailed in Chapters 7 and 8):
MEPO 3/2280
CRIM 1/482

John Christie and Timothy Evans (as detailed in Chapters 9 to 12):
MEPO 2/9535
MEPO 3/3147

John 'Acid Bath' Haigh (as detailed in Chapters 13 to 15):
MEPO 3/3128

Information that did not come from official police records is referenced in the *Source Attribution* section below.

SECONDARY SOURCES

A number of books were consulted in the writing of *Dark City*. Information on the Blackout Ripper case was derived from my previous book, *The Blackout Murders* (JR Books Ltd, 2006), which details the murders, investigation and subsequent trial of Gordon Frederick Cummins in their entirety. Other books relied upon include:

Booth, Nicholas, *ZigZag: The Incredible Wartime Exploits of Double Agent Eddie Chapman*, Arcade Publishing, 2007

Cherrill, Frederick, *Fingerprints Never Lie: The Autobiography of Fred Cherrill*, Macmillan, New York, 1954

Churchill, Winston S., *The Second World War, Vol. II: Their Finest Hour*, Houghton Mifflin Company, 1949

Fabian, Robert, *Fabian of the Yard*, Naldrett Press, London, 1950

Goodall, Felicity, *Voices from the Home Front: Personal Experiences in Wartime Britain 1939–45*, David & Charles, 2004

Kennedy, Ludovic, *10 Rillington Place*, Victor Gollancz Ltd, 1961

Marston, Edward, *Crime Archive: John Christie*, the National Archives, 2007

Orwell, George, *Decline of the English Murder and Other Essays*, Penguin Books, 1965

Priestley, J.B., *All England Listened*, Chilmark Press, 1968

Read, Simon, *The Blackout Murders*, J.R. Books, 2006

Simpson, Keith, *Forty Years of Murder*, George G. Harrap & Co. Ltd, 1978

Thomas, Donald, *An Underworld at War: Spivs, Deserters, Racketeers and Civilians in the Second World War*, John Murray, 2003

Tullet, Tom, *Murder Squad*, the Bodley Head Ltd, 1979

Ziegler, Philip, *London at War*, Alfred A. Knopf, New York, 1995

ARTICLES

'Paratrooper Loses Murder Case Plea', *The New York Times,* 17 January 1945

'Protests Against Hulten Execution Mount; Britons Raise Voices on Behalf of Soldier', *The New York Times,* 8 March 1945

'Soldier is Hanged as London Slayer', *The New York Times*,
    9 March 1945
'Vampire—A Man Held', *Daily Mirror*, 4 March 1949
'5th London Victim in Home of Murder', *The New York Times*,
    29 March 1953
'Antonio Mancini: The Life and Death of a London Gangster',
    New Criminologist, December 1995

PUBLISHED TRANSCRIPTS

Trial of J. G. Haigh (Edited by Lord Dunboyne), William Hodge and
    Company, Ltd, 1953
Trial of Jones and Hulten (Edited by C. E. Bechhofer Roberts), Jarrolds
    Publishers (London) Ltd, 1945

PERIODICALS

Murder Casebook, Vol. 5, Part 72 (A Marshall Cavendish Weekly
    Publication)

SOURCE ATTRIBUTION
Preamble
Details of robbery and Captain Binney's death. Thomas, pp. 293–95;
    Simpson, pp. 119–20.
'Both his lungs …' Simpson, p. 120.
'At the end of 1944 …' Thomas, p. 295.
'Total war …' Priestley, p. 115.

1: What the Psychic Saw
3,500 firewatchers. Ziegler, p. 210.
Bombing of Bank, Marble Arch and Balham stations. Ziegler, p. 117.
'All you could hear …' Ziegler, p. 117.

2: A Skeleton in the Cellar
'These were the times …' Churchill, p. 316.
Looting of bombed houses. Goodall, pp. 148–52; Thomas, pp. 76–85.
Murder Squad history. Tullet, pp. 9–10.
'The County Police …' Ibid., p. 9.
Murder of Leonard Moules. Simpson, pp. 45–47; Cherrill, pp. 71–76.

'Mercilessly clobbered.' Simpson, p. 45.

'I have never lost the thrill ...' Ibid., p. 26.

Conversations between Dashwood and Silverosa, and statements made in their confessions.

Cherrill, pp. 71–73; Simpson, pp. 46–48.

'Hard luck, George.' Simpson, p. 48.

'Don't worry.' Ibid.

Simpson finds execution has been 'expeditiously carried out'. Simpson, p. 70.

'I was only thirty-five ...' Ibid., p. 58.

Chapters three to five are based on the author's previous research into the Blackout Ripper case as detailed in his book *The Blackout Murders* (J.R. Books, 2006). Reference to Detective Chief Inspector Edward Greeno's reputation as the 'Edward G. Robinson' of Scotland Yard is derived from Booth, p. 23.

6: The Luton Sack Murder

Details for this chapter came from Cherrill, Simpson and Thomas.

'Whatever rings she may have been wearing ...' Cherrill, p. 199.

Organisation of Scotland Yard's various departments. Fabian, pp. 195–96.

'I don't think her own mother ...' Simpson, p. 96.

Details of autopsy, Simpson, pp. 97, 98.

'The first object in any murder inquiry ...' Cherrill, p. 199.

Chapman's interview with Manton reproduced in Cherrill, p. 202; Simpson, pp. 101, 102.

'I decided that the kitchen ...' Cherrill, p. 202.

History of fingerprint detection. Read, pp. 10–11.

Manton's statement to police quoted in Cherrill, pp. 204–05; Simpson, p. 102.

Manton's trial testimony quoted in Simpson, pp. 102–03.

7: Dreams of Molls and Mobsters

The case of Antonio Mancini is derived from *New Criminologist* December 1995, and Thomas, p. 271.

All information in this chapter pertaining to Jones and Hulten is derived from the case files.

8: The Cleft-Chin Murder

George Bernard Shaw's letter to the *Sunday Times* reproduced in *Murder Casebook 72: Blackout Killers*, p. 2,590.

'I've done everything I can ...' *New York Times*, 8 March 1945.

Violet Van der Elst's protest. Ibid., 9 March 1945.

'You let the girl go ...' Ibid.

'Don't touch me.' Ibid.

'I'd be better off dead ...' Ibid.

9: A Body of Lies

All information from this chapter is derived from the case files except for: 'Detectives are prepared to take it apart brick by brick.' *New York Times*, 29 March 1953.

'... to wrest from it all its grim secrets.' Ibid.

10: The Killer Inside

Details on Christie's childhood, subsequent years and time as a War Reserve Constable. Marston, pp. 5–14.

Christie cultivating his friendship with Muriel Eady. Kennedy, p. 55.

'For Let' sign going up at 10 Rillington Place. Ibid., p. 64.

Timothy Evans biographical details. Ibid., pp. 60–63; Marston, pp. 23–28.

11: The Man Downstairs

Evans move into Rillington Place. Marston, pp. 30–32; Kennedy, pp. 64–66.

Tension between Beryl and Timothy. Kennedy, pp. 66, 67.

Joan Vincent startles Christie. Ibid., p. 76.

Evans fired from his job. Marston, p. 43.

Joan Vincent confronts Christie. Ibid., p. 42.

12: An Innocent Man

Evans visit to Wales. Kennedy, pp. 91–93.

Letter from Mrs Probert to Mrs Lynch. Marston, p. 47.

Evans turns himself in. Kennedy, p. 98.

Police inspect drain outside Rillington Place. Ibid., pp. 101–02.

Evans return to London and questions raised by confession. Ibid., pp. 115, 118, 127.

Evans stands trial. Marston, pp. 58–63.

'Ridiculous.' Kennedy, p. 169.

'At that time, this fibrositis …' Ibid., p. 169.

'The last time you were in trouble …' Ibid., p. 172.

'I was upset pretty bad sir …' Ibid., p. 186.

Christie tries to dissuade McNeil from purchasing Rillington Place. Marston, p. 69.

Building purchased by Charles Brown. Ibid.

Tensions with neighbours. Ibid., p. 71.

Stay in St Charles' Hospital. Ibid., p. 72.

'… remarkable capacity for dismissing …' Marston, p. 93.

13: The Vanishing

All information from this chapter is derived from the case files.

14: Acid and Blood

Haigh's family background and burgeoning criminal career is taken from Dunboyne.

Haigh's quoted writings are derived from entries reproduced in Dunboyne.

Mrs Lucy Phillipe's encounter with Haigh. *Daily Mirror,* 4 March 1949.

Simpson findings in the sludge outside Haigh's workshop. Simpson, pp. 197–98.

15: Body of Evidence

Simpson's examination of sludge is taken from trial testimony and Simpson, pp. 198–99.

'We eventually extracted …' Ibid., p. 198.

'A groove in part …' Ibid., p. 199.

'The Vampire Killer will never …' *Daily Mirror,* 4 March 1949.

Bolam's appearance in court reproduced in Appendix II of Duboyne.

Haigh trial testimony reproduced fully in Duboyne.

Afterthought

'dramatic and even tragic qualities.' Orwell.

'no depth of feeling in it.' Ibid.

About the Author

Simon Read, a native Briton, currently lives and works in the United States. An award-winning writer, he is the author of eight works of nonfiction, including *Human Game: Hunting the Great Escape Murderers*, *Winston Churchill Reporting: Adventures of a Young War Correspondent* and *The Case That Foiled Fabian: Murder and Witchcraft in Rural England*.

Visit him online at www.simonreadwriting.com.

Index

If you enjoyed this title
from The History Press

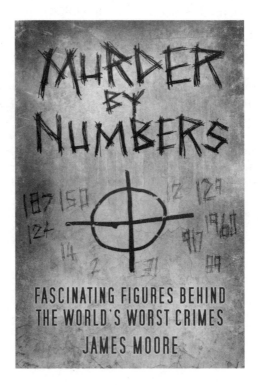

978 0 7509 8707 3